Nomenclatural Poetization and Globalization

Edited by
Adaku T. Ankumah

Langaa Research & Publishing CIG
Mankon, Bamenda

Publisher:
Langaa RPCIG
Langaa Research & Publishing Common Initiative Group
P.O. Box 902 Mankon
Bamenda
North West Region
Cameroon
Langaagrp@gmail.com
www.langaa-rpcig.net

Distributed in and outside N. America by African Books Collective
orders@africanbookscollective.com
www.africanbookcollective.com

ISBN: 9956-792-99-3

© Adaku T. Ankumah 2014

DISCLAIMER

All views expressed in this publication are those of the author and do not necessarily reflect the views of Langaa RPCIG.

The Editor

Adaku T. Ankumah received her PhD in Comparative Literature from the University of Wisconsin-Madison with a minor in drama. Her dissertation and initial research interests focused on revolutionary playwrights from the African Diaspora, such as Kenyan Ngugi wa Thiong'o, Martiniquais writer Aimé Césaire, and African American Amiri Baraka, who use their creative efforts to work for the destruction of what they consider to be the colonial/capitalist foundation of post-colonial Africa. Ngugi's play *The Trial of Dedan Kimathi*, a play that examines the arrest and trial of one of the famous leaders of the Mau Mau revolt against the British in Kenya in the 1950's, has been the subject of her published research. She has also done research on the role of women in revolutionary theatre, voicelessness of African women, and gender and politics in the works of African women authors like Mariama Bâ, Ama Ata Aidoo and Tsitsi Dangarembga.

Professor Ankumah's recent research interest includes the writings of women in the African diaspora. This includes research on memory in literature and its role in helping those dealing with painful, fragmented pasts forge a wholesome future in Edwidge Danticat's *The Dew Breaker*. She has also examined memory and resistance in the poetry of South African performer and writer Gcina Mhlophe. She recently co-edited, with Bill F. Ndi, Benjamin Hart Fishkin and Festus Fru Ndeh, *Outward Evil Inward Battle: Human Memory in Literature,* and with Bill F Ndi and Benjamin Hart Fiskin: *Fears, Doubts, and Joys of not Belonging.*

Authors

Adaku T. Ankumah is an Associate Professor of English at Tuskegee University. She holds a Ph.D. from the University of Wisconsin-Madison. Her areas of interest include women's literature (with a focus on African and Diaspora women) and the short story genre.

Antonio J. Jimenez-Munoz is lecturer at the University of Oviedo, Spain. His research takes on the influence of Romantic literature and culture upon the present. His main line of research deals with the influence of Romantic legacies in modern poetry and art and particularly the material continuity of Romantic modes of expression in contemporary art-forms. His fields of interest are Literary Criticism, Theory, and World Poetry. Before his current position, he was a Teaching Fellow at the universities of Kent at Canterbury-UK (2001-2004) and Hull-UK (2004-2006), after graduating in English Studies at the University of Cordoba (Spain) in 2001.

Benjamin Hart Fishkin, Assistant Professor of English at Tuskegee University specializes in teaching Nineteenth Century British Literature. He holds a Ph.D. from the University of Alabama where he served as a Junior Fellow in The Blount Undergraduate Initiative. In his research, he has emphasized Nineteenth Century British Literature through each phase of his education. Prior to earning his Doctorate from the University of Alabama in May of 2009, he obtained a BA in English and Film from the University of Michigan, Ann Arbor, and an MA from Miami University, Oxford, Ohio where he examined the interest of Charles Dickens in the theatre and how the stage influenced his novel writing. He has published *The Undependable Bonds of Blood: The Unanticipated Problems of Parenthood in the Novels of Henry James*. He co-edited *Outward Evil Inward Battle: Human Memory in Literature* with Adaku T. Ankumah, Bill F. Ndi and Festus Fru Ndeh, and *Fears, Doubts and Joys of not Belonging* with Adaku T. Ankumah and Bill F. Ndi. His recent research interest now include amongst other things the problems of marriage and the American family, and the relationship between the Blues and the single-parent home in the works of William Faulkner, August Wilson, and F. Scott Fitzgerald. Professor Fishkin joined Tuskegee University in the fall of 2009. Before taking up this position at Tuskegee University, Professor Fishkin was a Junior Fellow in The Blount Undergraduate Initiative at the University of Alabama. He has won several distinguished awards, including the Buford Boone Memorial Fellowship, the Oregon Shakespeare Festival Scholarship Award and the George Mills Harper Graduate Student Travel Award.

Bill F. Ndi, Associate Professor of English and Foreign Languages at Tuskegee University, Tuskegee, Alabama, USA, earned his Doctorate from the University of Cergy-Pontoise in 2001. He is a poet, playwright, storyteller, literary critic, translator, historian of ideas and mentalities as well as an academic who has held teaching positions in several universities in Australia, France and elsewhere. His areas of teaching and research comprise among others English Languages and literatures, French, Professional, Technical and Creative Writing, World Literatures, Applied/Historical Linguistics, Literary History, Media and Communication Studies, Peace/Quaker Studies and Conflict Resolution, History of Internationalism, History of Ideas and Mentalities, Translation & Translatology, 17th Century and Contemporary Cultural Studies. He has published extensively in these areas. His publications include numerous scholarly works on Early Quakerism and translation of Early Quaker writings. He has also published poetry and plays in both the French and the English languages. Professor Bill F. Ndi has 15 volumes of poetry of which 4 are in French, a play and 4 works in translation.

Blossom N. Fondo is Senior Lecturer in Postcolonial Theory and Commonwealth Literature at the Higher Teacher's Training College of the University of Maroua, Cameroon. Her publications have appeared in the *IUP Journal of Commonwealth Literature, Labyrinth: A Journal of Postmodern Studies* and *Kaliao; The Multidisciplinary Journal of the Higher Teachers' Training College Maroua,* and *Reflections on World Literature* edited by Nilanshu Agrawal. Her main areas of interest are postcolonial feminist theory, Anglophone Caribbean, African and African-American Literatures. She is currently working on a monograph on the representations of history in the postcolonial novel with a focus on the novels of Michelle Cliff.

Emmanuel Fru Doh holds a Ph.D. from the University of Ibadan and has taught in colleges and universities in Cameroon and the United States since 1990. Poet, novelist, social and literary critic, his research interests, with a remarkable interdisciplinary approach, include Africa's literatures, cultures, and politics; the African diaspora; and colonial and postcolonial literatures. Besides fictional and poetic works, Doh has published numerous substantial scholarly works, including *Africa's political Wasteland: The Bastardization of Cameroon*, and *Stereotyping Africa: Surprising Answers to Surprising Questions, Anglophone-Cameroon Literature: An Introduction, The Obasinjom Warrior: The Life and Works of Bate Besong*. Also worthy of mention is a significant book chapter in *Fears, Doubts, and Joys of not Belonging:* "Bill F. Ndi's Social Angst and Humanist Vision: Politics Alienation and the Quest for Freedom in *K'cracy, Trees in the Storm and Other Poems*". He is currently teaching in the Department of English at Century College in Minnesota.

Gloria Nne Onyeoziri is a professor of French at the University of British Columbia. She published *La Parole poétique d'Aimé Césaire* (L'Harmattan, 1992) and *Shaken Wisdom: Irony and Meaning in Postcolonial African Fiction* (University of Virginia Press, 2011). Other recent publications include "In the Face of the Daughter: Feminist Perspectives on Métissage as a Gendered Concept in the Works of Maryse Condé" (in *Emerging Perspectives on Maryse Condé*, African World Press, 2006), "Gisèle Pineau et l'oralité mondialisée" (*Nouvelles études francophones*, 2012) and "Willful and/or Imposed Alienation in Recent African Emigration Narratives: Chimamanda Adichie's *The Thing Around Your Neck*, Fatou Diome's *Le Ventre de l'Atlantique*, and Henri Lopes's *Une enfant de Poto-Poto*" in collaboration with Robert Alvin Miller in (*Fears, Doubts, and Joys of not Belonging*, Langaa-RPCIG, 2013).

Richard Evans is assistant professor of English at Tuskegee University in Tuskegee, Alabama. Educated in classics at the University of South Carolina, the American School of Classical Studies at Athens and Columbia University, Dr. Evans holds a Ph.D. in comparative literature with research interests in ancient and medieval literatures, theories of translation and linguistic relativity. He has published numerous academic book reviews, essays promoting the study of Classical Greek in schools, and articles on Greek and Roman authors in the Dictionary of Literary Biography

Robert Alvin Miller teaches French and African Studies at the University of British Columbia. He has published studies on J.M.G. Le Clézio and other francophone authors including Simone and André Schwarz-Bart, D. T. Niane and Aminata Sow Fall. Recent studies include "Interface and Erasure in Le Clézio's 'Mondo' and Gatlif's *Mondo*" (*International Journal of Francophone Studies*) and "Communes hippies et autres communautés improvisées chez Maryse Condé et J.M.G. Le Clézio" (in *Diasporiques*, F. Paré & T. Collington, eds., Ottawa: Éditions David, 2013)), and "Le Clézio et la voix des femmes: à la recherche du transhégémonique" (*Les Cahiers J.-M. G. Le Clézio* 6: 2013).

Stephen Magu is an Assistant Professor of Politics and International Relations at Hampton University in Hampton, Virginia and Adjunct Professor of Government at the Robertson School of Government at Regent University in Virginia Beach, VA. His publications have appeared in journals such as *Cultural Encounters, Conflicts, and Resolutions: A Journal of Border Studies*, the Journal of African Studies, *The African Journal of International Affairs and Development*, in the edited volume *Africa Yesterday, Today & Tomorrow: Exploring the Multi-dimensional Discourses on 'Development'*, the *International Journal of Political Science and Development* and in the forthcoming book, *Soft Power Strategies in US Foreign Policy: Citizen Diplomacy of the Peace Corps* by Lexington Books. His main interests are democratization in emerging markets, social and economic development in a global world, regionalism and cultural norm in modernity. Stephen is currently working on a second book, *The Black Man's Burdens*.

Table of Contents

Introduction.. xi

Chapter One: Interpreting Names and Naming as Social Force: An Historico-Philological Comment
Richard Evans.. 1

Chapter Two: Liquid Realities: Romantic Transience and the Use of Names in Emmanuel Fru Doh
Antonio Jimenez-Munoz.. 21

Chapter Three: Colonial Violence and Postcolonial Amnesia: A Reading of Michelle Cliff's *Abeng*
Blossom Fondo.. 35

Chapter Four: Names, Power Relationships and Influences in Francis B. Nyamnjoh's *Married but Available*
Benjamin Hart Fishkin... 57

Chapter Five: Ironic Onomastic Strategies of Calixthe Beyala and Chimamanda Adichie
Robert Miller & Gloria Onyeoziri..................................... 83

Chapter Six: The Politics of Names in the Age of Globalization: Examining the Socio-Political Consequences
Stephen Magu.. 99

Chapter Seven: The Global Reader and Names in Literary Works by Peter W. Vakunta, Bill F. Ndi and Emmanuel Fru Doh
Bill F. Ndi... *123*

Chapter Eight: All in a Name: Nomenclature in Francis B. Nyamnjoh's *The Travail of Dieudonné* and Bill F. Ndi's *Gods in the Ivory Towers*
Adaku T. Ankumah... *145*

Chapter Nine: Names and Nomenclatural Distortions as Dramatic Technique in Anglophone-Cameroon Literature,
Emmanuel Fru Doh... *169*

Chapter Ten: Character Nomenclature, the Bead-string in Thomas Jing's Tale of an African Woman,
Adaku T. Ankumah, Benjamin Hart Fishkin, & Bill F. Ndi.. *195*

Introduction

In a world continually marked with talks and rumors of and about globalization, along with the principal claim that the world is becoming a global village, one is tempted to investigate the centrality of names from the perspective that globalization has generated new terminologies. A global village, indeed, should warrant effective intercultural listening, understanding, and communication for a peaceful co-existence within this village. Yet, one of the keys to legitimizing peaceful coexistence is the acknowledgement of one's existence. This acknowledgement comes through an often ignored social fact, which is the name. Leah Milne claims that "a child is not alive… until it is named" (357). In the same vein, any refusal to address one by his or her name could easily be a source of grave conflict in such a world purporting to be a global village. Emphasis must be made here of the fact that names, naming rites and ceremonies are the principal elements that make the heart of any village to beat to the rhythm of peace. Hence Claire A. Culleton's assertion that "names prescribe and maintain our behavior, freezing in time and space our personalities; and because names can both order and stifle, codify and smother, characters in fiction often rebel against such nominal systematization" (72).

Names play a significant role in all cultures; we were reminded of this recently when England and the rest of the world waited with bated breath for the naming of the Prince of Cambridge, George Alexander Louis, son of the Duke and Duchess of Cambridge and third in line to the throne. In African cultures, however, where names take on an even greater significance, generally they are not bestowed on the individual without some type of ceremony. Wole Soyinka, Nobel laureate and keynote speaker at the 2013 CODESRIA-Guild of African Filmmakers-FESPACO Workshop underscores the significance of naming by modifying William Wordsworth's famous line, "The child is father of the man" to state the significance of naming in Africa: "[T]he name is father to the child." He notes the "careful thought" that goes into the process, even a "sense of history, hopes and expectations" which accompany the process. His conclusion is that "[c]hild naming, on this continent, is itself a creative act" ("A Name"). For this reason, some transplanted Africans in the West are surprised when asked to provide names for their babies *before* leaving the hospital. To them, the significance of naming is lost when they are asked to simply fill out a sheet of paper with the name chosen for the baby. Some names are honorific, conferring honor to elders living and dead, while others embody the hopes and aspirations of the family, just as others acknowledge the family's gratitude to the supreme deity for prayers answered.

Furthermore, names are essential to determining one's cultural identity. They indicate who belongs as well as who does not belong. A person's moniker determines the difference between who can immerse him/herself in a culture and who must look in through a pier glass. The present title, *Nomenclatural Poetization and Globalization* takes the role of a social anthropologist and explains, translates, and delineates where this border is drawn and how it can be broken in the age of globalization. While it does not adhere to the standard structure or format, this book is a dictionary about power. It addresses the fine line that exists between who has it, how they obtained it, and how they hope to protect and keep it.

The subject of naming has been researched and commented upon before. But a name is more than an utterance and the authors of scholarly texts look carefully at how they are formed and what they stand for. The editor is aware of this book's antecedents. Anne Ferry's *The Art of Naming* is a study of sixteenth century English poetry. This is an historical work in which Ferry is concerned with grammar and etymology. Accordingly, she spends time on metaphorical construction and parts of speech, and in the process, like a scientist, probing, dissecting, weighing and x-raying the English language. What she does not do, perhaps because the book was published more than twenty-five years ago, is to deal with the international aspect of names in the age of globalization and how cultures migrate from one place to another. In Percy Hide Reaney and R.M. Wilsons' *A Dictionary of English Surnames* the reader has a book that is essential for family historians. What is of interest, here, is how names have been changed, developed, and "sculpted" throughout the ages. *A Dictionary of English Surnames* is a wonderful and comprehensive reference book, but it is limited to one region: the book only presents British surnames. This raises questions about how to study this academic area if one is elsewhere? What about names from the Caribbean, from Cameroon, from Nigeria, from Kenya or from the ancient Mediterranean and Near East? If the reader were only interested in English surnames, as may have been the case during the rule of Queen Victoria, then Reaney and Wilson should be recommended, but if the reader were interested in the global and intercultural, then *Nomenclatural Poetization and Globalization* hopes to fill this gap. *A Dictionary of Period Russian Names*, by Paul Wickenden of Thanet, is excellent for those interested in name roots and personal names, but it presents a similar problem. This can be useful to see the units of how to build a Russian name, but its power is limited and stops at the border of a map whose fault lines are constantly behind and redrawn. The study before you has no such barriers.

Furthermore, the desire to understand literary names has spawned various volumes on onomastics. Leonard R. N Ashley, an acclaimed expert in personal names, published a 1989 book, *What's in a Name?* which was revised in 1995. He followed it with *Names in Literature*, published in 2003. The first book, written more for a general public than for scholars in the field, examines names and their origins, not only in terms of persons, but also places and businesses. The second book examines literary names in Western literature, from the classics through the Renaissance and Shakespeare to the modern. There is a proliferation of articles in the area on onomastics in Victorian literature, especially names in the works of Charles Dickens. Recent works in literary nomenclature includes Alastair Fowler's *Literary Names: Personal Names in English Literature*, a book which chronicles the use of names in literature from as far back as Homer, Spenser, Shakespeare, Milton and more recent as Dickens and Nabokov. Colin Burrows, who disagrees with Fowler's take on anagrams since he believes people find in anagrams what they want to see, sums up the work as "nonetheless something of a marvel. It shows why names in literature matter, and how they participate in some of the most delightful and tantalizing [sic] qualities of literature itself" ("I, Low Cur").

Meanwhile, nomenclature in literature has gained currency globally in recent years. In America, for example, the American Name Society, an organization which started in 1951 has the goal to promote the study of names, to "find out what really is in a name, and to investigate cultural insights, settlement, history, and linguistic characteristics revealed in a name" (ANS Website). Scholars in onomastics seek to respond to love-struck Juliet's age-old question to Romeo, "What's in a name?" She claims that a rose by any other name will still be a sweet-smelling flower; thus Romeo can simply "doff" his name, which is her enemy, and assume another, which is more appealing, so they can get married. In a pre-structuralist response which sees words as arbitrary signs, Juliet sees the act of naming as a random process based on the whims and caprices of parents. For deconstructionist Jacques Derrida, the act of naming itself does violence to language. As he writes in the chapter on "The Battle of Proper names,"

> There was in fact a violence to be named. To name, to give names that it will on occasion be forbidden to pronounce, such is the originary violence of language, which consists in inscribing within a difference, in classifying, in suspending the vocative absolute. (113)

To use the words of Antonio Sobejano-Morán in his title, there may be "ambiguity and destruction" in the way some authors arrive at names, but in the reader's mind, there is still a "connection between the arbitrariness of the sign and the naming process in literature" (31). However, is a name simply a word that can be substituted or interchanged at will?

Literary onomastics, therefore, is not quite so simple; for a name carries with it culture and heritage, character and aspirations, plot and theme. Authors, therefore, spend more time choosing character names. Citing a 2011 interview conducted by Black and Wilcox, Baker-Smemoe et al. note that these authors found that authors chose "names with personal significance," including doing research to find "names that are unique or significant, and choosing names with phonology that appealed to the authors." They conclude that "choosing names in fiction may have even more social significance than selecting names in general" ("Naming Practices"). The same idea has been noted earlier by one of the scholars in literary onomastics when he writes, "An artist's naming of his or her characters frequently involves calculated and conscious choices in order to deliver a message through the onomastic medium" (qtd. in Nguyen). Thus the names of characters are not simply a means of distinguishing one character from another. These names aid thematically in advancing plot, introducing irony, shaping identity, and even the absence of a name in a literary text can speak volumes about the character. As Butler suggests, "Even the lack of a name for certain characters has a purpose within literature, signalling [sic] covert information about the social or personal attitudes towards such characters" (13). In this light, names or no names, the author advances different aspects of the literary work.

Taking the reader back to the days of the Old Testament, names and character seem to go together; thus the psalmist could say in reference to God that "those who know your name will put their trust in you" (Psalm 9:10). To know the name of the Almighty is to know His character and attributes. Names are therefore important in establishing identities, especially in postcolonial nation-states where names establish ethnic affiliations. With the dawn of globalization and interest in multiculturalism, understanding names in literature has become even more pressing as global readers seek to appreciate literatures from various parts of the world.

People all over the world fear one thing above all else. What keeps people from their sleep at 3:00 AM is their thought that they might fade away. The localizing parochialism of this human fear is the flaw of so many books on the subject of naming. A name brings with it an important and universal recognition--if one wills, a lack of anonymity -- which Francis B. Nyamnjoh, of the University of Cape Town, qualifies as "visibility" (706). This is an area not touched upon in many other books on name. Visibility is not used here in the Arthurian sense i.e. in a physical sense, but in a social and psychological one. Status and wealth, while different, are very important. Most people want what stereotypical gangster films indicate to be "respect" or a knowledge that they "count" or that they matter. A name, like an actual house or structure or family, must be maintained, claimed, retrofitted, polished and (when possible) augmented. Social anthropologist, political scientist, philosopher, sociologist and intellectual, Pierre Bourdieu refers to a "house" (his emphasis) as something very precise and specific. "The "house" (*la maison*), both lineage and patrimony, lives on while the generations that personify it pass away…" (15). It has a reputation, a social currency and a value. This volume then is concerned with how such an entity "floats" on the free market and what is its role within the social order in a global world. Will a wave of daily interaction raise a name to new heights or will the absence of such a hydraulic lift cause the bearer of the said name to suffer? At first glance this may seem to be a misappraisal. After all, doesn't Juliet Capulet, in William Shakespeare's *Romeo and Juliet*, question "What's in a name? …" (II, ii, 1-2). In other words, isn't a calling card of no significance? The accomplishment, and not the title or the wrapper or the packaging, is what counts. With respect to experts in the field of love in Verona, contemporary global literature rejects and repudiates Shakespeare's dramatic assertion. Names mark an individual, just like Cain's scar in *The Holy Scriptures*. Just like a fingerprint and blood type, names last forever and cannot be wiped away. A baby's birth name, in this case, can be likened to that of a chemical compound within a DNA molecule. A name is irrevocable. It stands for more than merely identification. This may account for Claire Culleton's assertion:

> Names prescribe and maintain our behavior, freezing in time and space our personalities; and because names can both order and stifle, codify and smother, characters in fiction often rebel against such nominal systematization. (72)

Names have an impact on the text in question, be it a poem, a play or a novel. *Nomenclatural Poetization and Globalization* advances how a name can change a character. In other words how can a person fade away, and what is society's role in that change? Going by philosopher and philologist, Michel Foucault's insistence that language is one of the ways by which a person can be controlled, a person is

> [...] a vehicle for words which exist before him. All of these contents that his knowledge reveals to him, as exterior to himself, and older than his own birth, anticipate him, overhang him with all their solidity, and traverse him as though he were merely an object of nature, a face doomed to be erased in the course of history. (313)

From the quotation, the phrase and word "older than" and "anticipate" seem to indicate that the individual is powerless. The name will take the corporeal body and cover it, shape it, and overwhelm it, whether or not the flesh is willing. Think of a blacksmith hammering and pounding a hot piece of iron. That is the power of naming. A person is a vehicle for words and not the other way around. The name can serve as a blueprint, a map or a travelogue. From the moment a baby is christened, not born but christened, a concrete history "overhang(s)" it. He/She, like a child in Greek mythology, has very finite control over its destiny. In Arthur Miller's *The Crucible*, the seventeenth century farmer knows that his name is of tremendous value. A "proctor" is supposed to take care of or act for another. It brings with it qualities that are not negotiable, as John Proctor would have it:

> "Because it is my name! Because I cannot have another in my life! Because I lie and sign myself to lies! Because I am not worth the dust on the feet of them that hang! How may I live without my name? I have given you my soul; leave me my name!" (143)

The Crucible is about a town, Salem, in the throes of a spiritual crisis. The church abuses its powers and misapplies God's rules. Is it any wonder that the name "Salem" has been forever tarnished and linked to this abuse of power? A true theologian knows that a christening ceremony is not about the decision-making during which a parent or parents decide upon a specific name. It is a ritual that has to do with purification and that which shall be left after the flesh is gone. The spiritual component raises the stakes. Miller presents a name as the very last piece of value, something that is equivalent to actual life itself. Without it, the character is not only naked, but prostrate. John Proctor presents and participates in a great reckoning. In an attempt to preserve his family, he is willing to confess, even though this will be a false confession, but he is unwilling to do so before the public of Massachusetts, knowing full well that this taint will adhere itself to the Proctor surname forever. This action will besmirch his children and his children's children, hence the phrase "after the flesh is gone." The fact that he is an innocent man whose permanent and immortal identity is under attack makes any sort of restorative compromise repugnant.

Though these works are valuable resources for scholars in onomastics, these works published in the west are focused on western writers; there has not been much scholarly attention on onomastics in Africa. Bertie Neethling, in his book on names among the Xhosa in South Africa, notes the paucity of scholarly works on onomastics as late as 1976. According to him, this small number of works in this area caused "the serious names scholar [...] to wait until the twenty-first century" (n. pag.). Thus, this publication aims at providing scholars in literatures of the world with the tools that they need to decipher names in literature. It should interest scholars in African literature, giving them other ways to look at literary nomenclature. It is in line with Butler's note that "[names] are but one part of a text, and cannot be examined without consideration of other textual implications and motives" (13). The works represented in this volume examine not just the names but also other language and subversive issues which come through the use of names in literature from the ancient literature of the Near East and Mediterranean to contemporary Anglophone-Cameroon literature. It is in view of this that this introduction would borrow from Roland Barthes, the necessity for his book, *A Lover's Discourse* which shares a lot in common with nomenclatural poetization in a globalized world. Barthes highlights that his subject like that of the present book "is today *of an extreme solitude.*" He further points out:

> ... it is completely forsaken by the surrounding languages: ignored, disparaged, or derided by them, severed not only from authority but also from the mechanisms of authority (sciences, techniques, arts). Once ... driven by its own momentum into the backwater of the "unreal," exiled from all gregarity, it has no recourse but to become the site, however exiguous, of an *affirmation*. That affirmation is, in short, the subject of the book which begins here... (1)

Drawing on naming and nomenclatural contexts as significant factors in the development of literary texts since the earliest literatures of the ancient Near East and Mediterranean worlds, Dr. Richard Evans explicates, in the first chapter, the importance of personal names and their cultural contexts for accurate intercultural communication as looming large in a world flattened by globalization and contracted by intense communication today. He hypothesizes that for the present-day global reader of contemporary texts, the significance of names, embedded within a particular social or cultural context, may prove difficult to appreciate unless they are approached with educated interpretive skill and awareness. And through a journey back into the implication of names and naming in a variety of ancient texts, global readers, using an historical and a theoretical frame of reference, would arm themselves with tools for approaching unfamiliar nomenclatural patterns in texts of the diverse literatures of the modern world as well as better clarify the understanding of such texts.

In the second chapter, "Liquid realities: Romantic transience and the use of names in Fru Doh," Dr. Antonio Jimenez-Munoz examines the use of names by a major voice in Anglophone-Cameroonian literature. Through a critical examination of his poetry in collections such as *Not Yet Damascus* (2007), *Oriki'badan* (2009) and *Shadows* (2011), and his political writings such as *Africa's Political Wastelands* (2008) and *Stereotyping Africa* (2009), the chapter elucidates how, through names, Emmanuel Fru Doh's poetization speaks volumes about the conditions and spirits of Cameroonians both at home and in the Diaspora. The pervasiveness of names and naming in Emmanuel Fru Doh's works serves the function of inadvertent metaphors which are consistently recurring in his writing. This chapter explores the various functions of such use of names in Emmanuel Fru Doh's poetry and essays and illuminates his rich, personal conception of what a name entails. Also, juxtaposing Doh to the Romantics who emphasize on place naming as a trope, Dr. Jimenez-Munoz expounds on Emmanuel Fru Doh's poignant act of calling attention to the naming of people and collectives as a way of transience. Where Romantic poetry and theory aim to inscribe a name into nature, this chapter argues that Emmanuel Fru Doh seems to precisely do the opposite, highlighting the arbitrariness of names by reflecting that a given name is subject to change. Going beyond nominalisms, names are not only apprehended as a reflection of an inner soul, but they also serve as the key element in acts of remembrance, in the creation of artificial realities and the performance of often unfair actions in the name of others. Ultimately, a name, for Emmanuel Fru Doh, is a liquid, passing state of affairs, and not something hard and stable. A name reflects a given reality at a given time, but one which is both arbitrary and subject to rapid change, even in the case of humans and what goes by their names.

The third chapter springs from a statement by Jamaican writer Michelle Cliff that she named the protagonist of two of her novels (*Abeng* and *No Telephone to Heaven*) "Clare Savage" to highlight not only her light skin but especially the enduring legacies of colonialism. Consequently, Dr. Blossom Fondo investigates the nomenclatural practices and their implications in colonial and post-colonial violence. Accordingly, this protagonist's name, Clare Savage, refers to a mind "bleached of the past" by the savagery of the colonial contact. This chapter focuses on Michelle Cliff's use of the name Clare as an embodiment of the material effects of colonialism, precisely the cultural and physical violence that resulted in a state of amnesia and other related pathologies which amount to the obliteration of the past of the colonized. The chapter shows how Clare's body is a symbol, par excellence, of both the savagery of colonization and the occlusion of a sense of the past on which the present and the future needs to be anchored.

Dr. Benjamin Hart Fishkin's "Power Relationship and Influences in the Novels of Francis B. Nyamnjoh" exposes Nyamnjoh's focus on the French- and English- speaking provinces of modern-day Cameroon. Names are about more than solely identification for this writer. A name, this chapter contends, is eternally true and genuine. In *Mind Searching* he purposely restates and refutes Shakespeare's "What is in a name?" from *Romeo and Juliet*. And the author finds circumstantial name changing particularly repugnant. Fishkin shows that a name has energy. By closely reading *Married, But Available,* he underlines names as echoing the protagonist's misunderstanding of power, religion, and sexuality. In short, Nyamnjoh's universe challenges social science methodology to require more than categorization and identification when it comes to approaching names. Fishkin posits that names, according to Nyamnjoh, mark an individual just like a fingerprint, a blood type, or a sequence of chemical compounds within a DNA molecule.

The fifth chapter by Robert Miller and Gloria Onyeoziri, "The Ironic Onomastic Strategies of Calixthe Beyala and Chimamanda Adichie," ushers the reader into names as meaning carriers which, as a result, are open to the charge of irony. They explicate that if a character's name "means" something in the language of the text or in the language represented indirectly by the text, then that name may also carry the shadow of implied double meaning. Also, the authors reveal what comes out of this double meaning: satire, playful allusion, ridicule or suggestive contradiction. To do so, they dwell on the works of Calixthe Beyala and Chimamanda Adichie. This chapter portrays, on the one hand, that the ironic onomastic strategies of Chimamanda Adichie, found in her "traditional woman's narrative," "The Headstrong Historian," are rooted in the naming practices of Igbo language and culture where children are frequently named by (sometimes elliptical) sentences carrying proverbial, spiritual or practical claims to wisdom and understanding. This chapter explains how in Adichie's story a woman's voice is inscribed into the assumptions and presumptions of patriarchal traditions and colonial domination. The names given, taken and refused by various characters reflect the struggle of retelling and subversive reflection on imposed, fractured and contended senses of identity. For these authors, naming is not only a struggle pitting Igbo names against "Christian" names, but a subtle game where each act of "renaming" becomes an ironic response to a previous act of naming.

On the other hand, Calixthe Beyala's "novel of tradition," *Les arbres en parlent encore*, highlights the apocryphal and surprising names of her major characters which are more closely connected to the French language. Nevertheless, the overall effect of these names is one of subversive and satirical representation of the social, historical, and political worldview that shapes the Issogo community in its experience of German and French colonization as well as its entry into postcolonial times. All in all, the onomastic approaches to meaning by these two authors differ both in terms of cultural practices and tone. From the reading of these texts, this chapter suggests a strong link between naming, discursive disruption of cultural and historical instances of authority, and the insertion of a self-affirming female voice into the narrative of colonial and postcolonial experience. In short, the chapter therefore illustrates and explains the need by these two contemporary African women authors to rename and sometimes de-name the signposts of their conflicting cultural heritage.

Dr. Stephen Magu, in chapter six, examines naming conventions and processes as representative of identities, ethnicities and nationalities. Names turn out to be incontrovertible sources of perennial conflicts especially in postcolonial nation-states. Capitalizing on the significance of names, naming conventions and related cultural aspects, this chapter brings to the fore the fact that names are central to individuals' socialization throughout their lives. The chapter then opportunely interrogates the importance and consequences of naming given the present geopolitical dispensation and increasing globalization in our world, one in which national, territorial, and communal identities are losing their importance due to globalization, human rights, democratization and modernization. It establishes that, despite advances in this world with the nation-state based collective as the primary purveyor of political power, names and their associated ethnic identities remain the primary building blocks within the nation. They are instrumental to the formation of individual and group identities, and ultimately the nation's. In short, the chapter demonstrates how globalization has not diluted ethnic-based identities and in some aspects, has magnified *otherness* to the detriment of the unitary nation-state.

Chapter seven examines names in the poetry and prose genres in Anglophone-Cameroon literature. With a particular focus on some poems by Vakunta and Ndi as well as a novel, *The Fire Within* by Doh, Bill F. Ndi explores names from the perspective of the global reader and his or her appreciation of works by such authors without proper understanding of how names are used poetically. This study highlights the uncontested significance of having a good grasp of the writers' poetization of names in the emerging Anglophone-Cameroonian literature. It also points out that a keen appreciation of names clarifies understanding of the works and makes sense to the global reader as character and name are indissociable. Names within this literary framework have helped to substantiate the ways in which both names and naming shape and influence the lives, thoughts and thinking of a people in general and most specifically the writers who translate them into their creative venture. Some of the critical questions this chapter has addressed include the following: what place do names from this microcosm hold within the modern globalized and globalizing cultures? Can names from this receding culture stand the heat of the dominant hegemonic cultures? Are names just primary markers of identity or literary and semiotic signs adding to and shaping the understanding of these works of literature?

"All in a Name: Nomenclature in Francis B. Nyamnjoh's *The Travail of Dieudonné* and Bill F. Ndi's *Gods in the Ivory Towers*" by Adaku T. Ankumah reminds readers that names like Big Brother from George Orwell's *1984* or Sula Peace from Toni Morrison's *Sula* or Atticus Finch, the lawyer in Harper Lee's *To Kill a Mockingbird*, or Celie from *The Color Purple* by Alice Walker are conscious creative acts not random or erratic processes in art. Using the African writers' understanding of this, the author elucidates through the works of some Anglophone-Cameroonian writers how writers spend much time thinking through the process of naming characters because of the impact names will have on their respective text. Central to this chapter is Ankumah's claim that names have the potentials to relay important information about literary elements such as plot, character, or theme to the reader. She looks at the richness of names in a novel by Francis Nyamnjoh, *The Travail of Dieudonné* and in a one-act play by Bill F. Ndi entitled *Gods in the Ivory Tower*. Drawing upon the fact that both authors capitalize on naming to advance their works, Ankumah concludes that to appreciate the richness of the theme, plot, and characterization of the works of these authors, the reader must understand character names and the power they hold in deciphering these texts.

In this chapter, "Names and Nomenclatural Distortions as Dramatic Technique in Anglophone-Cameroon Literature," Emmanuel Fru Doh engages in an exploration of the use and the significance of names and nomenclatural distortions as dramaturgical devices in Anglophone-Cameroon drama. He achieves this by examining certain works from Anglophone-Cameroon that have best put this practice into effect. Accordingly, the chapter examines a play each from Victor Epie Ngome, and Bill F. Ndi and three plays from Bate Besong, an avid consumer of onomastics. Central to this chapter is the claim that without a proper grasp of such nomenclatural distortions, meaning and dramatic effects are either dampened or forever lost.

The concluding chapter, "Character Nomenclature, the Bead-string in Thomas Jing's *Tale of an African Woman*," springs from the phenomenological concept positing that the central structure of an experience, a name inclusive, is its intentionality and its being directed toward something, as it is an experience of, or about some object. Consequently, Ankumah, Fishkin, and Ndi direct the experience toward a name by virtue of its content or meaning together with appropriate enabling conditions. Thus, this chapter highlights names in Jing's novel as carrying with them "worth" that serves both as vehicles for structuring the plot and as carriers of the author's central concerns. Questioning the *raison d'être* of the names that various characters bear, and their actions, is the trigger to the investigation of Jing's characters' underlying actions. The name is a string holding the beads (i.e. plot structure, theme, characterization, setting, novelistic artistry, etc.) in place.

If a name is powerful in an allegedly homogeneous Near Eastern and Mediterranean community or a homogenous seventeenth century American community, imagine how much more complicated the subject becomes in a globalized world hundreds of years later. In a world of globalization, heterogeneity is the hallmark. People travel back and forth between African and European cities like Lagos, Yaoundé, Kinshasa, Cairo, Casablanca, Algiers, London, Amsterdam, Brussels, Frankfurt, Berlin, Copenhagen, Paris, etc. Amongst these travelers, some see fancy shirts and cute cell phones, and they want them just like others hear foreign sounding names, especially those of celebrities and want to appropriate or use them. The implication of this is that authentic or traditional nomenclature is seemingly fading away. Increasingly, according to the social and cultural anthropologist, Nyamnjoh, the traveler desiring of such fancies is "cheating on or being unfaithful to [his/her] culture, identity and belonging. It is like subverting the boundaries within which one is confined" (707). This volume addresses these erosions of cultures and also establishes that there is a relationship between a person's name and how he/she is disciplined, limited, restrained and kept in check. Included in this study is how a person's name keeps him or her in check or on the correct path—just as a law, rule or principle. Can a name be an issue when a young person wants to get married? Is there a connection between a person's name and his or her wealth, success or prominence in the community? What role does a name play in global peace or conflict resolution? What does seem to be a constant is that modernity has brought with it more than a handful of unpleasant surprises. These are a new set of problems that traditional onomastics does not easily recognize. Increasingly people find themselves unconnected and unacquainted with the world in a way that their grandparents and great-uncles and great-aunts would never have been. The way they behave with their peers is different. Their value systems are foreign. Everyone has forgotten how to be contemplative and, in his or her haste, has overlooked the relationships that are truly important. Yet, we are reminded by Litz, A. Walton's contention on Joyce's art that "No piece of information was too irrelevant to its place in the comprehensive pattern" (5). Starting with nomenclature, therefore, there is a possibility for restoring order in such a globalized world.

Works Cited

Baker, Wendy, et al. "Naming Practices in J. R. R. Tolkien's Invented Languages." *Journal of Literary Onomastics* 3.1 (2014): n. pag. Web. 12 Aug. 2014.

Barthes, Roland. *A Lover's Discourse,* New York: Hill and Wang, 2010. Print.

Bourdieu, Pierre *The Bachelor's Ball* Chicago : U. of Chicago P., 2008. Print.

Burrow, Colin. "I, Lowborn Cur." Rev. of *Literary Names: Personal Names in English Literature,* by Alastair Fowler. London Review of Books 34.22 (2012): 15-17. Web. 15 Aug. 2014.

Butler, James Odelle. "The Power & Politics of Naming: Literary Onomastics Within Dystopian Fiction." MPhil. Thesis. U. of Glasgow, 2009. Web. 12 Aug. 2014.

Culleton, Claire. *Names and Naming in Joyce.* Madison: U of Wisconsin P, 1994. Print.

Derrida, Jacques. *Of Grammatology.* Baltimore: Johns Hopkins UP, 1976. Print.

Ferry, Anne *The Art of Naming* Chicago: U. of Chicago P, 1988. Print.

Foucault, Michel. *The Order of Things: An Archaeology of the Human Sciences,* New York: Vintage, 1994. Print.

Miller, Arthur. *The Crucible,* New York: Penguin (Penguin Plays Non-Classics Edition), Penguin Books. 1976. Paperback. Print.

Milne, Leah. "The Importance of Naming in *Beloved* and *The Poisonwood Bible*." *CLA Journal* 55.4 (June 2012): 352-369. Print

Neethling, Bertie. *Naming Among the Xhosa of South Africa.* New York: Mellen, 2005. Web. 15 Aug. 2014.

Nguyen, Phong. "Naming the Trees: Literary Onomastics in Susan Warner's Wide, Wide World." *Studies in American Fiction* 34.1 (Spring 2006): 33+. *General OneFile*. Web. 16 Aug. 2014.

Nyamnjoh, Francis B. "Cameroonian Bushfalling: Negotiation of Identity and Belonging in Fiction and Ethnology." *American Ethnologist* 38.4 (November 2011): 701 – 713. Print.

Reaney, P.H. and R.M Wilson. *A Dictionary of English Surnames*. New York: Routledge and Kegan Paul, 1991. Print.

Shakespeare, William *Romeo and Juliet,* New York: Harcourt-Brace, 1968. Print.

Sobejano-Morán, Antonio. "Ambiguity and Destruction Through the Naming Process in *Reivindicación del Conde don Julián* and *Recuento*."*Literary Onomastics Studies* 15 (1988): 31-37. Rpt. in *Contemporary Literary Criticism*. Ed. Jeffrey W. Hunter. Vol. 133. Detroit: Gale Group, 2001. *Literature Resource Center*. Web. 16 Aug. 2014.

Soyinka, Wole. "A Name is More than the Tyranny of Taste." CODESRIA Guild of African Filmmakers FESPACO Workshop: *Pan-Africanism: Adapting African Stories/Histories from Text to Screen*. Ouagadougou, Burkina Faso. 26 Feb. 2013. Address.

Wickenden of Thanet, Paul. *A Dictionary of Period Russian Names*. Normal, IL: Free Trumpet Press West, 2000. Print

Chapter One

Interpreting Names and Naming as Social Force: An Historico-Philological Comment

By
Richard Evans

Personal names and nomenclatural procedures, a socio-linguistic category, vary from nation to nation and ethnic group to ethnic group, presenting a vast array of social, political, and cultural complexities as well as challenging pluralistic societies in their political, social and educational aspects. These challenges, especially with regard to names and naming in Australia as an example of a large multicultural society, are probed and analyzed in a recent book on implication of names in the educational sector, *Framing My Name: Extending Educational Boundaries* (Kumar, Pattanayak, and Johnson). Meaningful discussion of so diverse and expansive a topic requires some limitation, some approach to manage the multiplicity of variation in names and naming. Although several critical theories are cited by the authors of its various chapters, the editors of *Framing My Name* have noted speech-act theory as an overall controlling orientation, stating: " ...we recognize language as having a constructive and performative power in addition to its indicative function" (xiv). Even as this view of the social functionality of names is especially useful for appreciating names in a societal context, the theoretical approach here will extend and broaden some of the considerations of *Framing My Name* by commenting on certain significant literary examples of names from the Bakhtinean perspective of the socio-ideological nature of languages within the dynamism of heteroglossia (*Dialogic Imagination* 288-298). Bakhtin argues that any given, natural language is replete with an active mixture of special, ideologically loaded sub-languages that are oriented towards each other in a dynamic stratification and that these languages operate in relation to each other as the users of the language construct concrete meaning from instantiating those special languages of ideology. Thus, as a language of heteroglossia, personal names, within a given culture or ethnic group as well as across cultures and ethnic groups, function within their own specific ideological boundaries and orientations.

Although the ideological meanings of personal names sometimes may be understood more immediately from within a given culture or group than from an culturally or ethnically distant perspective, there exists a very real and practical problem of an appreciation and comprehension of the particular ideology or uniqueness of personal names by outsiders of a given culture; this problem is especially acute as the world is flattened by globalization, and local areas, even remote ones, are incorporated into this expanding global horizon of intellectual and literary interaction (Cf. Chapter Seven by Ndi, "The Global Reader and Names in Literary Works by Vakunta, Ndi and Doh"). A further pragmatic requirement for effective international understanding in business, commerce, trade, journalism, law, diplomacy as well as in areas of scholarship, science, literature and art calls for an appreciation of personal names as a foundation of efficacious intercultural communication as argued extensively in *Framing My Name*. Clearly personal names are quite basic to individual and cultural identify and their appreciation goes far in bridging cultural distance among members of distinct national and ethnic enclaves. Pointing out appropriate etiquette for name usage in the publishing world, an article published in *Science Editor,* "African Names: A Guide for Editors," by Bernard Appiah, emphasizes the necessity for correct usage of African names (precisely because of their differences for Western ones) in both the printed and oral sources of scientific journalism in order to avoid offence to authors with non-Western names:

> If you talk to someone who has an African name, ask him or her for the correct pronunciation. "Nationalistic" Africans may not take it kindly if you "Westernize" their names. I have an African friend who will even write the phonetic pronunciation of his name to help foreigners pronounce it well (17).

Negative feelings and reactions aroused by mispronunciation or other forms of name distortion generalize beyond Africa or African sensibilities as my own personal experience teaching as an Anglo in a Spanish-speaking country illustrates. When I was working as a professor in Mexico at the University of the Americas and the National Autonomous University of Mexico, there were, of course, certain legal formalities for work visas and other pertinent documentation required by the Mexican authorities. My Anglo-Saxon name, Richard Louis Evans, was not an official appellation satisfactory for the traditional Spanish nomenclatural framework. At every step of the bureaucratic process, I was informed that my name was Richard Evans *Thomas*, Thomas being my mother's maiden name, which she herself did not use. No amount of argument or display of a passport could change the minds of the Mexican officials from insisting on framing my name in terms of their particular, Spanish nomenclatural system. Until that point, I had never been required to think about my name as a source of personal identity, much less called upon to defend it. Of course, I was aware of the fact that the Mexican officials were only showing bureaucratic zeal and not willful insensitivity; nonetheless, I would have preferred to leave my name, by which I had been called all my life, just as it appears on my birth certificate and passport. These sorts of problems with distortion and reconfiguring of names, particularly it seems, of Oriental names in Occidental cultural settings, are fairly common although such annoying changes point out the practical side of diplomacy in intercultural communication and suggests a need for an awareness and a sensitivity to personal as well as national name usage (Pattanayak 65).

Beyond the immediate pragmatic need for approaching names carefully in the international arena, we understand that personal names and naming procedures are, in fact, an ideologically distinctive linguistic category in any given natural language: "From our infancy, we learn that our name is what registers us into the album of the social world, ultimately the *lingual world*" (*Framing My Name* 9, with my emphasis). We can place personal names and naming comfortably within the theoretical domain of languages of heteroglossia as characterized by Bakhtin. This theoretical designation advances a powerful hermeneutic scope for intercultural comparison of personal nomenclature both in worlds of daily living and literary texts. Beyond an immediate need to appreciate names for good intercultural relations, a psychological and social requirement for effective intercultural communication, a more speculative consideration presents itself. When we compare proper names from ethnicities or cultures other than our own, this investigation *from outside* offers a theoretical perspective that can capture significant meaning beyond that understood solely from within a particular ethnic or national community by that community itself. Here, outsidedness of view, whereby one's own linguistic structures are self-consciously and dialogically confronting those of other language systems or linguistic categories, is termed, in Bakhtinean terms, dialogized heteroglossia. Bakhtin posits an excellent example to clarify the hermeneutical concept of dialogized heteroglossia, an analogy that can demonstrate the interpretative power of the intercultural or inter-ethnic comparison of proper names and nomenclatural procedures.

According to Bakhtin's example in *The Dialogic Imagination,* let us suppose an illiterate peasant in large, multi-lingual environment. (Bakhtin is thinking of Soviet Russia in the 1930's and 40's.) This hypothetical peasant functions in several different languages in his daily life: he goes to church in Old Church Slavonic; he sings in one language and speaks to his family in another language; he writes official petitions in yet another, more formal (paper) language. While the peasant goes about not especially aware of distinctions and limitations of the languages he uses, the languages remain for him unanalyzed, i.e., monologized. But when our hypothetical peasant develops an awareness of the special properties and limitations of each of the languages that he uses, these languages become dialogized in his consciousness, and he develops the ability to choose a given language for a particular purpose (295-296). For the philosophically aware linguist and critic, the space between these various languages of the peasant, as they can be actively compared for distinctiveness and difference, suggests many broad interpretive possibilities, ranging from socio-historical stylistics all the way to linguistic relativity. Bakhtin argues that cultures, engaged in dialogic encounters, generate new perspectives that are not available solely from the inside of the cultures themselves:

In the realm of culture, outsidedness is a most powerful factor in understanding. It is only in the eyes of another culture that foreign culture reveals itself fully and profoundly (but not maximally fully, because there will be other cultures that see and understand even more). A meaning only reveals its depths once it has encountered and come into contact with another foreign meaning: they engage in a kind of dialogue, which surmounts the closedness and one-sidedness of these particular meanings, these cultures. We raise new questions for a foreign culture, ones that it did not raise itself; we seek answers to our own questions in it…. (*Speech Genres and Other Late Essays* 7).

Moreover, explicit in the Bakhtinean example of the peasant's languages is not only a synchronic comparison of the quotidian modern languages of the peasant but also a diachronic comparison of medieval Church Slavonic with the spoken, modern languages. An analogy can be made with this example of the peasant's various languages to the plethora of personal names and nomenclatural processes in various cultures of the world, both present and past. Because of historical monuments, documents and literary texts, we are not confined in our search for wider understanding of this significant socio-linguistic phenomenon of personal names to contemporary intercultural zones only. The literary and historical record can be mined as a source of significant understanding since names in literary texts often reflect the usage of names in real life circumstances. By looking in from the outside, diachronically as well as synchronically, at the names and naming contexts of varied cultures and ethnic groups in recorded documents, we can find ways to understand the social force of personal names not only in terms of how a given culture develops an ideology of personal names, but also in terms of how the naming practices of a given culture illuminate practices of other cultures. Such information can be gathered and stored for use in literary and cultural analysis of personal names throughout textual history into the present. Historical examples may contribute to expanding and deepening contemporary understanding of the force of names in social life and their reflections in literary texts of various cultures. Of especial note is the distinctiveness with which certain past and present cultures treat personal names. Since not every cultural group places the same importance on personal names, the cosmopolitan reader needs to be alert to hints about the particular significance of these names when she reads texts in historically or cultural foreign cultural domain: "Furthermore, this analysis of names within a literary framework would help substantiate the ways in which names and naming shape and influence the lives, thoughts and thinking of a people" (Ndi in *Framing My Name* 22).

Most types of personal names enter social reality through pronunciation; they enter into the dialogue of one of world's various languages, gathering ideological overlays and become oriented within the heteroglossia of those languages. Some names are international in carrying power and are situated more widely within the polyglossia of many languages. There has existed, however, since ancient times one name which long since has ceased to be pronounced out of reverence and respect: It is called by its Greek designation, the *tetragrammaton*, a sequence of four Hebrew letters, *Yod, He, Waw, He*, that religious Jews do not articulate and the articulation of which can only be supposed at this point in history *(The Jewish Encyclopedia)*. This sequence of Hebrew letters pictures rather than suggests a pronunciation for the name of the Judeo-Christian God. The letters can be written, and often are, but their original sound is a matter of broad academic speculation. This name has been one of greatest social force, uniting or dividing millions of humans all over the globe, but its authentic sound has not been heard in any human dialogue since Antiquity. This name is unique in that it is a visual symbol only rather than a sound symbol as well as a visual sign. All other names which will be discussed are dialogically oriented in language: The *tetragrammaton* is uniquely silent. Perhaps the refusal to sound this name is an indication of a belief that this name stands before time, outside of time and before human dialogue existed, for there were no names, no dialogue, before creation and time began.

Names and naming, both generic and personal at the beginning of time, were a preoccupation in two significant ancient Near Eastern creation narratives, the Babylonian *Enuma Elish* and the Hebrew *Genesis*. First, in the philologically complex and dense Babylonian poem, *Enuma Elish*, from the later second millennium of the Bronze Age, the world evolves from primeval chaos into a naturally and politically ordered construction through the birth of gods, humans and the rise of their ultimate overlord, Marduk (Foster 436-38). The poet focuses on names and naming so that the narrative opens with an explicit statement that in the beginning there were no gods with names and the ending of the poem is capped distinctively with an elaborate rehearsal and detailed explanation of fifty divine, power names of the Babylon's supreme god:

> When on high <u>no name</u> was given to heaven,
> nor below was the netherworld called <u>by name</u>....
> When no gods had been brought forth,
> Nor <u>called by names,</u> none destines ordained....
> (Tablet I, 1-2, 6-7; Foster's translation in *Before The Muses*, with my emphasis added)

Clearly, the poet in the introduction of this cosmogonic narrative, associates a god's creation, existence and destiny in and of themselves with having a name: "The poet evidently considers naming an act of creation.... For the poet, the name, properly understood, discloses the significance of the created thing" (Foster 437). Here, a name is not simply a label or reference of identification but necessary for existence. In Bakhtinean terms, the ideological orientation of the primal names of the older gods in the *Enuma Elish* is not metaphorical or symbolic; it is reality that no name indicates no existence. This basic meaning of a name is the most elemental significance that a name can conjure and makes sense for gods within mythological theogonies and still holds true for all individuals before their births. (We will later refer to a weaker, metaphorical or symbolic non-existence when Odysseus gives the Cyclops, Polyphemus, his deceptive pseudonym, *Outis,* meaning no one or nobody, as a trick to disguise his true identity.)

The climax of the *Enuma Elish,* in the latter part of Tablet VI and all of Tablet VII, catalogues fifty power names of Marduk that explicitly express his acts and functions:

> "Let us pronounce his fifty names,

"That his ways shall be (thereby) manifest....
(Tablet VI, 121-122; Foster 472-473)

There follows a running catalogue with a long list of divine names (Marduk, Marukka, Marutukku, Mershakusu, Lugaldimmerankia up to fifty) and explanations of their functions according to Babylonian theological and etymological principles, summarizing Marduk's ultimate supremacy:

The great gods called his fifty names...
they made his position supreme.
(Tablet VII, 143-144; Foster 484)

These fifty names, actually fifty-one, are not labels nor mere assertions of existence as opposed to non-existence as the naming at the beginning of poem had indicated that by having a name, a thing has an existence. The fifty names of Marduk, in distinction to declaring his mere existence, are the confirmation of his superior authority over all living gods and men and the culmination of his narrative of ascendancy over the cosmos. These names, then, are both signs of his status and the instruments of enacting power itself as the explanation of one of his names, Asaluhi, indicates:

Anshar gave him an additional name, Asalluhi.
"When he speaks, we will do obeisance,
"At his command the gods will pay heed.
" His word shall be supreme above and below,
"The son, our champion shall be the highest.
(VI, 100-105; Foster 472-473)

Marduk, signaled by the new name Ashalluhi, has become supreme god, and that name requires all other gods to bow and harken obediently his commands. In the contemporary, post-Christian West, we tend to dismiss the magical power of the reciting of the names of gods as a liturgical practice grounded in the ancient world, but such customs are not yet dead in religions of the world. In the Hindu religion of India, the divine name of Rama is still considered a supernatural force and the names of the monkey god,

Hanumaan, are recited by devotees in forty verses, called *Hanuman Chaalissa*. Divine names enter the linguistic world, carrying the hopes and prayers of the religious faithful who wish to win favor or succor from another dimension beyond the human realm (Pattanayak 69). The recitation of these divine names provides psychological support and social bonding for worshippers,

Second, parallel to the theological explanation of Marduk's cosmological empire in the *Enuma Elsih,* is another theistic justification for cosmic and social order developed in the early Hebrew tradition through its creation narratives in *Genesis*. There, too, naming and names play a significant role in establishing divine order, but additionally, naming opens the possibility of communication between human and God and between human and human. Whereas the *Enuma Elish* stresses naming as coextensive with existence itself and power of the gods, the first creation narrative of *Genesis* suggests naming after creation, *Genesis* 1: 3 and 5: "Dixitque Deus: Fist lux. Appellatque lucem Diem et tenebras Noctem...." Hence, naming the elements follows their creation in preparation for the creation of the human (*Genesis* 1:27) and God's direct communication with his new creature in verse 29, "Dixitque Deus...." Logically, for God to communicate to humankind, He had to have names and labels for the items of the universe. The ideological orientation of all these labels was benign, for the benefit of the human, as we are repeatedly told during the first creation narrative:" Et vidit Deus quod esset bonum."

In the second creation narrative in Chapter 2, a different naming scenario presents itself. Here, the male human, is shown all the animals created by God and granted the discretion of naming these animals himself; man is creating the language of names for communication with God and for the organization of the world around him, *Genesis* 2.29: "Appellavit Adam nominibus suis cuncta animalia...." These names would not have been personal names but the generic nouns by which the animals were labeled and ordered. The first truly personal name which Adam designates is that of his newly created spouse, *Genesis* 2:23. Adam gives a significant name to this spouse, a name which reveals her origin as "de viro sumpta est," taken from the man. In Latin, this word is *Virago*, to us known as Eve. The ideological orientation of this Adamic naming is practical, functional and focused on clear communication with God and his fellow human being. Since there would be only one language at the beginning of time and few communicators, active layering of ideology onto names would be minimal, a unique situation for names in human history. Adam, whether the first man or emblem of the inception of humankind, starts the process of naming in the human realm that ultimately "...plays a significant role in distinguishing as well as binding together objects, individuals, communities and cultures" (Pattanayak 70). What develops later grows from very elemental naming and basic communication into more textured and diverse interplay of ideological systems.

The ancient Near East locates not only the first stories of creation and naming, but the first rulers who wanted their names memorialized for future generations and thus devised methods of preserving their names for posterity. From the Bronze Age onward, there was a custom of building the names of Mesopotamian rulers, stamped on baked bricks or cones, into the foundations and walls of temples. The ruler's name quite literally became a part of the building and would be preserved, although typically not seen, for the life of the structure. The purpose of these foundation and wall bricks and cones was to secure immortality for the named ruler who was dedicating the building (Hayes 51-58). It is, indeed, notable that a name could be thought of as a physical object whose efficacy transcended the immediately visual display such as that of a statue or monumental inscription. The following is one simple example of an inscriptional foundation tablet from a construction of king Ur-Nammu, carved on stone and buried in the foundations of a temple of Enlil in Ur. Here is the text of the highly formulaic inscription:

> Ur-Nammu,
>   king of Ur,
>   king of Sumer and Akkad,
>   the man who built the temple of Enlil.
> (Hayes 105)

The ideology of celebratory immortality informs the purpose of writing down Ur-Nammu's name on stone and, thus, the name becomes not a symbolic memory but a literal object meant to be dug up at a later time of reconstruction or repair, to be touched as well as read for recollection. "Building inscriptions in general were not designed to be read by the builder's contemporaries; rather, they were designed to be read by future rebuilders of the building, who would most likely be kings themselves. Ultimately, these buildings and their inscriptions can be thought of as attempts by the rulers to attain immortality" (Hayes 52). This immortality was seen as the immorality of a stone or clay object, not just a recollection in words.

Homeric kings and heroes shared with the Near Eastern counterparts a desire for fame of their names, but they relied more on memorialization in songs of poets. In Book IX of the *Odyssey*, Odysseus narrates his encounter with Cyclops in which the details of Polyphemus' reception of Odysseus, his cannibalistic feast and grotesque guest-gift, his proposal to eat Odysseus last of all, constitutes a dramatic parody of the conventions of *xenia* type scene flavored with an anthrophogetic perversion of the normal reception of guests (Reece 130,137). Naming the guest is a fixed feature of the xenia ritual in Homer, and significantly, the names of Odysseus, embedded in this episode, are crucial elements for not only the narrative of the guest scene but also for further development of his homecoming narrative. Odysseus' ruse of a false name, "Nobody," his boasting declaration of his true name while he sails away from the Cyclops' island, and Polyphemus' curse, effected through pronouncing the hero's name, structure the drama of the guest-reception scene and further motivate the action for the rest of the *Odyssey* as well as represent the social function of names in Homeric society.

The Greek audience of the *Odyssey* has been clearly instructed in the proper manner of guest reception against the backdrop of the education of Telemachus in Books I-IV in which we see Telemachus graciously and hospitably received by Nestor, Book III, and by Menelaus, Book IV. Of particular note is that Odysseus is narrating his own story about Polyphemus at the Phaeacian court where he himself has been courteously welcomed and is being entertained by Alcinous according to appropriate *xenia* form in a sharp counter-example to his previous treatment by Polyphemus and others along his journey homeward. Moreover, the ancient audience knows ahead that Odysseus will shortly return to Ithaca where the hospitality-violating suitors await sure comeuppance from the returning war hero. The parodic features of the Cyclops' grotesque feasting on the raw flesh of Odysseus' men, the offer of the cannibalistic guest gift, to eat Odysseus last, have a uniquely predictive force for the fate of suitors back on Ithaca when linked to the blinding of Polyphemus and the boasting revelation of "famous name," Odysseus. Not only does the Cyclops' scene reinforce the major persistent aspects of Odysseus' character, cleverness and boldness, more precisely, it sets up an audience expectation for how Odysseus will deal ultimately with the suitor violators of hospitality who are wasting his own household. As Odysseus punished the Cyclops for his incivility and by ingenuity escapes from monster's clutches, so he will escape the dangers in his own house and punish the suitors. A detailed analysis of the guest-reception type scene by Steve Reece finds the particular details of the Polyphemus guest reception somewhat different from the most typical hospitality ritual. After the standard **arrival** element (*Odyssey* IX, 182), there is no typical reception or supplication at the door because the Cyclops is not yet home (*Od.* IX, 131). Odysseus and his companions enter the cave and help themselves to cheese while waiting for the Cyclops to return. When Polyphemus does come into the cave and finally sees the Greeks, he **demands their identity** before offering food (*Od.* IX, 250-255), clearly placing the question about a guest's identify out of normal sequence in the hospitality ritual: food first, then identification (Reece 132). When asked for his identity, Odysseus does not offer his name as in a typical guest reception scene but answers with general information and begs, in the name of Zeus, for the rights of guests and suppliants (IX, 259-271). Instead of offering his guests food as required by the laws of hospitality, the Cyclops (239) denies that he has any respect for Zeus, protector of strangers, and immediately eats his own gruesome dinner, smashing the heads of two of Odysseus' companions and devouring them raw: ".... he cut them up limb by limb...ate them entrails, flesh and marrowy bone alike." (Lattimore, *Odyssey*. IX, 291-93). During the next days, the Cyclops feasts on Odysseus' men two more times while Odysseus plots escape and vengeance.

After the Cyclops' third cannibalistic serving, Odysseus, in order to put the ogre to sleep, offers Polyphemus some special wine (*Odyssey,* IX 347-354). At this point, the narrative foregrounds two of the most central and memorable elements of the entire episode. First, Odysseus gives the Cyclops his false name of Nobody: " 'Cyclops, you ask me my famous name.... Nobody is my name. My father and mother call me Nobody...' " (364-367). The irony of the false name dramatizes the importance of true names, in contrast, as a means of knowing the power of the person with whom one is dealing. Certainly, Polyphemus would have been on his guard had he known that Nobody was the hero, Odysseus, rather than an actual nobody. Next, after hearing the name, the Cyclops, in return, offers his (per)version of the requisite *xenion*, the ritual guest-gift given by host to guest: "Then I will eat Nobody after his friends, and the others I will eat first, that shall be my guest gift to you" (369-70). As the scene moves toward its climax, Odysseus acts to save himself and his comrades by blinding the drunken ogre's single eye with fire-hardened, olive stake as the monster howls out in pain for help to his fellow Cyclopes, yelling that "Nobody" is harming him (IX. 408) so that his fellow Cyclopes go away, having been fooled by a false name. This ruse of the name, Nobody, is a memorable scene in Western literature as the human hero defeats anti-human monsters and confirms the essential character of the tricky Odysseus who uses wit as well as heroic brawn to overcome adversity in the face of monstrous savagery.

The next morning, Odysseus and companions escape the Cyclops' cave, clinging to the bellies of sheep. As they depart in their ship, Odysseus boastingly calls out his true name:

> Cyclops, if any mortal man ever asks you who it was
> that inflicted upon your eye this shameful blinding,
> tell him that you were blinded by <u>Odysseus, sacker of cities,</u>
> <u>Laertes is his father, and he makes his home in Ithaca.</u>
> (*Odyssey,* IX, 503-505 with my emphasis)

Odysseus does not offer his name courteously for identification as he might have done in the guest-reception ritual; this naming is a boast of vengeance and an assertion of the heroic stature of

Odysseus as "sacker of cities," punisher of Polyphemus. Aristotle in *Rhetoric* 2, 3, 1380 b 22, opines that Odysseus gives his name since the Greeks did not consider vengeance complete unless the punished party knew who had inflicted the revenge and for what injury (Stanford, 364, note on line 504). Although Odysseus has a very different character from Achilles, he is still a first-rank hero of the Trojan war who lives by the heroic code announced in *Iliad* XI, 784: "to fight always in the forefront and be preeminent above others...." To win and to be known to win constitutes the essential nature of such Iliadic heroes so Odysseus would wish, according to his dominant predisposition, to proclaim his victory with his famous name, *onoma kluton* (*Odyssey* IX, 364), at first disguised as *Outis*, now openly declared as a memorial of his revenge. Here Odysseus' name stands as an emblem of his homecoming mission and foreshadows his vengeance on the suitors as often "[n]ames become a way of telling the world who and what we are, where we stand and where we are heading to" (Ndi in *Framing My Name* 20).

The first two namings of the episode are given by Odysseus as he refers to himself, but the third time Odysseus is named by Polyphemus in order to curse the mortal who wounded him by burning out his eye. The language used for the curse by the Cyclops is formulaic, conforming to the precise formulation a the prayer to Apollo by his priest in *Iliad* I, 36-43, when he calls upon the god to strike the Greeks for refusing to accept the ransom of his daughter. Polyphemus prays to his father, Poseidon, to destroy or, at the least, delay the homecoming of Odysseus:

> Hear me, Poseidon....
> grant that <u>Odysseus, sacker of cities, son of Laertes,</u>
> <u>who makes his home in Ithaca,</u> may never reach that home;
> but if it is decided that he shall see his own people...
> let him come late, in a bad case, with the loss of all his companions....
> (*Odyssey* IX, 528-535 with my emphasis)

Polyphemus provides the *onoma kluton*, the famous name, of Odysseus exactly with the same identifiers that Odysseus has given. Odysseus' name, a surrogate for his person, is used to call down an imprecation that is, in fact, fulfilled by Poseidon as to its second stipulation that Odysseus arrives home, deprived of all of his companions. Odysseus' true name has been changed from a champion's boast to a curse of a shipwrecked sailor. Poseidon's relentless persecution of Odysseus, fulfilling the curse of Polyphemus, motivates the narrative of the hero's homecoming, disguised as a beggar. The boasting name and the cursed name are integral to this narrative movement since both punishment of Polyphemus and Odysseus' survival of the Cyclops' curse have a predictive import for the ultimate punishment of the suitors and the restitution of Odysseus' kingship in Ithaca. As the *Odyssey* concludes, Odysseus has triumphed with the aid of Athena; Zeus intervenes with his thunderbolt to block a final battle between Odysseus and the aggrieved relatives of the slaughtered suitors and so confirms Odysseus's justice and kingship (XXIV, 531-48) as Athena, in the form of Mentor, consolidates a peace pact. Thus, Odysseus is ultimately vindicated with respect to his previous revenge on the Cyclops, despite his subsequent persecution on account of Polyphemus' curse, and finally with respect to his execution of the suitors and renegade serving maids. Odysseus has balanced the scales of justice, restored his home to good order and thus completed his homecoming narrative. Unlike Agamemnon, his life and his name are secure.

    Homeric warriors accept the power of reputation to confer undying glory, but not every warrior is willing to accept the heroic code that invests the name with its power to offer this immortality. In Book VI of the *Iliad*, 119-236, two heroes, Glaukos and Diomedes meet in the space between the Trojan and Greek armies for single combat. One warrior, Diomedes, is already well known to the audience from his *aristeia*, just narrated in the previous battle book, Book V. From the text we can adduce that he was also recognized by his opponent who asks for no information about him. Diomedes, on the other hand, requests from his unknown challenger identification on the pretext that he does not wish to fight against some god, fighting in disguise. The response of Glaukos to Diomedes' query offers Homer the opportunity to introduce one of the *Iliad's* most memorable similes and a pathetic reflection on human mortality. Rather than immediately boasting of his heroic family linage, Glaukos confronts the inevitability of death and powerlessness of any name, even the distinguished name of a heroic family, to ameliorate its extinguishing finality:

> High-hearted son of Tydeus, why ask of my generation?
> As is the generation of leaves, so is that of humanity. The wind scatters the leaves on the ground, but the live timber burgeons with leaves again in the season of spring returning. So one generation of men will grow while another dies. (145-150)

Immediately following this simile, Glaukos recounts his distinguished linage from his great-great Grandfather, Sisyphos to his father Hippolochus. By naming his ancestors in sequential order from Sisyphus, Glaukos, Bellerophontes to Hippolochus, Glaukos confirms the truth of his previous statement that one generation passes and another grows up just like the leaves, thus diminishing his name before the inexorability of death. While part of the simile speaks to the inevitability of human passing, another part relates human life to the insignificance of forest leaves, blown away by seasonal winds, to be replaced by the next spring bloom. Herein lies, I believe, the focal analogy of the simile: Glaukos' list of distinguished ancestors will not prevent his death no more than any of them in their family chain has escaped it. Diomedes, too, is subject to the same end and trivial insignificance before the effacing power of death. With this bold rejection of the glorious immortality through a heroic name, Homer challenges the ethos of the pursuit of glorious victory or death on the battlefield and immortality of reputation. Likewise, Achilles in Hades pathetically remarks to Odysseus, rejecting of the aims and accomplishments of his own life choice of *kleos aphthiton* at *Iliad* IX, 413, unending glory:

> O shining Odysseus, never try to console me for dying.
> I would rather follow the plow as a thrall to another man...
> than to be king over all the perished dead. (*Odyssey*, XI, 488-491)

Glaukos' simile suggests that the ancestral names function effectively for the living only as a reminder of mortality, not a badge of honor or a reason to boast; a name, although highly important in the daily tumble of life, has no ultimate meaning *sub specie aeternitatis*.

Names often add narrative direction, color and tension to literary texts; in other cases, names of characters may serve as a pivotal symbol in a text as does the name, "Faith," in Hawthorne's well-known "Young Goodman Brown". Name as symbol, for example in the case of "Faith" in "Young Goodman Brown," does not require that the essence of the character be the same as the meaning of the character's name but only that the name offer clues to the challenges and tensions in play within the narrative. There is a type of name which goes beyond some symbolic function in the text, beyond a label or identification to the very essence of that character as Ndi suggests that literary "[c]haracter and name are more often than not indissociable" ("The Global Reader and Names"). The Old Babylonian *Gilgamesh* provides a telling example embedded in the structure of the Old Babylonian language itself: "Who is your name?" Gilgamesh my name am I" (Lambert 469). Here, the equivalence of the name and the person suggests a deeper connection of name to character than a mere label or tag of identification.

Likewise, Sophocles, in *Oedipus, the King*, reveals a similar intimate link between Oedipus and his name in the exchange between Oedipus and the messenger from Corinth. As Oedipus discovers finally that he is the "swollen foot" killer of Laius, his true father, from the shepherd who named him, his name and naming coalesce to reveal definitively to himself, in all its horror, who he has been and now is. The Greek text is totally clear on this point: ...*onomasthes...hos ei*. You were named ...<u>who</u> you <u>are</u> (*Oedipus Rex*, 1136). Oedipus' name carries his destiny because, as many names do in various societies, it involves his *ontology*, his naming at birth, his family history and his social position (*Framing My Name* 3). But more, it is who he is at the moment of the revelation and who he has been all along, though all unknowing of the fact. Oedipus' tragic reversal of fortune turns on his name which is exposed, at last, as his doomed essence.

Knowledge of various diachronic uses of names in historical documents and literary texts contributes to a better understanding of names and naming in contemporary cultures around the globe by enhancing overall polyglossic consciousness of the reader. The global reader must deprovincialize herself with an awareness of languages and cultures other than her own since "[o]nly polyglossia totally frees consciousness from the tyranny of its own language and the myth of its own language" (Bakhtin, *Dialogic Imagination* 61). So in the contemporary, flattened global world, names and naming from local cultures and in local texts are polyglossically positioned for appreciation by the global reader who is linguistically aware.

Works Cited

Appiah, Bernard. "African Names: A guide for Editors." *Science Editor* 33.1 (Jan.-Feb. 2010): 15-17. Web. 17 March 2014.

Bakhtin, M.M. *The Dialogic Imagination*. Trans. Caryl Emerson and Michael Holquist. Austin: U of Texas P, 1981. Print.

_____. *Speech Genres and other Late Essays*. Trans.Vern W. McGee. Austin: U of Texas P, 1986. Print.

Biblia Sacra. Print. *Clementina Vulgata*.

Foster, Benjamin R. *Before the Muses: An Anthology of Akkadian Literature*. 3rd ed. Bethesda: CDL Press, 2005. Print.

Hayes, John N. *A Manual of Sumerian Grammar and Tests*. 2nd ed. Malibu: Udina Publications, 2000. Print.

Homer, *The Iliad of Homer*. Trans. Richmond Lattimore. Chicago: U. of Chicago P, 1951. Print

Homer, *The Odyssey of Homer*. Trans. Richmond Lattimore. New York: Harper and Row, 1965. Print.

Homer, *The Odyssey of Homer*. Ed. W.B. Stanford. Vol. I. London: St. Martin Press, 1959. Print.

Kumar, Margaret, Pattanayak, Supriya, and Johnson, Richard. (Eds.) *Framing My Name: Extending Educational Boundaries*. Champaign IL.: Common Ground, 2010. Print.

Ndi, Bill F. "Names, the envelopes of destiny in the Grasslands of Cameroon." Kumar, Pattanayak and Johnson. (Eds.) *Framing My Name: Extending Educational Boundaries*. Champaign IL.: Common Ground, 2010. Print. 19-30.

_____. "The Global Reader and Names in literary Works by Vakunta, Ndi and Doh."

Lambert, W.G. *Babylonian Creation Myths*. Winona Lake: Eisenbrauns, 2013. Print.

Pattanayak, Debi. "Establishing the Space of Naming." in Kumar, Pattanayak and Johnson (Eds.) *Framing My Name: Extending Educational Boundaries*. Champaign IL.: Common Ground, 2010. Print.61-71.

Sophocles. *OT. Sophoclis Fabulae*. Ed. A.C. Pearson. New York: Oxford U P, 1924. Print.

"Tetragrammaton." *The Jewish Encyclopedia*. 1901-1906. Web. 20 March, 2014.

Chapter Two

Liquid Realities: Romantic Transience and the Use of Names in Emmanuel Fru Doh

By
Antonio Jimenez-Munoz

Western cultural traditions from Socrates to Ferdinand de Saussure have conceived the implicit but arbitrary relation between referents in the real world and the words we use to name them. The act of naming is seen as inextricably linked so that the name and the reality it represents are hard-coded into the use of the language by a community. Philosophers tend to stress the fact that only context can elucidate reference and the arbitrary nature of names, although at the same time they highlight the importance of realizing that names act as reference to themselves. For theorists, such as Gottlob Frege, a language can only mean if its nouns are taken as something stable, so that "the rising sun is not new every morning" but the word *sun* also expresses a relation "of a thing to itself, and indeed one in which each thing stands to itself but to no other thing" (56). It was only in the latter part of the last century that pragmatists, such as John Searle, stressed the fact that names can be used more flexibly as tokens of such relations between speakers, so that "anyone who uses a proper name must be prepared to substitute an identifying description" (168). These views contrast a monadic conception of naming as strong identification with a referent with the use of that term by a given individual. Other theorists like Saul Kripke have laid emphasis on the act of naming itself. They consider naming as a ceremony that fixes the reference of a proper name by ostension i.e. an act or process of showing, pointing out, or exhibiting. According to Kripke, a name and its referent are "not, in any intuitive sense of necessity, a necessary truth" (74), despite being used as such by a community of individuals. Even within social larger contexts, names can always mean anything else for individuals who decide so or have such an intention.[1]

There are two different conceptions of meaning at work here. The first and more rigid one conceives meaning as a link between a name and its referent (meaning as significance). In other words, names mean by pointing at particular, fixed realities in the case of simple proper names, and unique realities in the case of proper names. Names thus can mean because their nature as references is fixed for the users of a language, so that, for example, a banana always points to a certain type of fruit. The second view accepts that language can be used more flexibly; meaning can also be conceived as the use people make of linguistic signs not to point at a given reality, but to interpret anything real. This view highlights meaning as making sense. In the case of proper names, these would "have meaning only in an extremely minimal sense—one in which different names have nearly the same meaning, no matter what they refer to" (Soames 56). This would entail that names not only point at a given reality, but also that they become meaningless per se. Words, and literature to an extent, would become void of meaning as works of art would be self-enclosed in their own autotelic signification. In such a case, neither a poem nor its referents would mean anything outside the poem for a reader other than the author himself or herself.

That quintessential lack of meaning is not congruent with the use of names in any context, whether literary or not. Richard Rorty argues that Continental pragmatists, in their attempt to move away but not break with the philosophical tradition, have "lumped real problems together with pseudo-problems" (xvii), issues which are "problems arising in connection with language" (130) rather than real-life difficulties. These are problems for a metaphysical ideology which "arose in the context of the seventeenth century image of the mind as a Mirror of Nature, and of skeptical problems about testing the accuracy of representations of this Mirror" (334).

---

[1] Searle would later narrow down that "intentional content associated with a proper name can figure as part of the propositional content of a statement made by a speaker using that name, even though the speaker's associated Intentional content is not part of the definition of the name" (*Intentionality*, 256).

This deterministic view of language and literature must be resisted. Art, we must re-emphasize, does not necessarily mirror nature. Its use as a social means of communication facilitates a connection which is as meaningful as gleefully partial. Therefore, a poem becomes the place where meanings are exchanged but also negotiated. In this negotiation, however, when poets use a name they are more than pointing to a referent, be it a person, place or thing; they signal as much as they qualify, oppose or define these entities according to context. I would like to call the attention to how highly synchronic these distinctions above are, as they revolve about names as pertaining to a particular place and moment. When transposing these Western tensions between language and reality to other parts of the world, such as Africa, this arbitrary relation between words and referents is complicated by social and cultural factors. Debra Walker King has noted that some African parents still decide waiting up to a month, or until the newborn chances of survival increase, to name their offspring (54). However, some uses of names are more diachronic. For instance, the ancient West African tradition of renewal by giving a child the name of a deceased relative to mark and celebrate the returning to their spirit to a new body can be but one example where names transcend the here and now. Names in African culture can be seen as a "shorthand for a wealth of discourses" (56) which varies from family history to resistance to oppression.

Some commentators, such as Herbert Gutman, readily link naming to resisting oppression (192). Others like Sharon Bernhardt stress aspects of identity, in the sense that "when one bestows a name upon a child that person is not simply naming the flesh of the child, but rather the name is for the person's soul" (7), a spiritual interpretation which is often said to be extended to animals, rivers and objects. It must be noted that this anthropological emphasis on a narrative of domination, to read African names as either a record of resistance to European oppression or the expression of identity, does a great disservice to African literature, and particularly to that written in English. Some poetic practice would also go straightforwardly in this folkloric vein of identity or denounce oppression, but other African poets such as Peter W. Vakunta are more poignant as they complicate this relation between name and identity. In the aptly titled poem "Identity Crisis," he unearths structures of power present in naming which are unable to repress the longing to exist beyond whatever name one has or is given:

> I don't quite know who I am.
> Some call me Frog
> I still don't know who I am
> My name is the Bamenda Man;
> My name is Enemy in the House.
> My name is the Biafran;
> My name is underclass citizen;
> My name is the black sheep of the family.
> Shut up!
> Don't bother me!
> Don't you know that I am at home here?
> You forget that I was born here.
> I shall fight to my last breath,
> To forge a real name for myself. (*Straddling the Mungo* 3)

That *real name* Vakunta yearns for is not one to be bestowed upon him, but one to be won by action. In other poems, such as "Bushmen," Vakunta would insist on the irrelevance of names for those at peace with themselves: "What's in a name? [...] Jab, I am a bushman, / living in communion with nature" (*Green Rape*, 41). This aspect of African naming as something not given by birth but something to be lived through is often overlooked, as nouns are not tied to a particular bestowing ceremony but reveal relevant aspects of the life of those who bear them. Also, as Vakunta shows in these poems, identity is not affected by naming; the distinction between that self-proclaimed name and those other external names assigned to the self is seen as uncomplicated. This is no case, as defined by Ian Hacking, of "dynamic nominalism" as the interplay of identitarian names and "our invention of the categories labelling them" (106) as identity and external naming/renaming go their separate routes. Similarly, interpreting Anglophone African authors as able to "subvert and refashion English in the attempt to express themselves authentically" (Booth 66) tells only one aspect of what is achieved by that subversion. For most African authors, Ngugi wa

Thiong'o writes, identity is reflected into language as a set of values which "are the basis of a people's identity" and language becomes culture, acting as

> the collective memory bank of a people's experience in history. Culture is almost indistinguishable from the language that makes possible its genesis, growth, banking, articulation and indeed its transmission from one generation to the next (14-15).

Language, for most African authors at home and in the diaspora, is part of a rich tapestry which exposes history, experience and legacy; the literary work is "a place where names create streams of metaphoric, metonymic, allegorical, and other meanings that avail themselves of multiple interpretive possibilities" (King 1), but that conception does not need to be reductive, as language can also be independent from life. As Emmanuel Fru Doh exemplifies, diction and language cannot rule over thought, feeling or character; even an altogether foreign language cannot prevent communication of powerfully felt ideas:

> Then there was Ferdinand Oyono of Napoleonic
> Tongue twisted into Elizabethan diction
> For us to understand, alas another African to us,
> Like the rest, had to speak in a tongue of the 'care
> Even with Kiswahili that could have been taught us
> Or Lingala the language of rhythms, this pain
> In the side of my identity (*Oriki'badan* 37)

This separation between word and message, which may seem anecdotal in the lines above, is but an indication that names and language can function outside the scope of Western determinism. In Doh's poetry, the pervasive use of names and careful precisions about naming acts serve the function of what Charles Mauron termed "métaphores obsédantes" (25) as obsessive, inadvertent metaphors which are consistently repeated in his writing. Exploring the various functions of such use of names in Doh's poetry and essays would help give homogeneity to his wide-ranging work.

Likewise, analyzing names and their contexts of appearance reveals a wealth of significations with illuminating implications towards the aesthetic interpretation of his poetry, as names in Doh are consistently linked to acts of remembering which highlight the difference between nouns and referents. Connecting these ideas to concrete passages helps unearth his distinct conception of what a name entails, particularly when contrasted with poetic tradition in English.

I have already made a case for modern poetry in English, which includes Doh's, to be interpreted as a legacy of Romanticism (35-37), but this does not mean that Romanticism exhausts all poetic possibilities for future poets. Romantic poets show tension between naming as representation paradigmatically. Critics like Frances Ferguson have pointed out how Wordsworth's "Lucy" poems "figure in little a variety of problems about poetic representation and naming" (532-533). However, Romanticism also establishes the inception of that representation in the self of the poet. As such, the act of naming becomes the act of creation, in which the poet is, in Aristotelian terms, "sowing around a god-centered flame" (151). For Coleridge, naming also becomes interpreting, so that as subjects name something, they also shape reality to an emotion:

> (And so, poor wretch! filled all things with himself,
> And made all gentle sounds tell back the tale
> Of his own sorrow) he, and such as he,
> First named these notes a melancholy strain.
> ("The Nightingale" 16-22)

Romantic poems have a strong sense of place – whether real or imaginative – and can be seen as "inscriptions" in which "any verse [is] conscious of the place in which [it] is written" as Hartman wrote (311). But the emphasis is not mimetic. Heidegger already acknowledged that one of the key aspects of the Romantic shift is that, since it occurred, artistic expression "attempts once again a transfiguration of beings, which as reacting against the thorough explaining and calculating strives only to evolve beyond or next to this explaining and calculating" (349). This troping of reality is not as much aesthetic as it is epistemological; Hartman notes that "when fugitive feelings are taken seriously [...] then the Romantic nature lyric is born" (40). Much of this transfiguration of nature is done, as these examples above show, through names and naming. This Romantic trait, as Paul Sheats noted, is key to understanding how Romanticism looked for deliberate engagement with readers, giving them what they were meant to covet: "Even as the poet concedes what this landscape lacks, he names what the reader desires: a conventionally picturesque landscape that is humanized by man or by the diminutive society of Virgilian bees" (155). This aspect of naming also has another side: naming also entails the figurative possession of the named. Analysing Wordsworth's "Tintern Abbey," Carol Bolton notes how the poet "can then take imaginative possession of [nature] by naming" (154) in a way that the real is not only represented but also appropriated through naming. However, in the context of the poem this appropriation has a tendency to verisimilitude, so that fictional and actual appropriation may cohere, as Wordsworth's final lines in "To Joanna" attest:

> Beneath this rock, at sunrise, on a calm
> And silent morning, I sat down, and there,
> In memory of affections old and true,
> I chiseled out in those rude characters
> Joanna's name deep in the living stone:
> And I, and all who dwell by my fireside,
> Have called the lovely rock, JOANNA'S ROCK. (79-85)

When contrasting this Romantic use of naming to Doh, these emphases on representation through naming, of transfiguration of the real seems not to be at work. However meditative his verse can be, it would be wrong to think of him as a poet of appropriation and self-referentiality. Instead, it is easier to notice, as mentioned above, the importance of naming as a transhistorical act which invigorates the soul of this poet, as birth perpetuates a lineage and connects newborns to their past, as in "Dicots":

> This new red feather
> Crowning my black skullcap.

> You made me come alive
> Like the festive drums during naming,
> And how we yearned for your
> Knock on the door of life,
> How we longed the screams
> Of arrival to savour (sic). (*Shadows* 52)

However, this more anthropological vein cannot occlude the fact that the poet is also reflexive about the loss of traditions. In "Of Changing Tides," the poet laments that the "tam-tams" are "no more at namings / welcoming and celebrating babies" (*Shadows* 6). In that sense, Doh is not merely transmitting the past, as he does not only convey cultural concepts but also qualify them actively. In naming, he does not only present a reality, but also mediates that representation through a subjective filter. He reflects in the sense of mirroring the real, but he also reflects in the sense of thinking calmly. This may seem deceptively common in poetry, but it must be remarked that most poets in the Romantic vein add a third aspect to that double reflection, that of reflection about poetry so that the poem becomes increasingly self-referential. Decidedly, Doh avoids this and manages to stay focused on a kind of poetry which is intrinsically narrative yet powerfully subjective. Not only most of his poems in *Wading the Tide* (1995), *Not Yet Damascus* (2007), and *Shadows* (2011) revolve around the telling and comment of personal/national experiences, but also *Oriki'badan* (2009) shows that Doh's life is central to his work. This is not only particular, but the consistent treatment of his subjects through a self-focalized voice. Rarely does he try to present a third party to convey his thoughts. Also, he uses simile when he can present facts through his experience and opinions.

The result is that his poetry extols a direct, undoubted honesty since we read his mind at work and, unlike the Romantic and the Postmodern, at no point *about* his process of thinking. In naming reality, Doh engages in an active process of remembering which contrasts with what Joseph Viscomi calls the "vacant mind" (46) of Romantic poets in relation with their surroundings. Doh is largely meditative, but he rarely engages in the "astonishment," "high delight" or "blessed mood" of a Wordsworth (31). Contrarily, his mind is never quiet and does not yearn for the "tranquil restoration" of oneself with nature, so that "with an eye made quiet by the power / Of harmony and the deep power of joy, / We see into the life of things" (38). At the same time there is a sense, however, that most of Doh's sublime or transcendental moments are not personal but communal. He shares his experience with the adamant intention to improve the minds of the nation (particularly in tune with his more political texts). In this fashion, an African experience of connection to the past through naming reveals more than the sense of union and community that Edmund Burke associated with the meaningfully beautiful. Doh's emphasis chiefly ignores self-perpetuation, the instincts Burke associates with the sublime, but replaces that with the communal perpetuation of a nation troubled by political, linguistic and cultural ailments. Doh names reality and he is not, as Wordsworth would in "Expostulation and Reply," listening passively to "the mighty sum / Of things for ever speaking" (25); instead, he actively criticizes those selfish attitudes which value the personal over the communal, as in "Strange Treasures":

> How now we treasure the wrong things,
> How now we celebrate mediocrity like fawning curs,
> Singing panegyrics in acknowledgment of marauders
> Of our nation's coffers;
> Carting car-loads of bleating sheep and goats at dusk
> To the kitchen of ogres distributing national thrones
> That amongst the chosen our names may be announced
> To man a position of power. (*Shadows* 40)

The linking of names to personal identity can be misinterpreted in the longing for permanence. In "Losing Track," Doh makes known how Cameroonians and most Africans are "like orangutans acclimatizing to new names / And associations, forgetting our roots" (Shadows 26), but Doh is more interested in this communal identity as the stepping stone for a better national future. His often harsh critique names atrocities, calls names, and uses naming to unearth realities, but I would like to call attention on his more poignant act of focussing on the naming of people and collectives as a way of transience. Where Romantic poetry and theory aim to inscribe a name into nature and thus identifies both, Doh seems to precisely do the opposite: to highlight its arbitrariness by reflecting how that given name is subject to change, and in doing so he deviates from poetic tradition in the sense that he dissociates name from identity quite explicitly. In Doh's *Oriki'badan*, which chronicles his education, the poet remembers people and he signals this essential difference between names and identity explicitly. He recalls details about "that lady typist whose name I never knew" or lecturers whose "nicknames as the sessions came and went" (11); he uses general references like "that Phonology lady […] as her name / Is lost in my crammed cranium tortured by time" but overtly compensates that forgetfulness with "But I remember her, as intelligent as she was beautiful" (12).

However, Doh increasingly shows that his conception of personal and attributed names is flexible, and that this allows for names to inscribe the self into tradition, but only in cases when such is deserved. When referring to his former teacher Isidore Okpewho, whom he calls "Bàbá" and "High Priest," he signals how his presence points to a lineage:

> This High Priest radiated confidence, and
> Traditional sophistication in all that he said
> And did. He took life with a certain ease
> As if to the pantheon itself he belonged,
> Obatala's son especially forged to keep his name
> And those of minor deities and distinguished heroes
> Resonating. (*Oriki'badan* 22)

It is not only that, as in earlier works such as "Birth Tidings," a name given to a newborn "guarantees continuity / Of the family name, of the clan /Of our people" (*Not Yet Damascus* 49), that a certain name be "Conveying calls to the cadaverous lips / Of my ancestors" or that, as in "The Traveller's invocation" the name "resound[s] in women's songs" and "The thanksgiving of people feted in your name" (*Not Yet Damascus* 34) but also something which is transitional as Doh gives examples of changes in naming which are independent from those changes of the self. Historical and personal evolution become identity; his concept of personal, communal or cultural character is in constant flux, which names reflect but do neither comprehend nor reduce. In a poem such as "Even Before Purgatorio," names can be translated into their literal meanings, or even their social functions, but these and the truth about them remain separated. In the poem, Doh shows how names and actions can be ironically deceptive, for someone who goes by a name with the meaning of love can hate ruthlessly, and someone with a pious name can be devastatingly evil:

> My name itself means love
> And you woman, nominally Zachariah's,
> [...]
> By the cross-roads, nocturnal palates you pacify,
> Chthonic queen, commanding hellish legions
> Bidding them destroy the innocent, destroy
> The weak—those who failed your ravenous
> Cash-palate—imposing curses, inflicting pain,
> Torturing God's innocent.
> [...]
> Now the master speaketh, the rhythm of divine
> Justice yours to dance to, right here on earth.
> Even before *purgatorio*, God's mercy.
> [...]
> Repent now woman even as the blows are
> Beginning to fall from my shepherd's sceptre. (*Shadows* 24)

In Doh, consequently, transient representations of identity become the place for social commentary and not what Andrew Bennet sees as a central Romantic trait, to "celebrate the momentary, the ephemeral, for its own sake, precisely for its transience [...and...] the fascination with the quotidian and ephemeral" (70). Doh's quotidian is despicable. In poems such as "This Rush Palaver," he criticizes recent attitudes heavily, doing so not by simple nominalization, but by the juxtaposition of the culturally-charged "palaver" with "Danfu" or "Moluwe," particularly also in contrast with a much more familiarly reduplicating "rush-rush":

> My people rush as if late
> Only to sit and wait like others.
> It is now our second name;
> See how they treat us…
> *Oya* slow down and enjoy life.
> Leave early to be on time;
> This rush-rush! (*Shadows* 18)

This constant mutability of names points to the liquid reality of identity and selves in modern societies, particularly those in turmoil: names change as do factions and mutability of opinion. Names are external demarcators, which for Doh cannot obstruct the truth. Otherwise stable pan-African referents such as Wole Soyinka can go, in people's minds, through all possible states, "as he is accorded all kinds of names, from hero / Through traitor, to teacher" (*Oriki'badan* 32), and yet with his word being able to turn "the Nile into blood, summoning toads into / The palace, all to free his people from bondage" (*Oriki'badan* 33). Going beyond nominalisms, Doh does not only apprehend names as a reflection of an inner soul, but also as the key element in acts of remembrance, in the creation of artificial realities and the performance of often unfair actions in the name of others. A name is, ultimately for Doh, a liquid, a passing state of affairs, rather than something hard and stable per se; it means little to nothing. A name signals a given reality at a given time, but one which is both arbitrary and subsequently subject to rapid change, even in the case of humans and what goes by their names.

Ultimately, Doh does not cast representation as problematic, but he reveals himself as a moralist who shows the fallacy of naming as the creation of a forged reality. In his poems, names and deeds aptly go their separate ways to stress the fundamental lack of logic of the real: names belong to the narrative and do not mean nor make sense. The only way to reflect the maddening truth of a country laden with such political and social difficulties is going beyond the smoke and mirrors of naming. He does so in order to establish a discourse with a chance of becoming relevant to his people, but in doing so he also goes beyond aesthetic conventions home and away. Avoiding preconceptions in the interpretation of his work is paramount to avoid that his forest of meaning be not seen for his trees of names.

Works Cited

Aristotle. *Poetics*. Sherbrooke: McGill-Queen's Press, 1997. Print.

Bennet, Andrew. *Romantic Poets and the Culture of Posterity*. Cambridge: Cambridge U. P., 1999. Print.

Bernhardt, Sharon. *African Names: Reclaim Your Heritage*. Cape Town: Random House Struik, 2001. Print.

Bolton, Carol. "Taking Possession: Romantic Naming in Wordsworth and Southey." in *Silence, Sublimity, and Suppression in the Romantic Period* Eds. Fiona L. Price and Scott Masson.. Lewiston: Edwin Mellen, 2002. 149-168. Print.

Booth, James. *Writers and politics in Nigeria*. New York: Africana, 1981. Print.

Derrida, Jacques. *Margins of Philosophy*. Chicago: Chicago UP., 1982. Print.

Doh, Emmanuel Fru. *Shadows*. Bamenda: Langaa RPCIG, 2011. Print.

_____. *Not Yet Damascus*. Bamenda: Laanga RPCIG, 2007. Print.

_____. *Green Rape: Poetry for the Environment*. Bamenda: Langaa RPCIG, 2008. Print.

_____. *Wading the Tide*. Bamenda: Patron, 1995. Print.

_____. *Oriki'badan*. Bamenda: Laanga RPCIG, 2009. Print.

Ferguson, Frances C. "The Lucy Poems: Wordsworth's Quest for a Poetic Object." *English Literary History* 40.1 (1973): 532-548. Print.

Frege, Gottlob. *Philosophical Writings*. Oxford: Blackwell, 1952. Print.

Gutman, Herbert G. *The Black Family in Slavery and Freedom, 1750–1925*. New York: Vintage, 1976. Print.

Hacking, Ian. *Historical Ontology*. Cambridge: Harvard UP., 2004. Print.

Hartman, Geoffrey. *Beyond Formalism: Literary Essays 1958-70*. New Haven: Yale UP., 1970. Print.

Heidegger, Martin. *Contributions to Philosophy (From Enowning)*. Bloomington: Indiana UP., 1999. Print.

Jimenez-Munoz, Antonio. "In Moments Like These: Emmanuel Fru Doh and the Mirrors of Romanticism." in *Fears, Doubts and Joys of Not Belonging* Eds. Adaku T. Ankumah, , Benjamin H. Fishkin, and Bill F. Ndi, . Bamenda: Langaa RPCIG, 2013. 31-54. Print.

King, Debra W. *Deep Talk: Reading African-American Literary Names*. Charlottesville: Virginia UP., 1998. Print.

Kripke, Saul. *Naming and Necessity*. Cambridge: Harvard UP., 1980. Print.

Mauron, Charles. *Des Métaphores obsédantes au Mythe personnel. Introduction à la Psychocritique*. Paris: Corti, 1962. Print.

Rorty, Richard. *Consequences of Pragmatism: Essays, 1972-1980*. Minneapolis: Minnesota UP., 1982. Print.

Searle, John R. *Speech Acts: An Essay in the Philosophy of Language*. Cambridge: Cambridge UP., 1969. Print.

_____. *Intentionality: An Essay in the Philosophy of Mind*. Cambridge: Cambridge UP., 1983. Print.

Sheats, Paul D. *The Making of Wordsworth's Poetry, 1785-1798*. Cambridge: Harvard UP., 1973. Print.

Soames, Scott. *Beyond Rigidity: The Unfinished Semantic Agenda of Naming and Necessity*. Oxford: Oxford UP., 2001. Print.

Thiong'o, Ngugi wa. *Decolonising the Mind: the Politics of Language in African Literature*. Nairobi: East African Publishers, 1986. Print.

Vakunta, Peter W. *Straddling the Mungo: A Book of Poems in English and French*. Bamenda: Langaa RPCIG, 2009. Print.

Viscomi, Joseph. "Wordsworth, Gilpin, and the Vacant Mind." *Wordsworth Circle* 38.1/2 (2007): 40-49. Print.

Chapter Three

Colonial Violence and Postcolonial Amnesia: A Reading of Michelle Cliff's *Abeng*

By
Blossom Fondo

Introduction

The relationship between style and content has been well established in literary analysis. Although writers may basically be considered as story-tellers, they fulfill this role through the use of language arranged in a specific stylistic manner and this is what is referred to as style. Most often, a writer's message, viewpoint or vision can only be arrived at through a careful and studied analysis of his/her style. Thus Gregory Currie in *The Nature of Fiction* explains that "style is so very important in fiction. It is not just a matter of literary elegance, it is a matter of the very identity of the fictional story itself. Style and content are thus not independent features of a fictional work" (123). The style, therefore, serves as the port of entry into the author's vision and explains why they have to be treated together. It is generally the interplay between style and content that delivers meaning in a work of art. Peter Barry in *Beginning Theory* has thus advised that "form and content in literature must be fused in an organic way, so that the one grows inevitably from the other. Literary form should not be like a decoration which is applied externally to a completed structure" (19).

This chapter is interested in the ways in which Jamaican writer Michelle Cliff in *Abeng* engages a specific stylistic device in communicating the content of the novel. Although the title of the paper suggests that it would handle the interplay between colonial violence and postcolonial amnesia, it will do this through an engagement with the writer's use of naming or the onomastic device and the related charactonym. Writers of fiction have been using names of characters metaphorically and symbolically for as long as fiction has existed. Sometimes, as this chapter shall illustrate, it is through the names of characters that a reader might gain insight into the author's message. One of the ways the subject of colonial violence and its effects is beautifully crafted in this novel is through the author's use of naming.

The colonial enterprise, whether it involved physical brutality or mental enslavement, was a violent process insofar as violence is not always physical. Most often, the symbolic violence of colonialism proved to be of a similar magnitude and impact as the physical violence, and in a general sense, physical violence is always backed by symbolic violence in the way of harmful ideologies, philosophies, and attitudes. The profundity of the symbolic violence that often accompanied the physical violence can be best appreciated in the case of formerly colonized societies which, many decades after attaining political independence, are still to declare *uhuru* for their cultures. Although subtle and most often invisible, symbolic violence is as real and harmful as any other form of violence (Duckworth 42).

However, this is not to diminish the extent of the physical violence that characterized colonialism. This is especially true of former slave societies whose colonization also involved their forceful physical uprooting under the most horrific conditions and implantation in an alien and alienating land. Rather it argues that underneath this gruesome physical violence was the more insidious mental, cultural as well as symbolic violence perpetrated by such colonial institutions as the school and the church. Thus for these slaves, victims of European capitalistic greed, the violence they experienced was total, where the physical violence subjugated the body and the symbolic violence imprisoned the soul. The physical violence of slavery literally dehumanized people, and the psychological violence led to the acceptance of an inferior status, the imbibing of Eurocentric distortions about their names, cultures, past and subsequently rendering the colonized not only physically displaced from their original homes but worse of all occupying a cultural no-man's-land.

Thus it was a collusion of these different forms of violence that resulted in the postcolonial condition of amnesia[2], of living "without a history," without a clear sense of the past. Fabian Klose quotes Michael Mann who characterizes "colonial rule as a reign of terror for the subjugated population" (92). This reign of terror was without doubt created by the excessive violence of colonialism. Toyin Falola in's *Colonialism and Violence in Nigeria* has defined violence as "the use of force to maintain control; and the use of humiliating words to generate violent reactions" (ix). This definition of violence highlights its most basic elements, but sometimes and especially in the colonial context, the use of force did not constitute the only form assumed by violence. Thus the idea of colonial violence is more encompassing as it brings together the various practices of the colonizers that negatively impacted the colonizers both physically and mentally. In this regard, Tirop Simatei's definition of colonial violence provides the perspective from which the subject will be approached. In his article "Colonial Violence, Postcolonial Violations: Violence, Landscape, and Memory in Kenyan Fiction," he stipulates that "colonial violence will here be understood to mean relationships, processes, and conditions that attended the practice of colonialism [...] and that violated the physical, social, and/or psychological integrity of the colonized" (85).

Michelle Cliff in her debut novel *Abeng*, shows the ways in which the slave trade, slavery and colonialism constituted gross acts of violence which seriously affected the colonized. Through her main character Clare Savage, Cliff exposes both this savagery of colonialism and the devastating effects on the psyche of the colonized. Clare becomes an embodiment of the action and consequences of this unfortunate encounter.

In handling these issues, Cliff uses a beauty of style which engages the use of the onomastics device. Onomastics is generally viewed as the study of the history and origin of people and place names. Within literary studies, this is more specifically referred to as

---

[2] Nigerian author Chinua Achebe has noted that the decades the European rule had an amnesic effect on Africa. He adds that the Europeans swept the Africans "out of the current of their history into somebody else's history." This has been the tendency of the hegemonic colonial system the world over.

literary onomastics and refers to the study of names in literary productions. The *Online Dictionary of Language Terminology* defines literary onomastics as "the sub discipline of onomastics that studies the use of proper names in literature. In particular, it focuses on the names of characters in fiction." Furthermore, Kyallo Wadi Wamitila in "What's in a Name?" intimates the following:

> In reading creative works, we tend to identify characters basically by the names given to them. It is on this basic premise that some character analysis methods tend to define characters by taking recourse to their names and sometimes identifying them in metaphorical terms or as speaking names. Names play a very central and important role in any exercise and so would certainly the names given to characters be of importance to us. (35)

Wamitila's view here underlines the idea that very often an author may name a character for a specific purpose. This finds confirmation in Cliff's use of names in *Abeng*.

In an interview with Schwarz, Cliff underlines that naming her protagonist Clare Savage was not merely to indicate her light skin (Clare being an anglicized form of the French Clair, meaning light complexioned); rather it was to show that hers is a "mind bleached of the past" through the savagery of colonialism and its various institutions. Thus Wamitila quotes Nesseroth who notes that "it is not surprising that theorists pay so much attention to naming in fiction since proper names are the nodal points through which actions and descriptions are interconnected" (qtd. in Wamitila 35).

This chapter intends to examine these aspects of colonialism as expressed in *Abeng* through the character of Clare Savage. Clare, according to this reading, is an incarnation of the violence of colonialism which resulted in the obliteration and occlusion of the past and culture of the colonized. This leaves them as beings without memory who perpetually quest for a past upon which to better understand their present circumstances and build a future. The discussions are guided by postcolonial theory which amongst other things seeks to uncover the effects of the colonial encounter as narrated in works of fiction. This is so because the idea of postcolonial amnesia is considered here as a material effect of colonialism as will be indicated in the proceeding discussion.

Clare Savage: the Incarnation Colonial Savagery

Cliff's protagonist Clare Savage is a descendant of former slaves and former slaveholders. Cliff begins her novel with naming so as to draw attention to this double heritage which constitutes the major conflict in her novel and this is seen in her naming of Clare's parents: her mother, who is a descendant of former or freed slaves, is named Kitty Freeman, and her father, the descendant of slaveholders, is named Boy Savage. The two names point to the main tension in the text, which is the animosity between the slaveholders and the freed slaves. Thus it can already be seen that through the names, she brings to light the various groups that constitute the Island and shows that the society being a slave society is predominantly made of freed slaves and former slave holders. In other words, *Abeng* focuses on the victims of enslavement and colonial rule and the victimizers who are the savage slave holders who dehumanized black slaves. Clare's father, Boy Savage, is the grandson of the infamous slave owner Justice Savage whose savagery towards his slaves was as well-known as it was unsurpassed throughout the Island.

Through Clare Savage, Cliff can be seen as narrating the savagery of the slave owners and the colonizers towards the slaves. As we have seen above, this savagery was not always physical, even if the initial act of transporting the slaves to the New World was an act of such vicious proportions that it has remained the scar of human history. Their subjugation was ensured through other means, which were of profound consequences. Thus one of the first acts of violence we come across in *Abeng* is this symbolic violence mentioned before and in this case, it involves the distortion of the past of the colonized. Thus, Cliff narrates that

> In school they were told that their ancestors had been pagan. That there had been slaves in Africa, where Black people had put each other in chains. They were given the impression that whites who brought them here from the Gold Coast and

the Slave Coast were only copying a West African custom. As though the whites had not named the Slave Coast themselves. (18)

This distorted information passed through the colonial school is a form of psychologically violence, which involves leading the colonized to view their past in a negative light. This type of information passed across to the colonized constitutes one of the major hallmarks of colonialism which is the distortion of the past of the colonized. This point has been well-captured by anti-colonial critic Frantz Fanon in his seminal book *The Wretched of the Earth*, wherein he notes that "colonialism is not satisfied merely with holding a people in its grip and emptying the natives' brain of all form and content. By a kind of perverted logic, it turns to the past of the oppressed people, and distorts, disfigures and destroys it" (210). So, instead of building up individuals through the communication of useful and truthful information, Cliff here presents the colonial school as a tool of colonialism aimed at fostering the colonial enterprise through the perpetration of Eurocentrism. Fabian Klose intimates in *Human Rights in the Shadow of Colonial Violence* that "the excessive use of violence was a basic element of colonial expansion and rule" (92). Cliff juxtaposes the two forms of violence-physical and symbolic-throughout the novel to show how, indeed, the excessive use of violence was the major characteristic of colonialism. She shows how these forms of violence complemented each other towards the consolidation of colonialism. Thus, in reference to the physical violence that pervaded the Island during slavery and colonialism, Cliff writes:

No one had told the people in the Tabernacle that of all the slave societies in the New World, Jamaica was considered among the most brutal. They did not know that the death rate of Africans in Jamaica under slavery exceeded the rate of birth, and that the growth of the slave population from 1.500 in 1655 to 311.070 in 1834, the year of freedom, was due *only* to the importation of more people, more slaves. They did not know that some slaves worked with their faces locked in masks of tin, so that they would not eat the sugar cane as they cut. Or that

> there were few white women on the island during slavery, and so the grandmothers of these people sitting in a church on a Sunday evening during mango season, had been violated again and again by the very men who whipped them. The rape of Black women would have existed with or without the presence of white women, of course, but in Jamaica there was no pretense of civility – all was in the open. (18-19)

This lengthy quote is warranted here as it fully captures the extent of physical violence which permeated Jamaican slave society. Cliff therefore opens her narrative by indicating the collusion of these two forms of violence in the domination and subjugation of the colonized through the use of names.

Throughout the novel, there is the intricate interplay of these forms of violence to which the colonized such as Clare Savage and/or her ancestors were subjected. In criticizing Hartman's premise about England's successful avoidance of Holocaust-like trauma, Step Craps argues that if England had been spared the extreme violence that the European continent did inflict on itself, this has not prevented it from exporting violence and suffering in the name of imperialism and colonialism (1). The slave trade and slavery constituted some of the most extreme instances of British violence towards the black race. Colonialism, imperialism and the slave trade were in themselves gross acts of violence and sustained through violence.

One of the most violent act encountered in the novel is slavery itself which brought Clare's ancestors to Jamaica. Cliff underlines as follows:

> The enslavement of Black people–African peoples–with its processions of naked and chained human beings, whipping of human beings, rape of human beings, lynching of human beings, buying and selling of human beings – made other forms of employment in the upkeep of western civilization seem pale. (28)

Cliff's rhythmic presentation of these gruesome acts to which slaves are subjected goes to portray the perpetuity and wide extent of their physical torture. Her repetition of the phrase "human beings" draws attention to the fact that such treatment cannot–should not–be meted out to humans, thus underscoring the dehumanization of these slaves. Cliff pursues the physical violence which defined the Jamaican colonial society through Clare's paternal genealogy–the Savages–singularly through the person of Justice Savage whose descendants could not even pretend that he had been a "benign slaveholder" (30), because of his well-established fame to the contrary. The mere fact of being a slaveholder can hardly be termed benign. On the contrary, it is a most barbaric act characterized by the commodification, dehumanization and depersonalization of people. So, for a slaveholder to be considered singularly violent can only show the degree of harshness with which he treated his slaves, and Justice Savage was just such an individual. The Savage malevolence is nowhere better captured than in the treatment he reserved for recaptured runaway slaves as Cliff recounts:

> The recaptured slave was strung up in front of the quarters, where the queen's justice applied the cat 'o nine tails to his or back. [...]. Usually about a hundred or so strokes. After the whipping, the slave had salt rubbed into the wounds on his or her back. Then the slave was hanged by the neck until dead, from the large silk cotton tree in the backyard. Finally the rebel was cut down and the justice dissected the naked body of the African man or woman into four parts. Each quadrant of this human body was suspended by a rope from a tree at a corner of the property, where it stayed until the vultures, called John Crows, or the bluebottle flies finished it off. They ate the flesh and the blood. The bones fell to the ground where they melded with the earth, fertilizing the cane with potash. (30)

The grossness of such an act cannot be overstated, but suffice it to note that these acts not only dehumanize the slaves completely, but terrorize and traumatize them as well. It also leads them to believe not only in their presumed inferiority but equally in their sub-humanness. The treatment accorded to people is usually a reflection of how they are regarded. Thus for Clare's maternal ancestors to have been thus treated means they were considered inferior beings who were violated in both life and death. Therefore it causes such individuals to develop a disdain for the identity that has attracted such mistreatment, which has branded them as inferior. In this case, it is their Africanness, thus it comes as no surprise when Cliff writes of Clare's ancestors that "[t]hey wanted to forget about Africa" (30). We, therefore, see the ways different forms of violence collude to destabilize the colonized. Cliff's use of naming for specific purposes comes clearly to light here as the name "Savage" underscores the major trait of Justice Savage. It points to the grossness of the violence unleashed on the blacks.

Debra Walker King in *Deep Talk: Reading African-American Literary Names* has noted that "on a deep level of understanding and signification a name bearer *is* what its name suggests" (35). And because he represents an entire group of people on the Island, which are the colonizers, it can be said that they are savages. Justice Savage's name, therefore, bears witness to the savagery of those who would appropriate civilization as their creation. Clare Savage, being the descendant of the Justice, can be seen as the embodiment of the victims of this savagery, of the violence of colonization seen in her fragmented state. Thus Clare Savage is a metaphor of this violence. She uses the name "Savage" to draw attention to the savagery of the savages. At the same time, it can also be read as a revisionist project in the measure wherein the colonizers had in the myriad representations of the colonized described them as savages against whom the presumed civilized Europeans were set. Thus, by naming a white character Savage, Cliff can be read in effect as interrogating the whole system of representation as well as the binary oppositions that characterized the relationship between the colonizers and the colonized. So whereas the colonizers had portrayed the colonized as savage based merely on their cultural and physical difference, Cliff shows who the real savages are through a picture of the savage acts the Savages (whites) were involved in. The disregard of the humanity of others, coupled with their subsequent objectification through enslavement, is an example of violence which is of a savage proportion. This goes in line with Wamitila's view that "characters' names […] can be used artistically to achieve a number of goals like encoding a central trait in a particular characters' signification, embracing crucial thematic motifs, ideology toning as well as even showing the writer's point of view" (35). Thus names for Cliff are not merely a form of identifying characters, rather they constitute an important device she engages to express her vision as well as bring out specific character traits. It is through Cliff's infusing the metaphorical element in naming that the names of characters become a "discursive and invasive force" (King 63). W.F.H. Nicolaisen has noted this about naming in fiction:

> [I]n such fictitious realities, the special function of names as symbols, as metaphor, as linguistic icons (…) is more central than anywhere else, successful naming – not just competent but felicitous naming – is an essential ingredient of literary craftsmanship. (140)

It is this craftsmanship that Cliff exhibits through her manipulation of names to pass across her message. In *Name and Naming* Felecan Oliviu attests to this when he notes that "regardless of the historical age in which they professed their "creed," writers have chosen for their characters names that have conspicuous suggestive potential, to be able to send their readers the message they intended" (xii). So, through the metaphorical engagement of the name "Savage," Cliff has successfully passed across her message of the violence of colonialism.

A significant source of symbolic violence experienced by Clare Savage is psychological. In this regard, her father Boy Savage plays a crucial role. In his obsession with whiteness-as-perfection, he drums continuously into Clare the idea that she is white and should therefore embrace and accept only this part of her. This is a form of symbolic violence because Clare is of mixed ancestry. By persistently impressing upon her the idea that she is exclusively white, he not only confuses her, but renders her psychically disoriented.

Her father's doctrines constitute a form of violence, and this is what leads her to pose a number of questions which all indicate her confusion. Further, it emphasizes the idea of whiteness as not only superior, but equally desirable. Such a doctrine concomitantly denigrates Clare's African ancestry. By portraying whiteness as the only fact of her racial make-up worthy of acceptance, her father is indirectly leading her to feel that blackness is inferior and should be shunned. With Clare being of mixed ancestry, such a biased teaching can only contribute to making her unstable. It fails to give her a complete picture of who she is and where she is from. It obliterates her African ancestry and disconnects her from an important part of her past. This is the symbolic violence of racism which is further pursued when Clare, on vacation at her grandmother's Miss Mattie, accidentally kills her prize bull, old Joe. The narrator intimates that "Maybe Boy thought that Blackness was the cause of his daughter's actions–and the irresponsibility he felt imbued *those* people–and now had to be expunged once and for all. On this Island so far removed from the mother country, a white girl could so easily become thrash" (149). It is shortly confirmed that this is exactly Boy's line of thinking when he makes arrangement for Clare to move in with Mrs. Phillips, a white supremacist whose leitmotiv is "colored people are not to be trusted, and that she had not one drop of the blood, not one stroke of the brush" (142). Sending Clare to live with such an individual only goes to further expose her to more symbolic violence of racism. When Clare seeks to know from her mother why she is being dispatched to Mrs. Phillips, her mother replies: "Child what you did was a very serious thing. Your father is right. Punishment is not punishment enough. You have to learn once and for all just who you are in this world. Mrs. Phillips is a lady and you are getting to the age when you will need to be a lady as well" (150).

It is important at this juncture to point out what Kitty's definition of lady is so as to have a clearer view of what Clare would be subjected to at Mrs. Phillips. This comes about as a result of yet another incident which glaringly portrays the symbolic violence of racism in Clare's school. During morning devotionals, a black girl named Doreen falls under an epileptic fit. Instead of rushing to her aid, as was the right and thoughtful thing to do, "[t]he headmistress sang louder, as if to convey to the girls that they must not stop, must work to cover the sound of Doreen's skull and face hitting against rock, and the low groans coming from inside her" (96). Finally, it is only the black physical education teacher Miss Maxwell who reacts and rushes to Doreen's aid. So, in the aftermath of this Clare tries to seek answers from her mother as to why none of the white teachers had stepped up to assist Doreen, to which her mother replied, "Clare, you know how Englishwomen are – they think that they are ladies" (98). Taking the cue from this, to be a lady, following the prevailing colonialist doctrine in *Abeng,* is to despise blackness. This explains why there is an exact coherence between this definition and the kind of person Mrs. Phillips, considered to be a lady, is one of those white supremacists who totally believe in the virtues of whiteness and the vices of blackness.

In the world of *Abeng,* what is closer to whiteness is therefore considered better and more desirable, thus to be fair-skinned was to be lucky. Cliff recounts of Clare thus: "But she was a lucky girl – everyone said so – she was light-skinned. And she was alive. She lived in a world where the worst thing to be – especially if you were a girl – was to be dark. The only thing worse than that was to be dead" (97). Such unchecked and senseless veneration of whiteness is a form of violence that has devastating effects on the colonized. With such a mindset of Mrs. Phillips, one can only imagine what awaits Clare as she goes to live with her.

It therefore, comes as no surprise when she freely uses such an offensive word as "niggers" in reference to blacks and in Clare's presence. Peter Imbusch has noted that such actions as Mrs. Phillips' constitute violence when he writes that symbolic violence is built into language and communication in the form of hate speech, words with a racist or sexist background aimed at injuring the personal ethnic or sexual integrity of a person (25). So Clare's sojourn at Mrs. Phillips', far from training her into becoming a lady, is rather geared towards the extirpation of her African ancestry.

Significantly as has been briefly seen above, the colonial school constitutes an important location for the refinement and dissemination of these fallacious doctrines. The school represents the terrain of cultural and psychic violence which distorts and perverts the perceptions of the colonized. The biased Eurocentric education only helped to foster the idea of one part of the world or certain kinds of people representing civilization and the other representing barbarism. It contributes to erection of such binary oppositions which portray the colonized as the inferior other of the "superior" Europeans. Thus, in talking about Clare's education, Cliff writes that "Clare had been taught at St. Catherine's School for Girls that Jamaica had been a slave society. The white and creole mistresses hastened to say that England was the first country to free its slaves" (30). Such scanty and biased education denies Clare and her mates the benefit of a truthful and complete picture of their past. Education is used as a means of warping the minds of the colonized and leading them to, ironically, glorify England. The details of their past, such as where they originate and the conditions of their forceful and savage transportation by the English to Jamaica are withheld from them. Of course, such information would run contrary to that propagated by England of it being the seat and torch-bearer of human civilization. So, instead of educating the children, they are more interested in brainwashing them. This brainwashing is in itself a savage act which constitutes the manipulation and mental enslavement of the colonized.

Instead of Clare's education leading her to appreciate her present through a knowledge and comprehension of it, what is found in *Abeng* is an education that serves to conceal the truth. Through a jumble of confused, confusing, and unrelated "facts", the violence of colonial education rather dismembers the past of the colonized. Given that Clare and her ancestors found themselves in Jamaica through the slave trade, her education should have given more space to this aspect. On the contrary, the education glosses over this issue and rushes on to project England as the benevolent abolitionist of the slave trade. England's leading role in the macabre trade is never mentioned, as is the kinds of societies they found when they arrived in Africa.

Therefore, there is an intricate interplay between the two forms of violence in the text. In fact, the physical violence is simply an exhibition of the symbolic which has refused to recognize the full humanity of a group in the society. The full extent of these different forms of violence is well illustrated on the eve of the liberation of the African slaves. Having failed to prevent this freedom, Justice Savage decides to burn them all to death rather than see them free. His act of burning them, a gruesome example of physical violence, is backed by the symbolic violence which is the act of refusing to acknowledge and recognize the humanity of blacks. Thus he claims that the slaves were his property and therefore his to burn.

The justice's unthinkable act of physical violence is in itself informed by a thought steeped in an unthinkable form of symbolic violence through which people by virtue of the darkness of their skin are denied personhood and humanity. This thought, which culminated in the enslavement of Africans, is the same thought which has pushed the justice to burn the slaves, considering them as mere objects, and it is the same mindset that caused Clare's teachers to ignore Doreen when she was is in distress. This coheres with C. David Mortesen's view in "Linguistic Constructions of Violence, Peace and Conflict" that "[a]cts of physical violence emerge from acts of symbolic violence" (337). Peter Imbusch in "The Concept of Violence" defines symbolic violence by making recourse to Johan Galtung[3], who has been instrumental in the introduction and definition of the term in contemporary discourse. He notes:

> Galtung defined cultural violence by extending his definition of symbolic violence to include those aspects of culture which can be used for justifying or legitimizing direct, illegitimate institutional (or structural) violence. Cultural violence is aimed at making other forms of violence appear just – or at least not unjust – and thus making then acceptable for society. Cultural violence functions by switching the moral connotations of an action from wrong to right – or at least acceptable or unobjectionable and is successful to the extent that it succeeds in obscuring society's perception of actions or facts as violence. (25)

This definition clearly outlines what arguments the Justice proffers before engaging in the savage acts. The racist mentality which made slaves out of individuals and refused to recognize their full humanity, rather viewing them as chattel cargo and the property of their slave master, is the symbolic violence that has justified the

---

[3] For a detailed definition and explanation of the concepts of cultural/symbolic violence, a good starting point may be Galtung's article "Cultural Violence" in Journal of Peace Research, Vol. 27, no. 3, 1990, pp.291 – 305.

physical violence of burning them to death. Here Cliff's use of charactonym[4] is quite effective as Justice Savage's name suggests his distinctive character trait, his savagery. Charactonym, a sub-set of onomastics, generally refers to an evocative or symbolic name given to a character that conveys his or her inner psychological or allegorical nature. One, therefore, notices a glaring coincidence between Savage's name and his character trait. The use of charactonym here also serves as a satiric device (Test 140) which satirizes the excesses of the slave holders. By thus giving her character a name that is especially suited to his personality (Lederer 13), Cliff questions and debunks the whole system of slavery.

Racism is, therefore, seen as a form of violence as it determines not only how individuals are perceived, but above all, how they are treated. In the world of *Abeng*, color is everything and instead of the school acting as a corrective to such teachings, it is rather there that they are incubated and passed on. The society is infused with these racist ideologies which determine who is privileged and who is despised.

Clare's mind stands as a representation of the collective consciousness of colonized Jamaicans, whose colonial experience denigrated their African past, hailing England as the land of glory whose ways were to be emulated and embraced. These racist, hegemonic teachings which glorify whiteness while concomitantly denigrating blackness is what Kelsey Wood in *Zizek: A Reader's Guide* terms objective violence which include racism, hate-speech, and discrimination (23). All the violence that permeates the Jamaican society of *Abeng* leads the colonized to disconnect from their past.

Clare Savage: The Embodiment of "A Mind Bleached of the Past"

Mortesen has noted that "unlike the overt outcomes associated with acts of physical violence, the hurtful and injurious effects of symbolic violence are often hidden from sight – as invisible damage of invisible wounds" (357). Clare, as an embodiment of the colonial

---

[4]It is also known as aptronym and aptonym and refers to a name aptly suited to its owner.

legacy of violence, carries such hidden wounds. Cliff's naming of Clare draws attention to these consequences: amnesia, trauma and fragmentation. Clare, by her very name, typifies a kind of void or emptiness. She functions as a text on which is inscribed the violence of colonialism. Her pale skin which her name represents denotes fluidity, absence of fulfillment, and self-definition. All of these are the material effects of colonialism. This emptiness caused by colonialism is a postcolonial condition. Clare, therefore, embodies the trauma of colonialism. Milena Bubenechik in *The Trauma of Colonial Condition* underlines that "colonialism encompasses a series of trauma for indigenous populations" (4), while Ogaga Ifowodo in *History, Trauma, and Healing* has underscored the specificity of colonial trauma by highlighting its difference from classical psychology. He writes:

> The specific nature of the trauma of the colonized is characterized not by the desire of the son for the mother nor the father's threat of castration – to follow the classical psychoanalytic paradigm but by the self-abnegating effect of racism and political domination. (10)

The name Clare captures this "self-abnegating effect." It carries with it the connotation of being deprived of its essence. So, the names Clare Savage illustrate the savagery (Savage) of colonialism as well as the emptiness, deprivation, trauma, and amnesia (Clare) which follow.

Due to the violence of colonialism on the colonized, these colonized are denied access to their past, find themselves in a world without history. Within this discussion, amnesia is not considered as a medical condition; rather it is an artifact or material effect of the colonial encounter that leads to a blurring of the past of the colonized. Postcolonial amnesia, therefore, refers to this lack of an objective knowledge of the past of the colonized, occasioned by the violence of colonialism which created a disconnection between the colonized and their past. So far, the discussion has shown the ways in which the colonial encounter contributes to clouding their past with the result being amnesiac individuals who do not have a clear picture of where they come from. This Cliff explains accordingly:

> They did not know about the kingdom of the Ashanti or the kingdom of Dahomey, where most of their ancestors had come from. They did not imagine that Black Africans had commanded thousands of warriors. Built universities. Created systems of law. Devised language. Wrote history. Poetry. Were traders. Artists. Diplomats. (20)

Colonial violence has ensured that the descendants of slaves would be ignorant of their past. As such, they do not know that theirs was a past of great achievements as well. Rather, their past is presented to them like one long stretch of dark emptiness with nothing worthy of intellectual inquiry. This is the reason why no mention is made of the accomplishments of their ancestors in the schools and in books. So they go through life with no past to identify with or look back to and with no achievements to be proud of. The past of England has overwritten that of the colonized. Cliff then explains the amnesia of these colonized Jamaicans:

> They did not know that their name for papaya – *pawpaw* – was the name of one of the languages of Dahomey. Or that the cotta, the circle of cloth women wound tightly to make a cushion to balance baskets on their heads, was an African device, an African word. That Brer Anancy, the spider who inspired tricks and tales, was a West African invention. Or that Cuffee was the name of a Maroon commander – the word had come down to them as *cuffy* and meant upstart, social climber. (20)

Cliff's repetition of the phrase "they did not know" underscores the amnesia which is one of the more devastating effects of colonial violence. The colonized have become beings without a memory, having no knowledge of their past and merely accepting what the colonizers present to them.

Clare stands as the embodiment of this postcolonial amnesia, this absence or lack of a memory of the past of the colonized. She is aptly named Clare, which, as discussed before, captures this amnesia, a kind of blankness, a void that has been created and is being exacerbated by colonial violence. Thus throughout the narrative, the reader accompanies Clare as she gropes through life seeking for pieces to fill the emptiness of her being created by the colonial encounter. It is the consciousness of incompleteness, of something missing that spurs her into this quest that runs through the novel. Cliff also names and positions Clare as such to represent the collective postcolonial amnesia that is an aftermath of colonial savagery. She personifies the legacy of colonial violence. The physical violence is expressed in her "mutilated" pale skin and the symbolic violence in her amnesia.

In Clare's society, there are no books available through which she can glean some information about herself, her past and the oppression of her people. So, conscious of this void in her, she decides to go in search for greater knowledge so as to comprehend her place and that of her people in the world. She turns to what is available to her and these are the books and movies about the Jewish holocaust. Since the Jews, like the Africans, had suffered untold violations at the hands of the Europeans, Clare believes that by studying this fact of history, she can answer some of the questions that beset her mind about her person and fill the gaps that have come to define her being. She feels an acute need to fill the gaps in her past through whatever means is available to her. Cliff therefore adds:

> Clare knew that Anne Frank had been Jewish. And that *they*, the Germans, the Nazis, had killed her – one dark-eyed girl – for being Jewish. Clare knew something of what had happened to the Jews of Europe under Hitler during the Second World War, the war her parents had been part of. (68)

The violence of Clare's biased education has made sure that she would go through life without a memory, a factual picture of her past. Her teachers have tactfully blotted this past such that it is only through a similar past of oppression that she can begin to have an idea of what could have happened in her own past. Clare, as an embodiment of the collective postcolonial amnesia, is ignorant of the extent of the brutality of the slave trade and slavery of which her maternal ancestry was victim. What is important to note here is that the ignorance of this specific aspect of her past serves the purpose of the British who have always presented themselves in the most superlative terms as the torch-bearers of civilization. Clare's mind, bleached and cleared of knowledge of the past, cannot imagine the extent of inhumaneness of the revered British towards her ancestors. The violence of the colonial classroom has almost completely wiped off the past of the colonized; so Clare's mind is cleared of her past as regard even her immediate ancestry. Through the reinforcement of this symbolic violence by her father, Clare's ignorance of her past is accentuated.

At other times, it is not just the colonial mechanisms that obfuscate the past of the colonized, but the trauma of the violence that makes the former slaves themselves not to want to revisit their past by talking about it. A good case in point is Clare's maternal grandmother, Miss Mattie, who, it is said, "did not speak about her own childhood to her children – or to many people for that matter" (141). It is as a result of this pained memory caused by colonial violence that Miss Mattie prefers to remain silent about her past. As a result, it is said that "her children knew nothing of this experience, or of the beatings she had received at the hands of the overseer for not moving fast enough through the long corridors of cane" (141). This is another opportunity that Clare misses to know about her past. So, whereas grandmothers have been known to play significant roles in filling the gaps of formal education, here Miss Mattie cannot fulfill that role. Her descendants are the victims of this. For her to talk about that past would mean reliving the pain of the violent treatment to which she was subjected. This is a memory she prefers to bury and forget about. As such, colonial violence in one way or another invariably leads to the occlusion of the past.

Conclusion

The above discussions have shown the various ways colonial violence resulted in postcolonial amnesia. This situation left the colonized, bereft of their past through the extreme trauma of the violence, unable or unwilling to revisit the pained past. In addressing this situation, Michelle Cliff has manipulated language with such complexity and dexterity in order to pass across her message. Through the engagement of the onomastics device and the related charactonyms, Cliff highlights the interplay between colonial violence and postcolonial amnesia. This chapter has considered amnesia as a major effect of the unfortunate colonial encounter that continues to impact the lives of the formerly colonized. Through the apt naming of the character, Clare Savage, Cliff reproduces this intricate interaction between colonial violence and postcolonial amnesia. Her protagonist "Clare Savage" as a result incarnates the message of her novel which brings to light how the savagery of colonial violence cleared the minds of the colonized of a sense of their past and left them as individuals lacking a healthy memory. The result of this is haunted and restless individuals groping desperately and feverishly in search for an understanding of that buried past. By engaging this complex system of naming, Cliff successfully portrays these aspects of her novel. A reading of *Abeng* has shown that colonialism went far beyond physical violence and engaged other less tangible forms of violence which played a recognizable role in the establishment and consolidation of colonial rule. This significantly helped in placing the colonized in discomfiting circumstances wherein they not only experienced trauma in very extreme forms, but also in the dismembering of their past. The discussions have shown the important ways in which the naming of characters can serve in transmitting the author's message and viewpoint. Within postcolonial studies, the onomastics device draws attention to specific aspects of colonialism or the resulting postcolonial condition.

Works Cited

Algeo, John. "Onomastics" in Tom McArthur (ed). *The Oxford Companion to the English Language*. Oxford: OUP, 1992. Print.

Barry, Peter.*Beginning Theory: An Introduction to Literary Culture and Theory*. Manchester: Manchester UP, 2002. Print.

Behdad, Ali. "Eroticism, Colonialism, and Violence". In Hent de Vries and Samuel Weber (eds.) *Violence, Identity and Self-Determination*. Standford: Standford UP, 1997. 201- 207. Print

Bertills, Yvonne. *Beyond Identification: Proper Names in Childern's Literature.* Tevastg: Abo Akademi UP, 2003. Print.

Bubenechik, Milena. *The Trauma of Colonial Condition in Nervous Conditions and Kiss of the Fur Queen.* Hamburg: Anchor Academic, 2013. Print.

Cliff, Michelle. *Abeng.* New York: Penguin Books, 1995. Print.

Craps, Stef. *Postcolonial Witnessing: Trauma out of Bounds.* New York: Palgrave Macmillan, 2012. Print.

Currie, Gregory. *The Nature of Fiction.* Cambridge: Cambridge UP, 1990. Print.

Druckworth, Vicky. *Learning Trajectories, Violence and Empowerment Amongst Adult Basic Skills Learners.* London and New York: Routledge, 2014. Print.

Falola, Toyin. *Colonialism and Violence in Nigeria.* Bloomington: Indiana UP, 2009. Print.

Fanon, Frantz. *The Wretched of the Earth.* Trans. Constance Farrington. Suffolk: Richard Clay, 1963. Print.

Felecan, Oliviu (ed). *Name and Naming: Synchronic and Diachronic Perspectives.* Newcastle on Tyne: Cambridge Scholars, 2012. Print.

Gray, Benjamin. *Face to Face with Emotions in Health and Social Care.* New York: Springer, 2012. Print.

Ifowodo, Ogaga. *History, Trauma, and Healing in Postcolonial Narratives: Reconstructing Identities.* New York: Palgrave Macmillan, 2013. Print.

Imbusch, Peter. "The Concept of Violence" in *The International Handbook of Violence Research Vol. 1.* Wilhelm Heitmeyer and John Hagan (eds). Dordrecht: Kluwer Academic Publishers, 2003, 13 -40. Print.

King, Debra Walker. *Deep Talk: Reading African-American Literary Names.* Virginia: UP of Virginia, 1998. Print.

Klose, Fabian. *Human Rights in the Shadow of Colonial Violence: The Wars of Independence in Kenya and Algeria.* Trans. Dona Geyer. Philadelphia: U. Penn. P., 2013. Print.

LaCapra, Dominick. *Writing History, Writing Trauma.* Baltimore: The John Hopkins UP, 2001. Print.

Lederer, Richard. *Crazy English: The Ultimate Joy Ride Through our Language.* New York: Pocket Books, 1998. Print.

Mortesen, C. David. "Linguistic Constructions of Violence, Peace and Conflict" in *Encyclopedia of Violence, Peace and Conflict Vol.2*. Lester R. Kurtz and Jennifer E. Turpin (eds). Watham: Academic Press, 333 – 344. Print.

Nicolaisen, W.F.H. "Structure and Function of Names in English Literature" in *Studia Anglica Posnaniensia* 18, (1986): 139–152. Print.

Simatei, Tirop. "Colonial Violence, Postcolonial Violations: Violence, Landscape, and Memory in Kenyan Fiction". In *Research in African Literatures,* 36:2. (2005):85 -94. Print.

Test, George Austin. *Satire: Spirit and Art.* Gainesville: UP of Florida, 1991. Print.

Wamitalia, Kyallo Wadi. "What's in a Name": Towards Literary Onomastics in Kiswahili Literature". In *AAP60*, (1999): 35 – 44. Print.

Wood, Kelsey. *Zizek: A Reader's Guide.* Sussex: John Wiley and Sons, 2012. Print.

Chapter Four

Names, Power Relationships and Influences in Francis B. Nyamnjoh's *Married but Available*

By
Benjamin Hart Fishkin

"The husband of another is sweet...the wife of another is sweet..." (Nyamnjoh 83). Love, power and consumption dominate every aspect of the research of Lily Loveless. As a doctoral student in Social Geography, Lilly specializes in the "irresistibly obscene" (Nyamnjoh 84). Her fieldwork provides the reader with a description of course study never before published in a graduate catalogue and this sets up an inherent contradiction; what are the results of her attempts to order and categorize behavioral relationships and why is a woman so infatuated with sex named "Loveless"? It is surely the desire of Francis B. Nyamnjoh to get his reader to perspire. This is part of his narrative style. But one only gets four or five chapters into *Married but Available* before he or she realizes this initial assessment is wrong. It is through pride and the power to subdue that the writer wants to see the reader sweat.

This process of cooling via evaporation is cleverly, and expertly, distributed between the literary characters and their reader. The characters sweat in earnest as they have passionate sexual affairs with everyone except with whom they should be sharing their beds and the reader sweats because of the thorny, irrational, crazy, and absurd problems that ensnare those who do just that. Is the voyeur happy to have avoided the latter or sorry to have been left out of the former? The ensemble of characters, with fascinating names such as, Wiseman Lovemore, President Longstay, and Chief Dr. Mantrouble, indicates that Nyamnjoh is talking about more than having fun on the side. The names are of literary importance just as Charles Dickens' *Hard Times* uses characters such as Gradgrind, M'choakumchild, Harthouse, Blackpool, Sparsit or Bounderby and Henry James's *Portrait of a Lady* uses characters such as Touchett.

The importance of naming to Nyamnjoh is subtext or rather precisely how that subtext threatens to explode. Will it tear the lives of the participants asunder or will it be some sort of inconvenience—like a hangover that is not severe enough to sway one off drink?

Names and naming are an important component of any literature. In fact, just reading a list of names in *Married but Available* aloud is enough to give away Lilly's, and thus Nyamnjoh's, conclusions about Social Geography. This creation on reproduction highlights the importance of names not only in Africa, but within the context of international travel and scholarship. When we first meet Lilly she is on an Air Mimbo flight to study abroad when the women directly to her right gives her a box of two hundred and fifty condoms. "Life is too sweet and too short to waste" she says (Nyamnjoh 7). Think for a moment how different this philosophy is from the American South where these words are composed, read and heard. Think of the Papacy, even though Lilly is not Roman Catholic, which has forbidden the use of condoms in disease-prevention efforts in a land devastated by HIV/AIDS and other sexually transmitted epidemics. Lilly's idea is "to snatch what was left of life" and to defy and unravel the tether of repressed living (Nyamnjoh 7). Are Westerners not restrained and unhappily limited by invisible chains of their own making? Nyamnjoh's *Married but Available* with the initials M.B.A. being probative as they are the same as a coveted degree involving business administration transcends these baffling problems with names.

If Juliet Capulet has never seen the importance in a name it is because she is in full blossom of her youth and has never been to the unpredictable land of Mimbo (10). The name Mimbo is one consonant removed from "Bimbo"; a less than complimentary term for an attractive female whose physicality dominates all. However, the presence of the letter "M" provides us with the male equivalent—a man who has no sense of obligation. The male seeks desire and gratification, to which I do not object, but does so without any forethought or planning, to which I do object. The women (often girls) are far more understanding and know precisely what is going on. This is supported by a Spanish saying that "a woman thinks more in a minute than a man does in a whole month." It is the women who are the thinkers. It is the women who are clever. The quiet, outwardly meek, precise machinery of the female mind undoes the brash, boisterous and unjustifiably confident male. The men, who are not strong, use alcohol to make them feel invincible. Think of an old-fashioned Swiss chronometer whose carefully calibrated gears automatically adjust for accuracy and stability. This is a mechanism that the men do not have. The social roles, if they are not reversed, create a class of women who are entrepreneurial and without guilt about their sexual exploits. The women are in charge. The men are dumb enough or blind enough (but not with love) to run headlong into one mess after the other.

There is a sense of tragedy mixed in with the lightness of Nyamnjoh's humor more to the effect of comic relief than anything else. The word Mimbo in Cameroonian Pidgin English also references alcoholic beverages and there are three types of tragedy that originate and emanate from the bottle. William Shakespeare's *Macbeth*, arguably the greatest tragedy of all, states through Macduff's Porter, four hundred years before Mimboland has deteriorated into dilapidation, that drink promotes these perverse effects. In responding to Macduff's question: "what three things does drink especially provoke?" He replies: "marry, Sir, nose-painting, sleep, and urine. Lechery sir it provokes and unprovokes. It provokes desire, but takes away the performance" (*Macbeth* Act 2, Sc. 3, Lines. 26-30). Alcohol may take away performance but it is no hindrance to procreation and the problems that are inherent with doing so irresponsibly. Everyone drinks constantly. Lilly refers to beer in terms of crates or cases of twelve twenty-five ounce bottles. The result is a confused, disorientated, and impaired thought process. There is nothing wrong with taking a drink now and again. In fact, in its proper dosage, alcohol is a safe social lubricant. However, Mimbolanders drink to excess, never considering the consequences elicited above by Macduff's Porter. It is easier to function on auto-pilot. If Ralph Waldo Emerson once said that the most difficult thing to do is to think (8), then the easiest thing to do is to drink, screw, and act without forethought. Mimbolanders drink and create chaos and then drink to lament the chaos that they have created. The song never ends and the cycle of self-anesthesia continues in perpetuity. The nation takes two steps back for every step forward, tripping and falling over obstacles of its own misconstruction.

The very name of the African country is a testament to male incompetence, male indifference and male self-destruction. There is a psychological "cancer", malady or short-circuiting in male thinking and it is growing, getting worse and about to metastasize. Do Mimbolanders behave recklessly because they are so named or are they so named because they animatedly and unabashedly pursue sex and drinking? In other words how do these people get their names in the first place? Surely a character named Dr. Sexwale is not named for his interest in oceanography. Lilly Loveless is so named because her father, a librarian, planned, reasoned and traced his family history so carefully. The result is a name that intentionally reaches back "…to a time when there was so little love in the world that people thought, would this child survive in a loveless world?" (Nyamnjoh 36). Bobinga Iroko's first words to Lilly are to tell her friend (Dr. Wiseman Lovemore) to love less. "The hazards are just too many" (Nyamnjoh 35). No truer words are spoken in *Married But Available*. To do so is no easy trick in a world where there are no happily married couples and there are no signposts to demarcate the divisions between love and sex. People, in Nyamnjoh's words, need to be tamed (Nyamnjoh 35). When it comes to appraising this mess Bobinga Iroko says "To love less you need a therapist, not a girlfriend" (Nyamnjoh 35). Names exist to tell people that there is so much wrong in Mimboland cum Cameroon that no one knows what to fix first. I am not objecting to sex and drinking, but at what cost? What price—an outcome measured in instability—is too much to pay? This thought never seems to enter the discussion. There is no discussion. It is as if the male never even considered that a woman—his woman—could be practiced at the art of deception and do it even better and with more skill than he. The husband has opened a door that cannot easily be shut. The name of a character seems to sum up behavior that is without nuance or subtlety. Lilly Loveless sums up what John Lennon said thirty years ago, claiming "Nobody Told Me". He said; "Everybody's making love and no one really cares" (John Lennon,). That is the problem with Mimboland. A woman in the Lulu Salon, again note

Nyamnjoh's ability to inject revealing humor through a seemingly "throwaway" naming detail, points out that the manipulative gamesmanship involving sex, consumerism and power are not about to change.

> …my husband was so predictably boring. No idea of foreplay. When he wanted it all he did was throw himself at me, desperate for one thing only. It didn't matter whether I was in the kitchen cooking, on my knees saying my evening prayers, or in bed deep asleep. He is passionate about instant sex, and doesn't care what I think or feel, as long as he sticks something somewhere. And now that I've found someone interesting, loving and tender making me happy by doing what he has never done in ways he has hardly imagined, he goes around complaining ignoring him in favor of a boy young enough to be my grandson. It's jealousy, pure jealousy. When he took me for granted and treated me like an old layer, he thought going out with younger flesh is his prerogative. Now that I am giving him a taste of his own medicine, suddenly he knows what it feels like not to be desired and respected… (Nyamnjoh 111)

The women do it better, literally, physically, and metaphorically. Nyamnjoh uses the palindrome "PIP" (to stand for "Party In Power") but it is the women who are in charge (Nyamnjoh 43). Isn't it an older sister in *Great Expectations* who beats Pip mercilessly? "Pip" an, abbreviation for Phillip plus Pirrip, is Charles Dickens' struggling, hurt, hero—always outdone by Estella. He is always reaching for the girl that is out of reach, leaping for a higher social class that does not deliver as promised. When he does rise financially and socially he deteriorates emotionally and loses his innocence to London's material pleasures. His moral descent is accompanied by financial debt, centuries before credit cards, which is also an African problem. All of his brothers, five in all, are dead, when the novel begins. Pip's personality is in turmoil, changing rapidly with each new stimulus. If in Shakespeare the readiness is all then in Dickens the unrealistic is all. What is asked for never yields the desired results. *Married But Available* tells us that men behave "…as if they were some super men or the Oliver Twist of sex, when we [women] know that ordinary men are in and out even before you've unzipped your skirt" (Nyamnjoh 280). Money does not solve his problems, it creates them to the point that he does not know if he is coming and going. The ultimate fantasy is love which he does not find. In terms of psychological health, which is where it counts, he should have stayed on the "farm" or "marsh" and eschewed the temptations of the city, but what young person can do that?

The use of the word "Party" is immediately recognizable. It is also a political party—politicians are almost always men. In these circles the women think with dispassionate reason, weighing one love off against another. Thank goodness paternity tests are rare, states senior journalist Bobinga Iroko, "...else man would be shocked to know how their wives lead them to take perfect strangers for their offspring" (Nyamnjoh 38). In an almost cruel form of extreme materialism "...the child belongs to he who owns the bed" (Nyamnjoh 38). This is the consumerism that shapes and dominates every relationship between men and women. Bobinga Iroko's name is very symbolic. Bobinga and Iroko are both types of trees that produce very desirable hardwood. Newspapers are made of paper and paper is made of trees. This influential writer and reporter for *The Talking Drum,* injects Lilly with a spark of excitement that she cannot find at the Muzunguland African Studies Institute in Livingstonetown. Surely this made up home front launching place for *Married but Available* is a reference to David Livingstone, the Scottish missionary and scientific explorer who helped colonize Africa during the later portion of Queen Victoria's reign. Bobinga and Iroko Trees are a representation of strength and stability. They have deep roots, and are found in Africa and are a source of growth and life. This has sexual implications as dictionaries and botanists frequently refer to both as a "tropical African hardwood" and Nyamnjoh's character playfully mocks at Lilly Loveless. He makes her aware of philandering, promiscuity and hypocrisy. The purpose of names is to shock the reader; to make him or her aware of the wide gulf between theory and practice.

While a pleasant and flirtatious man Bobinga Iroko is not what he seems. He readily discusses cheating and sexual promiscuity, but he rejects Lilly Loveless's advances. They dance too close and laugh too long at a nightclub in Sakersbeach, but it is he, in the classic role of the western woman, and not the biological woman, who says no. Bobinga Iroko is circumspect, not wanting to have sex with Lilly and create what Britney calls…"beautiful zebra babies" (Nyamnjoh 200). But why not? In a world where anything goes why is Lilly so unfortunate to have met the one man in Mimbolanders with integrity? Why is he inflexible and what does this have to do with the literary, political, and psychological importance of his name? The name Bobbingo Iroko is that of a crossbreed. The two toughest and most resilient types of wood from the rainforest ([re]form and [un]scramble his name when a "…timber tanker' loaded beyond capacity…" with both crashes into his Toyota. The resulting tragedy irreparably wounds his fiancée, Loveline, and compels him to change his name from Godlove and embark on a new course as an inflexible and resolute journalist. This is a realization that he can no longer submit to the vulnerability that love demands. He is so hurt and damaged and in immeasurable pain that, in calculated fashion, he elects to live above the fray with a body and a heart not ensconced in the world, but rather covered in the welcome numbness of ice having lost his "Love Line".

If we presume the names of Livingstonetown and Iroko to be arbitrary we are supposedly incorrect. Bobinga is also a hardwood tree referenced to and Francis B. Nyamnjoh is making a carefully constructed point. Names mark an individual like a fingerprint, a blood type or a sequence of chemical compounds within a DNA molecule. They identify and reveal not only the actor, but the framework of the very theater in which he or she performs. One cannot break free of his or her name. It is something that is carried, like heavy or over packed baggage, through the international airport of globalization where all of the signs and all of the public address announcements are in another language. Nyamnjoh's talent is that he places people in strange environments and, like any good anthropologist, notates how they assimilate into the unfamiliar. In a new culture they are either burdened, or reinvigorated, by a fixed identity that is not of their own making. The literary critic Claire A. Culleton states that failing to accurately depict someone's name is a form of "sedition" (Culleton 96). When a name is rejected there are psychological, emotional and moral consequences. "…[I]gnoring it, truncating it , replacing it, misspelling it, misprinting it, mispronouncing it, withholding it, disregarding conventionalized forms of it …" are what the colonizer does (Culleton 96). As a matter of record this has been going on for a very long time. It brings with it all sorts of baggage. A nation in this portion of Africa can be humiliated politically and so that it can be controlled economically.

Lilly's journey, while a geographic one, is every bit a passage or program of ideas. By stepping into the context of globalization she is searching for something that "…no empire can give you and no empire can take away" (West 172). This quotation by Cornel West also applies to a person's given name at birth. It demands a renewal of what West calls "democratic Christian identity" (West 172). No one has the moral authority, the economic means or the political will to take someone's spiritual power. That power is wrapped up in a system of naming: that system is nomenclature. The crisis in black America, and perhaps this is why so many African American children have uniquely spelled names, is that for too long this has been forgotten. Britney, Lilly's research assistant in Mimboland, has been given an English sounding name "Brit-ney" in the hopes that she will forget (and relinquish) her spiritual power. This is more a statement about the relationship between Africa and the West. What's more, when an African takes on the identity of a European—and so to speak "drinks the kool-aid"—she eagerly begins to emulate her oppressor. She does willingly what not even the most wide-reaching dominant hegemonic culture can do and runs headlong in the pursuit of her own inauthenticity. If Lilly Loveless exploits Africa it is Britney who hands unhesitatingly her the keys to the kingdom. She begins to shop, she begins to alter her body, she begins to see a hair engineer on a regular basis and she begins to send her money as a consumer on an odyssey back to the very nation that has corrupted her (Nyamnjoh 104).

The characters clearly, and overtly, point out idiosyncrasies in the names of their peers. Bobinga Iroko is asked [by Lilly] "…have you ever considered changing your name to 'Bobinga Iroko the Difficult'?" (Nyamnjoh 166). Surely this is because he is evasive, downplaying compliments and flattery so that he does not wind up in her bed. It is also a reference to wood that is "difficult" to cut, mould, or bend. He knows exactly what is on her mind and is unwilling to be bamboozled. When Mrs. Wiseman Lovemore meets Dr. Nosewordy Boiboibambeh at the University of Mimbo, and the two attend a conference abroad entitled "The Future of the African Breast in Literary Studies", the academic appeals on an intellectual level. The use of the word "wordy" is a hint of what this sort of relationship has to offer. "It wasn't his small office overflowing with papers that attracted me. It was I guess the glint in his eye when he saw me noticing his artwork on his walls. The work spoke to some sensitivity within him. That's what attracted me" (Nyamnjoh 242).

Attracted? Yes! Sexually intimate? No! As an academic, Boiboibambeh is of no interest to women like Mrs. Lovemore. A little deconstruction of his name here will, in the first instance, reveal, "Boiboi", a Cameroon Pidgin English word for a knave in the sense of a male servant and "Bambeh" yet another Cameroon Pidgin English word for indentured servant, therefore a semantic reconstruction of "Boiboi" plus "bambeh" will yield a male indentured servant. A further venture into his last name Nosewordy reveals more why Mrs Lovemore takes interest in him as he is nosy and wordy. He pries into the papers given to him by Mrs. Lovemore and comments on them. He is considered one who serves others, with little money, almost like what one calls an "Uncle Tom"—even though the term's original literary connotation is very positive and the term has since become one of controversy. His, the Stowe character's, is not always positive when used outside a strictly literary context. Nosewordy has people him, but belittle his accomplishments because nobody cares about them. Characters comment on names and reveal traits, before they even know the subject. This is not dissimilar to being drawn to a restaurant by chance because the lighting or décor is appealing. Even without looking at a menu one can often "tell" whether or not this a relaxing place to eat. Changing the pitch of the light, the background music, the fabric of the upholstery is just like changing a name. When Adapepe, the girlfriend of the also significantly named Burning Spear replete with a "colorful trademark Bob Marley hat", meets Britney we see a topic that is often underestimated by the slim portion of the populous that still reads books" (Nyamnjoh 263).

> "I'm here with Lilly Loveless, who is visiting from Muzunguland. I can't just leave her on her own."
> "Lilly what?"
> "Loveless," repeated Britney.
> "You mean Lovelace...like in Deep Throat?"
> "Lilly L-o-v-e-l-e-s-s," Lilly Loveless spelt out. "Strange name, I know."
> Adapepe smiled. "Then why don't you abandon it? We've got lots of names in Mimboland seeking to be adopted. Just tell Britney what size of name you want, and she'll arrange it for you" (Nyamnjoh (259 – 260).

Burning Spear, the "DJ" of Adapepe's heart, is a reference to the Jamaican roots and reggae singer (Nyamnjoh 283). The provocative play is part of the novel's texture. The character name "Burning Spear," when juxtaposed with the actual reggae artist "Burning Spear," denotes a spiritual connection. This transcends the physical and brings to the student strike a feeling that is unbound and without limits. Brought up on Curtis Mayfield, James Brown, and Marcus Garvey we (without any European help) have the unity of Pan-Africanism in music. This is an intentional counterpoint to Nyamhnjoh's Burning Spear as a striking campus leader setting the machinery and wiring of interconnectivity of Black Nationalism to the soundtrack of a Rastafarian beat.

"I smell trouble like burnt cooking," comments Lilly Loveless when she hears Britney's stories about relationships (Nyamnjoh 99). Britney, who also works as the receptionist at the Mountain View Hotel, is a research assistant with a treasure trove of anecdotes and information. She does not mince words. Love affairs are almost always business arrangements. They are encouraged by dollars, credit cards and presents. Shortly after they begin work on Lilly's research project Britney tells her boss, in a taped interview, about a love affair between a student named Emma and a man who has children but "...just can't resist what younger university, high or secondary school girls offer" (49). She is roughly twenty years of age whereas he is fifty-five. The male in this interview is named "Innocent." That says a great deal about naming because he is precisely the opposite of the term. There has even been a Pope named Innocent and who is more righteous, honest and forthright than he? Why don't the two simply go in a back room, meet with a team of lawyers and shake hands before proceeding to the more pleasurable aspects of their relationship? Innocent views a female like Emma as a prize to show off and this flies in the face of logic. No rational philanderer wants his wife to have proof of the fact that he has grown tired of the same old thing, but he does not even pretend to be secretive. He does not even go through the motions as he openly buys Emma "…expensive body lotions, perfumes, shoes, jewelry, clothes and airtime for the cute little cell phone he bought her as a birthday present" (Nyamnjoh 51). He is there to earn his wealth and she is there to display it. There are no common feelings of love and this causes all sorts of problems. His wife of thirty-five years is, understandably, unhappy and what is to become of his five children's education? Surely a man can see problems down the line and swerve to avert them with a bit of forethought, but that is not what Britney finds in her research.

When it comes to whether or not to remain in the marital bedroom the male gender, even the brightest and most intelligent professional among them, does not have any resolve. The result is chaos that even an artist like Nyamnjoh cannot order. Africa shall "never see the light of day under the leadership of its male species" (112). Cars are destroyed, women fight with one another, bills are not paid while individuals who pride themselves on being strong and capable prove to be frail and inauthentic. Men do this when they know full well the results that inevitably follow. Nyamnjoh says that this is "…the tonic to help people bear relationships that would otherwise be too burdensome to even contemplate" (Nyamnjoh 37). Even staining your name forever is worth the rush and the risk and the environment, rather than being upset, seems to take the matter in stride. The same culture that places so much sacred importance on how a child is named seems to be ambivalent about the ease with which that very same person is willing and eager to besmirch it. The owner is free and unencumbered to self damage his prestige, his religion, his class and his name in sub-Saharan

Africa and no one seems to be the slightest bit surprised. Another one of Nyamnjoh's characters is named Simba Spineless and the author is crass, but right on the money, when he depicts men as slaves to biology, or Darwinism, or both: "In Africa where divorce is not looked upon kindly, only adultery saves marriages" (Nyamnjoh 112). Is this not precisely what Oscar Wilde says, six thousand miles, and one hundred and twenty summers ago? "In married life three is company and two is none" (Wilde 7). While the relationship between Jack and Gwendolyn may be between two people, it is an intersection and a convergence of three names. (Four if one takes into account that Gwendolyn's name will change if she does indeed get married to Jack who is really Ernest.) To be her husband Jack must be both Ernest in name and earnest in behavior, character and identity. The word "earnest" is both ordinary, according to literary scholar Alastair Fowler, and "meaningful" when that very same combination of phonetic sounds becomes "Ernest" (Fowler 2). The name changes and so does the character's elasticity.

On the subject of aging, Nyamnjoh is as clever as the Victorian author when it comes to talking about love and sexual relation.

> What is the difference between 8 and 78?"
> I read on the internet that at the age of 8, you take her to bed and tell her a story. "
> "At 18...?
> "You tell her a story and take her to bed?
> "28...?
> "You don't need a story to take her to bed?
> "At 38...?
> "She tells you a story and takes you to bed.
> "48...?
> "She tells you a story to avoid going to bed."
> "What about 58...?"
> "You stay in bed to avoid her story?"
> "At 68...?"
> "If you take her to bed, that'll be a story!"
> "And at 78, both the bed and the woman are dead and buried?"

"Exactly! What story? What bed? Who the hell are you? (Nyamnjoh 86)

Note the mathematical template Francis B. Nyamnjoh provides and looks even further at how Lady Bracknell's set of conditions for Gwendolyn's boyfriends is every bit as calculated. Age is important. Physical address is important. Whether Jack smokes cigarettes or cigars is important. The only thing we, the reader(s), need is to fill in a name that brings with it the particular theme that fits the circumstance. In society's eyes Jack's very DNA changes when we associate him with a brand new name. He has a "proper" name, as Fowler would make note of, but is that name "proper" in terms of its other definition? (1). Is it appropriate or suitable? Does it conform? Nyamnjoh, in his wonderfully energetic look into people's sexual exploits does not need proper names. He needs common nouns. Words like "story" need nothing specific because everyone's story is the *same* story. Everyone wants to have sex. The proper names come later when each individual selects a course of action that he/she hopes will give him/her power—the power to take someone to bed. Their characteristics, connections and advantages determine their name or, alternatively, Nyamnjoh determines their name and, like a skilled operator of marionettes, guides them and watches them adjust to their own unique set of circumstances.

A name exists to reflect, adjust and enhance identity. It has a special, spiritual connotation that one ignores (or fails to notice) at his/her own peril. Nyamnjoh recognizes this attachment and conjures Lilly Loveless to reveal the evidence that supports this unbreakable chain. Her doctoral research involving "fieldwork," is new to her but it is not new to social and biological scientists (Nyamnjoh 1). The relationship between a person's name and a person's identity is anthropological (Culleton 31). It goes back many centuries and this fact is not lost on Nyamnjoh. The case studies we receive from Britney, Lilly's research assistant and receptionist at the Mountain View Hotel, all have to do with a relationship between two entities that is impossible to untangle. Nearly a century ago Sir James Frazer, in *The Golden Bough*, pointed out a fact that if read by Lilly Loveless at the Muzunguland African Studies Institute at Bruhlville might have saved her the cost of a return Air Mimbo ticket. The link we are talking about

> …is not a mere arbitrary and ideal association, but a real and substantial bond which unites the two in such a way that magic may be wrought on a man just as easily through his name as through his hair, his nails or any other material part of his person (Frazer 284).

And Ndũngi wa Mũngai, in the chapter "Immortality is in your name" in *Framing My Name: Extending Educational Boundaries*, points out that the name reveals the person and further talks about how a name embeds and immerses one into the minutiae of a given system. Names matter and the person who does the naming wields the power. He/she is the driver of the car, the Captain of the ship or the head decision maker. To this he writes:

Among the Gĩkũyũ people of Central Kenya where I was born, we tend not to talk in terms of 'my name' when we speak in our mother tongue. Instead, we tend to say 'I am called –'. This implies that it is others who give you a name to identify you with…A name tells a lot about you and acts as a window for others to peep in, as they attempt to know you. In some cases, the name can determine whether you live or die depending on who is peeping and what their intentions are… (*Framing My Name* 102).

Based on a name people presume behavior. A name says something about how a person will dress, speak, procreate, vote and earn a living. It says something about whether or not a person "dare[s] to enter in [or remains] weeping stood without" according to William Blake. (52)

If the name reveals the person, the person reflects society. In Mimboland one cannot help see danger, difficulty and disorder because the sexual relationships are not fundamentally stable. When a girl named Valerie ("girl" is Nyamnjoh's nomenclature) begins dating a medical doctor it seems, at first, that she has found the "Mimbolandian dream". The doctor buys her things, lets her stay in his up-to-date house (in terms of facilities) while this gives her prestige by association (Nyamnjoh 119). Is this not the same motivation that powers Gustave Flaubert's *Madame Bovary*? How did that work out? Not only does Valerie have an MD's spouse to consider she must also be wary of "other girls dating her doctor, and using every dirty trick in the book to win him over" (Nyamnjoh 120). Clearly the doctor, who is not innocent in this scenario, is making the most of his medical training. Pray tell, what was his specialty? In reality this is not a Cameroonian dream. It is a male fantasy where a man has a rotation of four girls (in addition to his wife) with all of the additional women less than half of his age. Valerie says that she cannot leave the doctor "because he supplies me with my needs…" (Nyamnjoh 121). One need not be an etymologist to see the relationship between "Valerie" and "value". The word "valuation" is a staple of Rupert Murdoch's *Wall Street Journal*. Nyamnjoh has taken a girl's name and turned it into a transaction. *Married but Available* reveals secrets that would make a Victorian blush. It drags out into the open the fact that no couple is together for love, affection and genuine companionship. When Valerie's teacher in Form Five in a Catholic School, Mrs. Fidelis, appears and is also dating the doctor it is clear that her name means something too. It is a misnomer. How can Mrs. Fidelis be party to an infidelity? "…fidelity is only skin deep" according to our author (Nyamnjoh 123). Africa is, in his words, an incubator, not for premature infants in a nursery ward, but for affairs. A moment of fun is quickly replaced with suffering, lasting hurt and bitter tears.

Lilly's landlady, named Desire, is one of the rare people who actually realizes that storybook love evaporates with youth. In terms of literature, no one in Mimboland has gotten to the nineteenth century. Desire's praise of the ideal, always using words like "companionship", "chemistry", and "beyond sexual attraction" quickly give way to relationships that are an "extractive industry" (Nyamnjoh 386). People grab and people take, all the while manipulating others. The language she uses to summate her soliloquies is "pursuing shadows" (Nyamnjoh 386). But what are these shadows and what do they have to do with love, power, sex, and desire. Sigmund Freud states that "satisfaction is obtained from illusions" (Freud 30 -31). Whereas Desire embraces reality people actively and eagerly run from it. Nobody wants any distance to exist between illusion and reality because this will "interfere with enjoyment" (Freud 31). In an attempt to enjoy, in the short term, the individual suffers, spends, confuses, misappropriates imagination and "...underestimate what is of true value in life" (Freud 1). This is a perpetuation of childhood fantasy where no one wants to do without the psychological, physical, and financial that someone else must pay for.

Names move people spiritually. In *Married but Available* they are revealing poetic devices. Nyamnjoh's ability to maneuver and manipulate them shapes the novel and keeps things lively. Given the subject matter this sort of "liveliness" is reminiscent of Geoffrey Chaucer. Chaucer uses nearly "2,000 names" in his writing (Fowler 15). The pilgrims would surely have enjoyed these kinds of stories. The sexual humor seems to be a perfect fit. The way in which Nyamnjoh's women gush over cute cell phones, shoes, boutiques and expensive clothing is part of the farce.

As if all of this is not enough remember the "thin light skinned black woman in a colorfully lacy top" who sits next to Lilly, at the window, of the Air Mimbo flight (Nyamnjoh 6). The unnamed woman has just completed a degree in reproductive health and is returning to Mimboland to teach HIV/AIDS prevention. Up to date scholarship is being promoted and introduced, but does anyone even care? Upon meeting the Honourable(sic) Epicure Bilingue, also an international airline passenger, Lilly exclaims "What a name!" (Nyamnjoh 7). The "bilingual" reference refers not to spoken language but to homosexuality, another topic which nobody wants to talk about. If people that are gay do indeed exist as "'...well-placed high ranking members of society'" the discourse is about how to remove them rather than understand them (Nyamnjoh 423). Bilingue is a "...maverick politician, member of parliament and of government with a taste for new ways of quenching old thirsts (Nyamnjoh 424). This is another element of modernity (and reality) that no one wants a part of. Bilingue is a touchstone, traveling as a political pilgrim, back to Africa, who organizes "Dens of Perversion that make Sodom and Gomorrah look like pre-historic child's play" (Nyamnjoh 424). This is a nation that is not comfortable in its own skin. The females are in context and belong in modern Africa, but does modern Africa belong? The continent is not the birthplace of consumerist ideals. *Married but Available* could not have been written in the nineteen fifties.

Somehow a culture which is not known for instant gratification has become a place where too much is never enough. In their book *Affluenza*, Clive Davis and Richard Dennisss state that people complete themselves "by acquiring things that compensate for our [their] perceived shortcomings" (13). But what possible shortcomings can the African have? The continent has wonderful natural beaches and resources. The land is nothing less than a "perfect paradise" (Nyamnjoh 71).

On the beach, women like Lilly Loveless and her assistant, Britney, "spread their towels side by side to start the day with liquid pleasures in the company of the sea. Lilly Loveless attached her curls at the back of her head while Britney let her long braids go free" (Nyamnjoh 115). They could easily be samples of the fieldwork in their own academic research. The notion of wanting to improve, and doing so through clothing and cars, is a concept that has been imported from the West. In 1884, at the very seashore, Sir Alfred Saker landed, in hopes of colonizing "Mimboland" i.e. Cameroon for the United Kingdom. In what Bob Dylan might have called "A Simple Twist of Fate", Alfred Saker landed just a day after the Germans had appropriated the territory as a colony. It is upon precise and unanticipated details such as these that fortunes are made and fortunes are lost. The beach—Sakerbeach—brings us home to the naming principle. We are too late, fallen if we were religious, and the pristine components of Africa that existed before cannot be put back together. Likewise, the possibility of romance between Bobinga Iroko and Lilly Loveless cannot truly blossom. It is too late as well. This materialism causes problems that were not there before. The need to consume is irredeemably harmful and causes all sorts of psychological and sociological problems. Issues such as love affairs, marriages, and family structures are thrown out of balance. Who would have thought that colonialism's greatest weapon was not the gun, the language or the currency, but rather the credit card. From the moment she arrives Lilly is introduced to "…the bumpy reality of a city hardly at peace with itself. The city's roads and refuse had been totally neglected, just as the air conditioning, toilets and other facilities at the nightmare of an airport. It was as if Mimboland had gone for decades without a government…" (Nyamnjoh 9). When she finally arrives in

Puttkamerstown, where the university is located, there is a fountain dedicated to Prussian legislator Otto von Bismarck. The clumsily disguised name is a tip off that this is Cameroon and that money and control emanate from elsewhere. The once luxurious Lodge of Puttkamerstown is a significant symbol of "…power and powerlessness…" whose clock has literally stopped ticking (just as George Orwell uses an intentionally incorrect time piece in *1984*. There is no genuine heartbeat, only a lack of self-reliance. Psychologist Tim Kasser reveals that materialism brings with it a tremendous, and unadvertised, cost (Kasser 72). Materialistic values get in the way of people being healthy and having healthy relationships with other people. All of this buying, in the long run, makes people unsure and insecure about whom they are. It puts distance between people and their names. This is a crisis of identity and self-perception. This is a lesson unknowingly proven by women who

> …cheat for various reasons, major amongst which is the need to live a life that is not theirs. The pressures on them to dress well, do their hair, buy this and that, be here or there in a class and in places above their means or attainments, push them into the open arms of affairs with men who are either pretending or honest about bringing them to consumer paradise (Nyamnjoh 80).

Nyamnjoh chronicles this unhappiness. He portrays people as objects. They are manipulated by other people. The men pursue sex—what those in Mimboland call "horizontal jogging" (Nyamnjoh 40). The women pursue money. That means luxurious apartments, hard wood floors, perfumes, track suits, trendy outfits and a plethora of other things they cannot easily afford themselves. The result is a lack of caring and relationships that do not have any sort of authenticity. African and African-American literature scholar Robert Phillipson calls this "the language of reification and commodification" (Adams and Mayes 224). In humanitarian terms people have failed miserably. A person's attributes—their hair color, their bank account balance, the brand sewn into the soles of their shoes—are what count. These conditions are then "traded" to satisfy wants and needs just like frozen pork bellies on the Chicago Mercantile Exchange.

In keeping with the tract on naming, it is no wonder that Francis B. Nyamnjoh calls one of his less than introspective characters Dr. Simba Spineless. He is missing what is truly important, peoples' inherent qualities, and he disregards them. The subject, characterized by kindness, self-esteem, satisfaction, healthy relationships and other qualities that can't be bought, is replaced by the object, something that is exchanged, given, received, and often confused with being a true connection to another person. Spineless's shiny new Prado, a fancy car he has received as a bribe, exists to help him sleep with women and he has a "…queue of university girls at his service every day…" (Nyamnjoh 40). In terms of priorities "…when Dr. Simba Spineless is determined to think, he thinks with his penis. He begs to differ with those who insist there must be more to a woman than being a writing pad" (Nyamnjoh 41). His attempts at authorship are prolific.

The "Reg of Mimbo", the doctor is a high ranking official at the university, has produced a dystopic novel, a crumbling marriage, and even more illegitimate children than he can count (Nyamnjoh 39). His first name, Simba, references the animation of Walt Disney. This is because the adult is a child. It is children who watch cartoons. It is children who have yet to form an identity. *The Lion King* entertains as a rite of passage that Simba Spineless has yet to experience. His maturation lies in front of him and, since he is fifty years old, this is a national crisis. The "spineless" surname means that he has no resolve. He cannot stick to solely one woman. He can't even keep the number of his sex partners in the single digits. *Married but Available* is a text that, while very humorous and very entertaining, is a curious study in chaos. The result is that Mimboland does not function properly. In the 1994 film version Simba the baby lion runs away and avoids his responsibilities and ignores the fact that he must one day become king. His namesake is ensconced in an equally idealistic jungle paradise. More than $400 million in international ticket sales travel back to Los Angeles in the hopes that it will stay that way.

Married but Available is a realist novel in which peoples' happiness is wrapped up in possessions. But there is one problem with this. Women are not things. There is more to them, and they have more to offer, than merely being people to have sex with. Something must have happened to change the African mindset. The traditions, the way people thought and felt prior to (roughly) the mid-nineteen sixties, have changed and have been transformed. In his book chapter "Balzac in Zanzibar", Robert Phillipson calls this new society "bourgeois individualism" (Adams and Mayes 222). It swoops in from the West and (and unlike the sankofar bird and more like a pterodactyl) it "attacks" the way people think. The word that often comes up is reconfigured, reoriented or reprogrammed (Adams and Mayes 222). No matter how it is named people have conformed to a brand new way of thinking. They learn to embrace "markets" and once introduced to this new way of thinking they cannot easily go back. In addition, just like a religious convert who has found a brand new way of worshipping God, be it Catholicism, Judaism, Hinduism or Quakerism, the newly initiated cleave to this new way of life with an ardent fervor that exceeds the expectations of those who have done the converting. Literary figures like Graham Greene and Gerard Manley Hopkins come to mind along with religious figures such as John Henry Newman, Saul of Tarsus and Saint Augustine. The new African, or should I say the African who has now been introduced and integrated into the world of commodities, aspires to buy more than a nineteen year old in Beverly Hills. If the nineteen year old is female, she is now susceptible and vulnerable to the man who can buy her things that she wants. In what Phillipson calls the developing economy of Africa in the twenty-first century money can buy absolutely anything and the emotional consequences of this are no less significant than the invention of the electric light (Phillipson 224).

If we look at these anecdotes inquisitively, and resist the urge to point the figure of judgment, we realize why Chapter Ten of Nyamnjoh's novel begins with Lilly having a stomach ache. The language the author uses, ostensibly talking about the washing of hands, is that people are less concerned about cleanliness than about "redistributing dirt" (Nyamnjoh 123). The language is loaded with meaning. Nyamnjoh says that Lilly may have "[fallen] prey to the practice" and one needs not be clairvoyant to interpret this subtext (Nyamnjoh 123). The water, in a plastic bowl, rather than a sink with running water, "was the same that had done several rounds of dirty hands" (Nyamnjoh 123). Why is dirt, dust or grime part of the package when it comes to making love? Could it be, as a comedian in the United States once said, that sex is only dirty if you are doing it correctly? Lilly, as someone who is young and from Muzunguland, views all of Britney's eavesdropping as shocking. She is, literally, "a shrinking violet"—a play on the "flower" that her name represents. She is considering cross-pollination. Her home country, like England in the eighteen eighties at the height of the rule of Queen Victoria, like the American South right now, which preaches monogamy only to practice serial monogamy or infidelity (like in the recent case of Louisiana congressional representative Vance McAllister in early April of 2014), and like the Ireland of James Joyce where families are frequently too large and ill planned because contraception is forbidden due to religious reasons, puts its collective head in the sand. The ostrich is tellingly referred to with the plural of the word "fowl" by Nyamnjoh (Nyamnjoh 123). "Fowl", being precisely identical in pronunciation to "foul", means full of dirt or mud. When scared the creature, which cannot fly, places its beak and its head in the sand to avoid any bad information. They have forgotten what the two women discussed at the very start; "Scholarship is not about subjectivities. Objectivity is paramount and a good researcher is one who sterilises[sic] her personal opinions" and truly opens her eyes in support of the facts (Nyamnjoh 49). Lilly's illness is twofold: on the one hand Muzunguland does not tolerate sex or any form of outward sensual expression. That is bad. On the other hand Mimboland is so accepting and sex so common and readily available that it has lost its meaning. That is bad. It is no wonder she keeps running to the toilet. Whichever step she takes she has a problem. Every move she makes eliminates a possible alternative. And the clock is ticking as Nyamnjoh intimates through a flashback replete with rhetorical questions exposing her rebelliousness against Victorian/Muzuguland conservatism:

> Lilly Loveless remembered thinking years ago, as she walked through a crowded shopping mall in her native Bruhlville: what would it be like to approach some relaxed-looking tall,

handsome, sexy young man her age and lay a kiss on him? Would he take advantage of a passionate kiss with a stranger? Would she earn herself a black eye? Would it be exciting, or disappointing? Both? What if she dazed him by flashing her tits to say: 'Be a man – take me, use me?' She fantasized about breaking some other intriguing taboos, such as sex with an extra man or woman in the picture, the way only exhibitionists or the porn industry know best. Was that too weird, too counter culture, too dark and wrong? Or was it a valid sexual exploration that she was ashamed of due only to society's wagging finger (Nyamnjoh 75)?

Any person who does not know where they belong is going to be hurt, marginalized, alienated, and in need of a very sympathetic ear. In Lilly's case her environment is so easygoing that her reaction to it is nothing like the past. It shapes her, changes her, and makes her question her upbringing. When Joseph Conrad does it he is colonizing. When Francis B. Nyamnjoh does it he is looking at the damage colonization has wrought. It is easy for Lilly to lose track of whether her sensational research emanates from Muzunguland or Mimbolnad. The two regions are so different that an accurate translation is impossible. People have been openly cheating and running around in Mimboland for so long that such discussions need not be articulated. They are redundant. Bobinga Iroko says "If you want fidelity love is not the game for you. Only a moralizing hypocrite or an idle social scientist would think of wasting money on a silly study like yours" (Nyamnjoh 37). Lilly's understanding of Africa is rooted in the colonial era, with all of the misconceptions, mistakes, and misjudgments inherent within. People do not philander because they are told not to philander. The nation is independent because, in 1960, it was declared independent. This is the horror, the brand new horror—the gap, chasm or pit between what existed a century ago in the Belgian Congo (when Conrad wrote *Heart of Darkness*) and the present (in Nyamnjoh's Mimboland *cum* Cameroon). Are we to live in the Victorian world of rules and limits or in the present world that is so relaxed with itself and who it is? Conrad provides us with the first hint of the environmental cyst of materialism. A cyst is a tough protective capsule or membrane which covers or surrounds a parasite in its gestative state. It is a cell or cavity that encloses reproductive bodies. *Heart of Darkness*, one of the first novellas that embraces European Imperialism as a subject, dives headfirst into the morbid squalor that will soon besmirch the lovely environs with plastic, labels, chaos, complexity and accountants with red ink who do business from other parts of the world and make the African feel like an unwelcome guest.

The word 'ivory' rang in the air, was whispered, was sighed. You would think they were praying to it. A taint of imbecile rapacity blew through it all, like a whiff from some corpse. By Jove! I've never seen anything so unreal in my life. And outside, the silent wilderness surrounding this cleared speck on the earth struck me as something great and invincible, like evil or truth, waiting patiently for the passing away of this fantastic invasion (Conrad 125).

To cure her physical and existential crisis Lilly must hear a message like this one. Is economic freedom, the kind of security Conrad speaks of, important or is the selfish desire to have more, that Nyamnjoh speaks of, important? In the midst of this conflict, and in need of peace, Lilly is brought to the hospital to seek treatment. She arrives at Mount Rebecca Hospital with Bobinga Iroko to seek an explanation for her troubles.

The occurrence in Lilly's stomach may seem a regular course or procedure. After all, people have stomach aches all of the time. Having a meal out in a public place in a restaurant or bar may indeed cause some sort of gastric distress. A small and inexpensive place, in a city like Douala for example, may not be accurately inspected by the African equivalent of the Food Safety and Inspection Service. There may be no one to ensure that the nation's commercial supply of meat, fish, and poultry are free from dirt, unsoiled, safe, and wholesome. Her lunches of Watafufu and Eru may be the problem. But they are not the problem. Her need for a remedy is not an aberration. There is no such thing as an innocuous detail when one is talking about literary discourse. The biologist E. O. Wilson states that those who actually do the research will tell you that "…they almost never find a phenomenon, no matter how odd or irrelevant it looks when they first see it, that doesn't prove or serve a function…" (*Psychology Today*, Interview, "E.O. Wilson Is on

Top of the World", September 1, 1998). That goes tenfold when one is researching, reading and writing about money, sex, and power.

Just like a mathematic equation which links two specific elements, there is a purpose behind the naming of the medical facility. Mount Rebecca hospital is not a random phrase, title nor appellation. Rebecca is the name of a prominent figure in the Old Testament. In terms of theological substance she is one of the four Matriarchs of Israel. She is always depicted in sketches, paintings and artwork holding a carafe or jar on her shoulder or being by a water well. Hence the reference to Lilly washing her hands in *Married but Available*. Rebecca is sought after as a potential wife for Abraham's son Isaac. In verse 18 of Genesis 24 she states "Drink my lord." And I will fetch water for your camels as well. She is a woman of great character and this one of the most emotional and love inducing scenes in *The Bible*. There is nothing like it in Muzunguland and Mimboland.

Lilly's pain, illness, discomfort and stomach ache have their antecedent in Rebecca. Our postgraduate student is in a quandary over the trouble she sees. She is always "not knowing what to make of Britney's stories (Nyamnjoh 154). Her conscience is always "telling herself not to be shocked by whatever would come next" (Nyamnjoh 141). But she is discombobulated and her stomach is spinning. This is a crisis. Nyamnjoh knows she is not the first woman to be so unsettled. Rebecca's pregnancy, after twenty barren years, is extremely uncomfortable. The course of this unsettled chaos is a mystery. "Why is this happening to me?" says Rebecca as she prays to God for answers (Genesis 25: 22). The word, phrase or image of a woman with stomach pain serves as an umbilical cord between the two women. They are connected by a tool or a literary device and it is a new one. The name Rebecca means to tie, to couple, to join and to secure. The babies Esau and Jacob are inside Rebecca's belly, fighting with each other constantly to see which of the two will prevail. "Two nations are in your womb; two people will come from you and be separated" (Genesis 25: 23). They are two conflicting ideas and philosophies. In time the two countries of Edom and Israel, one for each boy, will struggle just like the two countries that battle for Lilly's soul.

A scientist is a person who orders, categorizes, and classifies. If an epiphytic orchid grows non-parasitically it is the job of an expert researcher, in this case a botanist, to separate the epiphytic from those that are parasitical. Does one benefit at the expense of another or not? Since orchids are a symbol of love and beauty, and are colorful and come in gift baskets, it is easy to see that such a tropical, ornamental plant can reveal human characteristics. Lilly Loveless is a behavioral scientist. She is not so concerned about the different types of orchids, but she is concerned about the different types of people. She wants to investigate how people act while simultaneously remaining above the fray so her judgment is not impaired. What she does not expect is that what takes place in *Married but Available* will attract her and pull her in. The fieldwork for her PhD, which at first was thought to be an in-depth examination of other peoples' ethics, values and proclivities turns out to be a self-analysis. Her misadventure upends and disorients her and the longer she stays in Mimboland the more she must unlearn all of the lessons she has so carefully been taught at home.

Works Cited

Adams, Anne V. and Janice A, Mayes. (eds.) *Mapping Intersections: African Literatures and African Development No. 2.* Trenton: Africa World Press, Incorporated, 1998. Print.

Blake, William, "I Saw a Chapel of Gold" in *Selected Poetry.* London: Penguin Books, 1988. Print.

Conrad, Joseph. *Heart of Darkness and Other Tales.* Oxford: Oxford's World Classics, 2003. Print.

Culleton, Claire A. *Names and Naming in Joyce.* Madison: The University of Wisconsin Press, 1994. Print.

Emerson, Ralph Waldo. *Intellect: ,* Philadelphia: Henry Altemus. 1896. Print.

Fowler, Alastair. *Literary Names: Personal Names in English Literature.* Oxford: Oxford University Press, 2012. Print.

Fraser, Sir James. *The Golden Bough: A Study In Magic And Religion* I Volume, Abridged Edition. New York: The Macmillan Company, 1951. Print.

Freud, Sigmund. *Civilizations and its Discontents*. New York and London: W. W. Norton & Company, 1961. Print.

Hamilton, Clive and Richard Denniss. *Affluenza: when too much is never enough*. Crown Nest NSW (Australia): Allen & Unwin, 2006. Print.

Kasser, Tim. *The High Price of Materialism*. Cambridge, Massachusetts and London, England: The MIT Press, 2002. Print.

Lennon, John. *Milk and Honey,* New York: Capitol Records, 2010. Audio CD.

Nyamnjoh, Francis. *Married but Available*. Bamenda: Langaa Research and Publishing CIG, 2009. Print.

Shakespeare, William. *The Complete Works*. New York: Harcourt Brace Jovanovich, Incorporated, 1968. Print.

West, Cornell. *Democracy Matters: Winning the Fight against Imperialism*. New York: The Penguin Press 2004. Print.

Wilde. Oscar. *The Importance of Being Earnest*. New York: Dover Publications Incorporated, 1990. Print.

Wilson, E. O. Interview, "E.O. Wilson Is on Top of the World", September 1, 1998. Web May 5 2014

Chapter Five

Ironic Onomastic Strategies of Calixthe Beyala and Chimamanda Adichie

By
Robert Miller and Gloria Onyeoziri

If names carry meaning, they are also open to the charge of irony: if a character's name "means" something in the language of the text or in the language represented indirectly by the text, then that name may also carry the shadow of implied double meaning. Out of this double meaning can arise satire, playful allusion, ridicule, or suggestive contradiction.

The ironic onomastic strategies of Chimamanda Adichie, found in her "traditional woman's narrative" "The Headstrong Historian," are rooted in the naming practices of Igbo language and culture where children are frequently named by (sometimes elliptical) sentences carrying proverbial, spiritual, or practical claims to wisdom and understanding. As pointed out by Afam Ebeogu:

> virtually every name in the Igbo culture, as in many other African cultures, has a context. The contextual significance of these names implies that each of them is the product of some experience, which produces a creative exercise that gives rise to the name. Each of these names is, therefore, of some literary significance in so far as the human imagination has fashioned out the name within the framework of a particular true experience. Thus, each of these names is parahistorical, in the sense that it is the product of a creative imagination rooted in a historical fact. (137)

As Adichie seeks to inscribe a woman's voice into the assumptions and presumptions of both patriarchal traditions and colonial domination, the names given, taken and refused by various characters reflect the struggle of retelling and subversive reflection on imposed, fractured, and contended senses of identity. Naming is not only a struggle pitting Igbo names against "Christian" names, but a subtle game where each act of "renaming" becomes an ironic response to a previous act of naming.

Calixthe Beyala, in her "novel of tradition" *Les arbres en parlent encore*, makes a number of references to the native language of the ethnic community represented in the novel (the Issogos), but the names of many of her major characters are more closely connected to the French language. We are not told whether these "French" names such as "Fondamento de Plaisir," "Esprit de vie,""Opportune des Saintes Guinées," and "Édène" should be understood as translations of Issogo names, as nicknames created by the narrator herself, or simply as names reflective of the creative genius of the community they represent. Nevertheless, the overall effect of this array of apocryphal and surprising names is one of subversive and satirical representation of the social, historical and political worldview that shaped the Issogo community in its experience of German and French colonization as well as its entry into postcolonial times. Men's names could carry cultural value (such as the apparently Issogo name of the protagonist's father) or pompous ridicule (such as the colonial commandant Michel Ange de Montparnasse). Women's names reflect their own inanity (such as Gono la Lune), their potential complicity with their oppressors (such as Opportune des Saintes Guinées) or their multi-dimensional challenge to patriarchal authority (such as Fondamento de Plaisir).

Although their approaches to onomastic meaning differ both in terms of cultural practices and tone (Adichie using in "The Headstrong Historian" less obvious comic effect than *Les arbres en parlent encore*), both of these texts suggest a strong link between naming, discursive disruption of cultural and historical instances of authority, and the insertion of a self-affirming female voice into the narrative of colonial and postcolonial experience. It is therefore the goal of this paper to illustrate and explain the need by these two contemporary African women authors to rename and, sometimes, de-name the signposts of their cultural heritage.

Re-naming and De-Naming

Many elements of our life experience may seem to be given to us in the form of circumstance, culture and socio-economic background, but few of those elements stand out more decisively as a deliberate "gift" than a name. Although we may change our name(s) in various ways through the course of our lives, the naming that takes place either before or after our birth is generally understood to be an act in which we have little or no role to play. Claims and counterclaims of cultural belonging surround our birth. Many cultures construct official proceedings and rituals – such as baptisms and naming ceremonies – to oversee and regulate these claims, to ensure that all legitimate stakeholders, except perhaps we ourselves, are properly represented.

A colonized community is likely to experience this ontologically uncanny practice in an unusually fractured and disconcerting way. Édouard Glissant's novelistic cycle of the Longoué and Béluse families (beginning with *Le Quatrième Siècle*) offers a classic example of the ways in which the disruptions of the Transatlantic Slave Trade put in place generations of re-named families whose identities had to be reconstructed and renegotiated through political resistance, self-questioning and the endless, maddening search of intergenerational memory.

It should come as no surprise therefore that Adichie's "The Headstrong Historian," itself a story of postcolonial re-writing, should place so much emphasis and varies so much on the question of re-naming. There is a major difference, however, between the way in which the protagonist Nwamgba's son is re-named and her experience in relation to her two grandchildren's names.

Her son Anikwenwa (Ani has given the child) was named through a tacit agreement on the part of his parents to express gratitude towards the earth god Ani (202). The English name Michael is imposed by the Catholic priest Father Shanahan "because it was not possible to be baptized with a heathen name" (208), baptism being a condition for admission to the mission school and English language education. Nwamgba (whose name means "child of wrestling" or "wrestling child") fails to see in this change any threat to her son's identity: "His name was Anikwenwa as far as she was concerned; if they wanted to name him something she could not pronounce before teaching him their language, she did not mind at all" (208). There are at least two different ways in which we could interpret Nwamgba's ready acquiescence. Since we know that she has her own agenda in sending Anikwenwa to school – the training of her son in English that will enable him to challenge her adversarial in-laws in the colonial court system. She may have been unaware of the insidiously subversive trap hidden behind the transformation of Anikwenwa into Michael. According to this interpretation, Father Shanahan's act of baptism was a revised version of the parents' original act of naming, but one whose significance was capable of being concealed from the person who, as the original naming agent, had the most interest in preventing that revision. Another interpretation, however, would be that Nwamgba's true resistance to colonial acculturation, the resistance that will eventually reshape her granddaughter's understanding of history, does not lie in any pitched battle against the foreign aggressor but in the self-understanding that enables one to dismiss the nomenclature of the other as irrelevant to one's own symbolic universe. The wrestler's more subtle form of struggle lies in the refusal to envision defeat. If Michael is a name she cannot pronounce, it is necessarily, in Nwamgba's mind, a meaningless detail. The foreigners may offer some useful tools as means to power but do not have the power, according to Nwamgba, to undo the act of naming that was intimately related to her life, to that of her husband, and to her beliefs.

Nwamgba's encounter with re-naming reaches a climax when her name for her granddaughter Afamefuna comes into competition with the Catholic priest's choice of Grace:

> From the moment Nwamgba held her, the baby's bright eyes delightfully focused on her, she knew that it was the spirit of Obierika that had returned; odd, to have come in a girl, but who could predict the ways of the ancestors? Father O'Donnell baptized her Grace, but Nwamgba called her Afamefuna, "My Name Will Not be Lost," and was thrilled by the child's solemn interest in her poetry and her stories, the teenager's keen watchfulness as Nwamgba struggled to make pottery with newly shaky hands. (214-215)

The narrator has quietly inversed the order of re-naming by suggesting that Nwamgba's onomastic claim overrides the baptismal name. Like the ironist who often accidentally fails to mention the target of her irony, the narrator makes reference neither to Nwamgba's reaction to Father O'Donnell's decision nor to the incongruity of her son Michael's complicity in allowing a stranger to determine his daughter's name. The notion of grace itself seems to slip into Nwamgba's renewed hope of life as her gradual erasure from her descendants' memory is at least mitigated. In fact, both names are highly pertinent to Grace's life, considering her grandfather's family's apparent genetic predisposition to recurrent miscarriages. But just as grace does not slip into Afamefuna comfortably (the grace Nwamgba found in her granddaughter was probably not exactly what Father O'Donnell had in mind), Grace herself will practice something closer to de-naming by having her name officially changed to Afamefuna ("in a Lagos courthouse" 218) after her grandmother's death. While Onyeoziri suggests that this act can be seen as a way of inscribing orality, with its implicit self-affirmation, into an apparently transcendent written culture, the act of de-naming as such also has its implications. Nwamgba's naming of her granddaughter simply ignored the intrusion of colonial values, but Afamefuna had to undo a process of identity formation that had characterized, for the most part, her entire life experience, including her education, career and marriage, with nothing to go on but the marginalized presence of an aging grandmother. Yet, we read that Afamefuna, as she struggles to represent African history in a postcolony barely able to understand the value of that discipline, "would imagine her grandmother looking on and chuckling with great amusement." The act of de-naming is not only a "headstrong" effort to reclaim the traditional knowledge that the world took away from her when it named her Grace, but also a nod of complicity to a woman who refused to take a foreign culture more seriously than her own experience, critical thinking, and beliefs. As Ogwude points out, Adichie consistently "contrasts various life-styles within her social matrix, showing the wholesome and life-supporting alternatives as well as the negative and self-destructive ones" (119).

The name that doesn't seem to fit or seems to fit too well

Beyala's *Les arbres en parlent encore*'s onomastic strategy does not involve an immediately obvious process of naming, renaming and de-naming, but that nonetheless suggestively identifies characters according to the narrator's ironic intentions. In a sense, the naming and renaming has already taken place in Édène's creative reconstruction of the colonial world she remembers from her earliest childhood memories as the daughter of Assanga Djuli whose story "is none other than the story of Africa crouched between tradition and modernity" (7).[5]

One of the most striking names is attached to one of the most striking characters in the novel, Édène's stepmother Fondamento de Plaisir. The odd combination of Italian and French words used to name Assanga Djuli's second spouse reflects Fondamento de Plaisir's role as a pioneer among the Issogos in the importation of European consumer goods. Although Édène is silent on the origins of the name, one possible explanation would be that the foreign sounding names came attached to some brand name or marketing slogan used in the past by the astute businesswoman to attract clients to her revolutionary new line of products:

[Fondamento de Plaisir] supplied the village with products whose existence we knew nothing about before. As soon as she brought them tied up in her wrapper, she would go around the village beating on a saucepan: "New things from Urope! Come see the newest new things from Urope" [...] Then her goods would appear before our wondering eyes: cloths dyed to the color of birdkillers, *Douceur de Lune* talcum power, perfumes and soaps. (82)

Like her products, Fondamento has built her reputation and economic ascendancy on the mystifying attraction of foreign sounding words. As the meaning of her name suggests, she has established for herself a foundation of economic independence on the buying and selling of widely varying forms of pleasure. Sexual pleasure may be the most obvious of these commodities, but they also include the attraction of globalizing consumerism and the mystification of language. Fondamento herself, ironically, is in some

---

[5] All translations from the French in this study are our own.

ways deprived of the fundamental pleasure she trades in. Having no children, she is reduced to tears by Édène's vindictiveness on behalf of her jealous but highly fecund mother Andala and her attempt to "adopt" a child picked up somehow from the market ends in humiliating failure. As we see Fondamento de Plaisir build her commercial empire while gradually losing the battle for Assanga Djuli's affection to Andala, a more conventional and unimaginative spouse, we begin to understand that the pleasure-foundation in Édène's sexual economy is both precarious and treacherous, a foundation that allows a woman to affirm her independence in the community while at the same time insidiously sowing the seeds of her ultimate marginalization and exclusion.

Édène herself comes close to reproducing her stepmother's trajectory as she rebels against the physical abuse of an elderly husband imposed on her by her family, faces excommunication and estrangement from her parents, forms a shaky alliance with Fondamento, and fights in colonial court to protect her children from her ex-husband's patriarchal claims. The Edenic echoes of her memorial to her cultural past contained in her name are only partly contradicted by her own fate. On the one hand, her determination to honor her father's memory as "the history of Africa" enables her to understand (without accepting) the ostracizing effects of colonialism and patriarchy. On the other hand, her ironic treatment of her father's questionable legacy invites caution and skepticism on the reader's part when it comes to any precipitate celebration of "traditional Africa" Hitchcott (20).[6]

This line of analysis leads us to reflect further on the lavish name that Édène attributes to her suspected half-sister and life-long rival Opportune des Saintes Guinées. A woman is "opportune" when she appears on the scene at exactly the right moment. She is perfectly placed to benefit from given circumstances or to prove useful in those circumstances. The reach of Catholicism, under both German and French colonization of Cameroun, is strongly connoted by the expression "Saintes Guinées," making one of Africa's broad zones of traditional culture appear inherently

---

[6]Hitchcott emphasizes this highly skeptical treatment of "the oral tradition" as a central theme of *Les arbres en parlent encore*.

Christian.[7] Opportune's name places her at the forefront of European evangelization, both as the ideal recipient of Catholic values and the perfect vessel for their propagation. One of the Issogos' first converts, Chrétien No. 1, is attracted to Opportune, at the expense of his admirer Édène. Opportune seems to be everything that Édène is not: attractive to men, submissive to the patriarchal authority of Gazolo (Chrétien No. 1's middle-aged father to whom Édène is forcibly given in marriage by her own father), and open to the new Catholic faith.

Yet, Opportune is surprisingly unsuccessful in fulfilling the contract of opportunity that her marriage to Chrétien No. 1 seemed to imply. It is in fact the crisis in her relationship with Chrétien No. 1 that will lead to Édène's nearly lifelong estrangement from Gazolo, from her own parents, and from the Issogo community. After discovering (through Édène) that Chrétien No. 1 has been seen with another young woman, Opportune resists his advances. When Chrétien complains of the situation to his step-mother Édène, she makes the strangely inappropriate suggestion: "T'as qu'à la violenter," (277). The verb *violenter* is ambiguous in French in that it can mean to treat someone or something in a violent way (already shocking enough in itself), but can also be a euphemism for *violer* (to rape). Though Édène claims that she didn't think she was doing any harm in giving this advice, Chrétien No. 1 apparently understands the word in the second sense and tries to force himself on Opportune, and it is in defending the latter from this violence that she herself planted in Chrétien No. 1's mind that Édène will decide to stand up to Gazolo (her husband and Chrétien No. 1's father) to the point of beating him up and becoming an outcast.

Despite the epic character of Édène's wrestling match with Gazolo, her role as a woman resisting patriarchal oppression does not emerge unscathed from her duplicitous dealings with her half-sister. Her strong desire for Chrétien No. 1, and consequent jealousy, poorly serve any possible cause of solidarity in a common cause. To the extent that we can attribute the name Opportune des

---

[7] Whereas, as Augustine Asaah points out, in Beyala's work "toponyms and anthroponyms betray the novelist's will to blaspheme" (160). Asaah understands blasphemy in this context as the use of discourse to challenge the assumption that Africans are inherently more spiritual or religious than other people.

Saintes Guinées to Édène's creative work, it would appear that the latter sought to create a multivalent figure reflecting the exploitation of women, the hypocrisy of a "Christian" Africa and her own sense of being passed over because of her "masculine" strength of character to the advantage of a more attractive, but weaker, half-sister. The opportune nature of the "first" Christian's first wife is thus represented as an illusion for Opportune herself and an obstacle to Édène's fulfillment as Assanga Djuli's "true" daughter destined to tell the story of his legacy. The two mythical/narrative centers of creation – Eden and Guinea – are drawn by Édène's creative economy into competition for a shifting object of desire as Édène's focus gradually moves from Chrétien No. 1 to the affirmation of her own place in history.

Naming and the excess of meaning

In a study of Imanu Amir Baraka's *Dutchman*, in which they insist on the central relationship between naming and re-naming rituals and racial identity in African American writing, Greenfield and Pinchoff describe three ritualistic functions of renaming: ethnic cleansing ("ridding or confounding the racial and cultural identity of the self or the other through naming and/or renaming"); sexual and gender dissolution ("neutering, altering, or grotesquing the sexual identity of the self or other by naming and/or re-naming") and existential negation ("denying by naming and/or re-naming the existence of the self or the other in absolute, universal terms that stand apart from gender, racial, religious, or other forms of cultural 'self' and 'other' identification") (127). These rituals are part of a tradition that goes back to the earliest times of African American history and can be seen "as early as the 18th century" in Olauda Equiano's "asserting the primacy of his African name over his slave name" (123). It would thus not be surprising to find that elements of this three-part analysis would present significant parallels in postcolonial texts such as those of Adichie and Beyala that relate naming practices to a racialized colonial experience of identity loss.

The parallel is not absolute, however. While renaming and pre-emptive naming of Anikwenwa and Afamefuna by Fathers Shanahan and O'Donnell may be a racialized relationship of self and other, something akin to Greenfield and Pinchoff's ethnic cleansing, the overall narrative framework of these acts is less a back and forth of self and other than the story of two women's wrestling match with colonial history and its tendency to erase the memory of the part they have played in that history: Nwamgba reminds us of her part in the formation of Afamefuna's postcolonial vocation as a historian by affirming that her name (or her husband's name) will not be lost, while Afamefuna returns to the colonial archives to reassess the way that her grandmother's people responded to colonial oppression and seals that (re)search project with the return to her grandmother's name. The priests' naming rituals as ethnic cleansing are not forgotten nor are they recognized as irrevocable in their influence or even central to the headstrong historians' narrative.

Many of the ironic naming strategies practiced by Édène in *Les arbres en parlent encore* are directly related to the struggle between the colonized and the colonizer. The early German commandants are both rendered anonymous and ridiculed by labeling them as *Haut Dignitaire No. 3* or *Kommandant No. 3*. A black man acting in complicity with the German authorities in their imposition of oppressive taxation is called "Monsieur Taxes" and will eventually be hanged in an uprising against the German regime. On the other hand, Michel Ange de Montparnasse is ironically named after a Paris subway station as a caricature of the "good colonialist" who temporarily "goes native" only to treat his "African wife" Esprit de Vie like a servant to his "legitimate" French wife. Ethnic cleansing in the economy of Beyala's onomastics is a display of ridiculed claims to superiority punctuated by names suggesting the (not always unambiguous) possibility of socio-cultural leadership such as Fondamento de Plaisir, Assanga Djuli and Édène.

Both Nwamgba and Édène are associated with the effects of Greedfield and Pinchoff's second naming ritual: sexual and gender dissolution. Just as Lula in Baraka's *Dutchman* is given what Greenfield and Pinchoff call a "de-feminized" identity when Clay asks her if she is "a lady wrestler or something" (131), Nwamgba's name designates her as a wrestler, suggesting some awkwardness in the way that her gendered identity is perceived. Her father for example "found her exhausting, this sharp-tongued, head-strong daughter who had once wrestled her brother to the ground. (After which her father had warned everybody not to let the news leave the compound that the girl had thrown a boy.)" (199). Rather than leading to a "defeminisation" of Nwamgba by the other, however, Nwamgba's naming leads to a play on assumptions of what "traditional" gender roles in Igbo communities really were, a bemused reflection that Nwamgba herself takes up when the narrator reports her thoughts on discovering that the spirit of her husband has come back in the body of the girl Afamefuna: "she knew that it was the spirit of Obierika that had returned; odd, to have come in a girl, but who could predict the ways of the ancestors?" (214). By attributing the "oddly" gendered identity of her granddaughter to the ancestors, she associates the event with tradition, but with a tradition that is unpredictable, playful and surprising. Ebeogu points out that names such as "Afamefuna" "are given under circumstances in which the continuity of male progeny in the lineage is somewhat threatened. In some cases, the bearers of the names are the first-born males in the lineage; in some others they are not, rather they only strengthen the progeny already ensured by an earlier birth of a male child in the family"(140). Nwamgba inscribes the play of gender into the granddaughter's name as a permanent problem, a riddle for future generations: is the "my" of "my name shall not be lost" that of Obierika whose spirit has returned in the girl or that of the person who gave the name and in that sense speaks though the act of naming as a person seeking to be remembered.

Although the sexual and gender dissolution is less clearly marked in Édène's name (except perhaps to the extent that as a place name, Eden is inherently gender neutral), Beyala's narrator is also thought to be too strong for a woman and, at least in the early years before she leaves the village to join Fondamento de Plaisir in the city, too masculine in her physical appearance. But, as is the case of Adichie's Nwamgba, the perceived ambiguity of Édène's gendered identity is much more than a ritual of de-feminization. Édène's claim to strength at the expense of social acceptance is a representation of her struggle to be the history of her people that was otherwise assigned to a father whom she admired but who finally could not adequately complete the narrative the inspiration of which she was initially prepared to attribute to him. Hitchcott makes an important point when she states that in *Les arbres en parlent encore*, "Beyala foregrounds the fictional natures of both colonial history and the so-called oral tradition. What she suggests, then, is that neither offers a satisfactory site for the construction of postcolonial femininity" (22). However, to discount Édène's role as a speaking subject of oral tradition and memory, as if the irony and ambivalence of her words cancelled out the self-affirmation that they actually imply, would be to confirm her powerlessness before both gender dissolution and ethnic cleansing.

There is no obvious sense in which Greenfield and Pinchoff's third naming ritual of existential negation achieves any form of transcendence in either Adichie's or Beyala's narrative of tradition. Yet, both texts address this issue in subtle ways. In re-writing the history of the colonization of Nigeria, Adichie also revises the title of colonial narrative derived from the intertext of Achebe's *Things Fall Apart*[8]. The chapter from "her textbook" entitled "The Pacification of the Primitive Tribes of Southern Nigeria" will be re-written as her book *Pacifying with Bullets: A Reclaimed History of Southern Nigeria* (217). Her revision is doubly ironic in that she parodies the earlier title and in that she underlines the paradox of the use of violent means to bring peace. Afamefuna not only de-names herself from the "grace" of Father O'Donnell but (though we are not told whether or not she abandons her married name at some point) also withdraws from the symbolic renaming of marriage. She rejects her Cambridge-educated husband George Chikadibia "not because of the four miscarriages [she] had suffered but because she woke up sweating one night and realized that she would strangle him to death if she had to listen to one more rapturous monologue about his Cambridge days" (217). The miscarriages symbolically evoke the names of Obierika (who had a family history of miscarriages), Nwamgba (who struggled though miscarriages) and Ani (the earth god in gratitude to whom her own father Anikwenwa was named). The marriage naming she rejects; "George Chikadibia" may evoke the king of England through much

---

[8] This title closely resembles the book project that arises in the mind of the District Commissioner on discovering Okonkwo's body: the last words of *Things Fall Apart: The Pacification of the Primitive Tribes of the Lower Niger*. (148)

of Nigeria's colonial period. Chikadibia means Chi is greater than the *dibia*, but the Chi could be the God of the colonialist who is more powerful that tradition, or the God of our tradition who defends from ancient curses such as the tendency to miscarry associated with Obierika's family. Afamefuna has chosen to honor the memory of her grandmother, but ironically the name of the husband whose Cambridge narrative she rejects also seems to echo the situation of her life story. In this sense the onomastic structure of Adichie's story seems to point to a conscious choice by an African woman of her name and its history, while at the same time foregrounding a history of erased identities in which such a conscious choice is extremely difficult.

Édène's act of naming of herself and of those around her similarly suggests an ambivalent refusal of Greenfield and Pinchoff's existential negation. As she reaches the end of her story she explains the basis of her self-confidence:

> I hear the voices of the first Africas, I hear their storytellers and their legends. I hear the voice of Michel Ange de Montparnasse, I hear the rapes, I hear the screams of childbirth. Long minutes of silence follow. Then a jubilatory chorus getting louder and louder: the inviolate voice of the African imagination that no domination will ever bring into submission because it could never give it a name; these are the blended voices of the people of mixed blood that cry out: "We are humanity because we are *métis*." (410-411)

Admitting that she cannot understand the new world or decrypt its song, Édène realizes that she cannot prevent her story from becoming part of a humanity that is human because it is universal. At the same time, she recognizes the jubilation of voices that cannot be conquered precisely because they cannot be named. Given that so much of her creative imagination has been invested in names, one can hardly deny Édène the last word in her ironic claim to remember "the dreamed of time when the corn stalks were of silver and the ears of gold [...] unless that prestigious past of the black continent were just a juggler's trick" (411-412).

Conclusion

As we look more closely at the problem of names in these two narratives that purport to look critically, but not dismissively, at the problem of tradition in postcolonial Africa, we begin to realize that names themselves are closely bound up with that problem. How can we explain this connection? It is clear that at many times in the history of Africa and its diaspora since the time of the slave trade, naming has been a battleground of racial oppression, ideological power struggle, and the denial and affirmation of identity. It is also clear that on this battleground the names of women are often sacrificed, disparaged, or simply forgotten.

On the other hand, our reading of Beyala and Adichie also suggests that the metaphor of the battleground is not necessarily the best way to understand any of these three interrelated problems: names, tradition and the possible perspectives of African women. Not that there were no battles historically, nor that there are no battles in the present state of affairs. But, just as Michel Ange de Montparnasse misunderstood the nature and meaning of the battlefield on which the Issogos under Assanga Djuli declared war on the neighboring Isséles (76-79), falsely equating their war to the European tradition of mass carnage, we too could easily misunderstand the struggles of women characters like Nwamgba, Afamefuna and Édène without sufficient reflection on their contexts and concerns. When an Igbo mother and father sit down together to imagine the name of a child, as when an author sits down to imagine the name of a character, they seat themselves at the confluence of history and imagination in order to give the child that perfect name, a viaticum perfectly suited to a new history of a person in the world. What could be a more important and desirable gift? Contrastingly, what could be a greater emblem of human oppression than to destroy that gift in the name of some claim to racial, cultural or religious superiority? Yet what could be a greater delusion than to think that we could actually conceive of the "right" name for something so elusive and uncontainable as someone else's future? Narratives of tradition, when they are honest about the difficulties tradition poses for everyone, meet this problem head on because they know that to give "our" past a name, we have to relive that terrible moment of naming that dares to imagine who we are and who we could be. The ironic voice, because it refuses to guarantee its own claim to truth, is eminently suited to such a daring gesture.

Works Cited

Adichie, Chimamanda Ngozi. "The Headstrong Historian." In *The Thing Around your Neck*. New York: Knopf, 2009. 198-218. Print.

Asaah, Augustine. "Calixthe Beyala ou le discours blasphématoire au propre." *Cahiers d'Études Africaines* 46.181 (2006): 157-168. Print.

Beyala, Calixthe. *Les arbres en parlent encore*. Paris: Albin Michel, 2002. Print

Ebeogu, Afam. "Onomastics and the Igbo Tradition of Politics." *African Languages and Cultures* 6. 2 (1993): 133-146. Print.

Glissant, Édouard. *Le quatrième siècle*. Paris: Seuil, 1964. Print.

Greenfield, Thomas and Sarah Pinchoff. " 'Hopeless Colored Names': A Taxonomy of Naming and Re-naming Rituals in Baraka's *Dutchman*." *Names* 55.2 (2007): 123-137. Print.

Hitchcott, Nickie. "Calixthe Beyala's *Les arbres en parlent encore*."*Dalhousie French Studies* 68 (2004): 17-25. Print.

Ogwude, Sophia O. "History and Ideology in Chimamanda Adichie's fiction." *Tydskrifvir* Letterkunde 48. 1 (2011): 110-123. Print.

Onyeoziri, Gloria. "L'oralité transposée des femmes africaines : « The Headstrong Historian » de Chimamanda Adichie," in *Traditions oralespostcoloniales*, Luc Fotsing and Moustapha Fall, eds. Paris: Harmattan, 2014. 43-52. Print.

Chapter Six

The Politics of Names in the Age of Globalization: Examining the Socio-Political Consequences

By
Stephen Magu

Introduction

Names are basic individual and collective identifiers. Practically every human being has one. Individuals and societies often choose the length, meaning and other attributes that the name represents. Names have not only been used as identifiers, but also as a "method of differentiation" between different social classes, groups and during pre-modern times, as a justification for ethnic and racial superiority.

In a well-regarded scholarly work, Samuel Huntington argued that "the great divisions among humankind and the dominating source of conflict will be cultural...the fault lines between civilizations will be the battle lines of the future" (22). In his argument, Huntington further proposed eight distinct civilizations. A quick exercise in estimating the cultural differences can be quite aptly captured in the names and social conventions to be found within these "civilizations." Whether or not this argument is accurate, it is important to note the importance that Huntington intimates regarding the basis of nomenclature: culture and identity.

In this vein, examination of naming patterns in eighteenth-century Jamaica illustrates how slaves (and persons of African descent) were considered different. Burnard writes that Whites were listed by first name and surname; slaves were denoted by first name, sometimes accompanied by a modifier referring to age, occupation or ethnicity" (325). Names, in addition to serving the identification function, serve social, political, economic, and cultural functions. They also serve other personal functions; for example, Kolle, Dijksterhuis and van Knippenberg attribute individuals' self-esteem to names and find that some individuals have in the past used names to make life-changing decisions and finding a "positive bias for own name letter affects even important life decisions, such as deciding which place to live, which college to attend, or which career to choose" (671).

There is a strong emphasis on names, naming and the meanings of names. This takes on significant meaning principally in African communities. Names are indicative of ethnicity, of identity, of affiliation. This notion will be revisited later in this chapter. The import of names is not limited to only groups of persons with strong identification with ethnic group; indeed, the function of names can also be found in developed Western nations. In the United States, the use of the terms "Black" versus "African American" has been the source of much debate; identity, including racial identity, can be surmised from names. Martin notes, for example, that in the case of the United States, "Jesse Jackson announced that members of their race preferred to be called 'African American'" (Martin 83). Names have been leveraged by political leaders to appeal to perceived injustices and advocate for changes leading to different power dynamics, to assert particular identity (whether imagined or real) or to differentiate oneself from the "other."

Names, therefore, can have political meaning: as a function of belonging or exclusion and can subsequently become a social and political engagement with far-reaching consequences. This research argues that while names are primary individual identifiers (every individual has one), they serve social, political, economic and cultural functions. Names, as the basis of identity, play a very significant role in international relations. Because they are an inalienable part of individual and group identity, names have been instrumental to global catastrophes such as genocides and politicides, including those in Rwanda, Bosnia and most famously, during the Second World War's holocaust against the Jews in Europe – they were used as identifiers. The dearth of studies on the relationships between names, identity and especially political functions and outcomes overlooks one of the most significant sources of turmoil in the international system in the past hundred and fifty years. The present research recommends that greater attention be paid to the implications of names and their national identities in international relations.

Names in African Societies

According to John Mbiti, naming in African societies was important not only due to the ceremonial nature, but because of the meaning of names. Mbiti writes that "nearly all African names have a meaning; the naming of children is therefore an important occasion which is often marked by ceremonies in many societies" (115). Often, there were several, multiples or even tens of ceremonies each year, which gave meaning to communal life. The ceremonies not only propagated the specific culture of the community, but also prescribed different functions for the different sectors of the community. Ifi Amadiume, for example, writes that "the lineage group named each child born into the patrilineage and performed the naming ceremony. Any member who failed to perform the naming ceremony for his child was fined" (58).

Many African communities practiced (as some still do) elaborate ceremonies around the birth and naming of a child. Naming ceremonies were part of elaborate cultural traditions that affirmed membership, kinship and identity. There is also an active integration of all aspects of life in naming ceremonies: traditional, political and cultural aspects are evident. For example, Nyanzi, Manneh and Walraven record that, with respect to Gambia,

> according to Islamic tradition, the baby is given a name and prayed for by the Imam and the village elders seven days after birth. This naming ceremony is often collectively celebrated with prayers, jubilation, feasting, music, dance and fanciful dressing. Both maternal and paternal relations from far and wide join the family and villagers to witness the naming of the baby (49).

As Stella Nyanzi, Hawah Manneh and Gijs Walraven note, there was significant interest attached to the process of naming the baby, in the belief that the qualities of the person naming the baby (in some cases, the Traditional Birth Attendant), would "shave off the baby's hair, handing the child over to the elders and Imam to give it a name and pray for it", or in some cases, to give the child its name, which was considered one of the highest honors that a Traditional Birth Attendant could be accorded (49).

Naming ceremonies especially in African communities differ from society to society. With close to or over 3,000 individual ethnic groups, the disparities in the naming conventions, practices and ceremonies is huge. However, some general inferences can be drawn from different naming ceremonies. Hahn, Vedder and Fourie, for example, writing about the ethnic groups of South West Africa (again, in a rather generalized fashion), note that the naming ceremony was an occasion to bring together relatives, family and friends.

The father's best friend would play a major role in the child's naming ceremony, although the father would actually name the child. The "name chosen is generally that of the father's greatest friend, whether a relative or not, who is thereafter held in high esteem by the whole family. He also acts as a kind of god-father and after the naming, presents the child with cattle or other presents" (Hahn et al. 27). It is clearly evident then, that the naming more than provided the child with a name; it was an occasion to provide the child with financial resources.

Children in some African societies have an identity embedded in that of the greater society into which they are born. In other communities, it is often previously known what name a child will carry upon birth. As Yvan Droz observes, among the Kikuyu, a child had responsibilities to "give back the present of life"; therefore, "his/her main duty is to bear children for his/her parents and to devolve the 'traditional' family names" (116). There are more dire consequences which are tied into the individual and the societal conception of an individual.

This is especially important in the traditional communities, where individuals would spend most of their lives within kinship, age-group and other systems that imposed expectations on them. Droz attributes to this social identity-parenthood (and therefore naming) dichotomy among the Kikuyu: "children being the bearers of lineage names, it is the duty of every Kikuyu to name his or her children after his or her parents or bear the consequence of being cursed" (117). It is clear then, that the individual necessarily has choices about whether to have children, or how to name them, unless he or she is willing to bear the costs of being socially ostracized; "childless men and women cannot achieve this sense of accomplishment [being an accomplished person]" (Droz 117).

Some of the cultural practices have found their way not only into modernity, but also to communities that are voluntarily or otherwise displaced or absent from their ancestral lands and are found in foreign countries. Despite globalization of cultural experiences, there are aspects of African culture that have not been touched by "modern practices"; even in expatriate African communities, there is often a concerted effort to not only carry on with the ceremonies that mark African communities' lives on continental Africa, but to also perform certain ceremonies as best imagined and/or represented in the diaspora. D'Alisera chronicles the naming ceremony for a Sierra Leonean family in Washington DC, articulating the negotiation between the *there* and the here, the need to fit into the American narrative/identity (Amy) versus that of retaining the Sierra Leonean identity (Aminata) (16).

Naming, both as a ceremony and as a product, is decidedly an invaluable part of not only the individual in the African community, but also serves as one of the different steps of developing kinship, identity and propagation of the next generation in the African community. The importance of the name cannot be understated; its implications ought to be considered especially in the light of the modern nation-state, the perennial conflict especially in certain parts of the world (Africa especially), and given increasing interconnectedness through the globalization process. It is especially important to determine whether globalization and the modern nation-state are affected by such an individual choice.

Naming conventions

What's in a name? According to Martin, a name is practically everything, depending on the power relations and the implications the names carry. Martin writes that "names can be more than tags; they can convey powerful imagery. So naming --proposing, imposing, and accepting names--can be a political exercise" (23).

However, it is not evident that there is an active consideration of the implications of names during naming; implications and consequences are often realized many years down the road and are subject to other strategic, geographic, territorial and great power plays, for example the rise and/or strengthening of one group over another.

Mbiti sheds more light on names and naming conventions, especially in African societies. "Some names may mark the occasion of the child's birth. For example, if the birth occurs during a rain episode or the rainy season, the child would be given a name which means 'rain' or 'rainy' or 'water'" (115). Naming conventions, ceremonies and practices often had unforeseen outcomes, especially when continued in the age of globalized illnesses. For example, Wojcicki notes of practices "among the Ashanti of Ghana [where] after the birth of a child and at her/his naming ceremony, the child's grandfather will spit into the child's mouth to strengthen her/his spirit" (2016). Naturally, this has the potential to transmit certain illnesses, but does not necessarily take away from the importance of the naming festival. However, it is important to note that just as the practice, however originally conceived and based on the communal beliefs, the danger it exposes children to may find parallels with the implications of names in the larger societal context, especially when applied to politics and the management of common resources.

Nomenclature and conventions in the same have also produced an interesting socio-political outcome, one that is intimately related to the concept of the modern nation-state. Gachuhi recognizes this outcome, writing that "some tribal groups have naming customs which bring pressure to have many children so that there is a child to be named for each of the parents' parents, brothers and sisters" (5). Coupled with the problem of lower levels of income, education, health and urbanization, and cultural precepts that "include the notions that many descendents must be produced to ensure the survival of lineage" (118), there is a propensity for some communities to contribute significantly to the high population and fertility rates, which impact the distribution of resources amongst the country's population.

The politics of nomenclature and power relationships

Names and nomenclature, as seen previously, are an integral part of individual, group and even national as well as international identity. Kinship groups, communities, ethnicities and language groups form the modern-day nation. Indeed, nations have been described variously as "a large-scale solidarity, constituted by the feeling of the sacrifices that one has made in the past and of those that one is prepared to make in the future. It presupposes a past; it is summarized, however, in the present by a tangible fact, namely, consent, the clearly expressed desire to continue a common life" (Renan XVI) Other scholars suggest that "the term nation is by no means so clearly defined" (Jespersen 1), yet it is clear, for instance, that Switzerland and the United States are separate nations. Jeismann defines it as a unit that was a "draft, an artefact which was based on the will for collective action and commonality"(18).

However a nation is defined, it is not clear that African societies have, or had overcome the primary identifiers (communities, tribes or ethno-linguist groups) at the time of becoming "nations." As such, for most postcolonial African nations, after independence, the primary identifiers were paramount and also exposed communities to a division of resources based on the concept of the collective nation. Many of these countries spiraled into conflict. It is important, at the onset, to note that in most international relations literature does not articulate "theoretical or empirical connections between social construction of ethnicity and violence" (Fearon and Laitlin 847).

To argue that conflict based on ethnic? and socially constructed identities would almost automatically buy into the primordialist argument, well-articulated by Fearon and Laitlin (848 - 849) that assumes that conflict between two groups is inevitable based on A and B's unchanging characteristics. Fearon and Laitlin discuss the social construction of identity, but it is unclear if identity construction is done with the intention of using names as a power relationship. For example, a child born in the Kikuyu community does not determine its name; the name is previously determined by the societal naming norms .

Still, what is important to keep in mind is the fact that while construction of social identity may be voluntary, in many instances, the construction of the modern nation-state was not; this is especially true in the case of many African countries. A good example of the role of ethnicity in conflict can be seen in countries as diverse as Somalia, Cameroon, Nigeria, Rwanda and even in the Eastern European countries such as the former Yugoslavia.

Names as Colonial Power Relationships

In the African context, names are more than individual identities; in fact, they denote a group, culture and a collective phenomenon. As previously argued, naming conventions become a process of more than giving an individual a name; "diviners are consulted to identify which progenitor had reincarnated and this will guide the choice of a name. The ceremony, therefore, takes the form of a welcoming reception", thereby connecting the past, the present and the future, and simultaneously "preserving the memory of progenitors by clothing the ritual with religious garb and awe" (Kalu 116).

Names also identified the social status of individuals, a function of power and station in society. Newell notes that "over the course of an individual's life, he or she would accrue a variety of names and titles depending upon and reflecting social status, gender, generation, religious beliefs, achievements and standing in the eyes of the community" (21). It is, however, notable that over time, an individual could change his/her name, accrue more names and often, quickly change the name and adopt another.

The advent of colonialism had an effect on nomenclature and the conception of names. Colonialism was, of course, preceded by "exploration of the continent" by such explorers as David Livingston, Johannes Krapf, among others. Christianity preceded colonialism and, in many cases, opened up the continent for colonization. Yet, the whole attitude towards Africans by the missionaries was dismissive, often derogatory. For example, Johnson writes that most (of those missionaries) who lived among the natives, both in India and Africa, were more struck by their ignorance than by their potentialities (part 7). Of the Indians, one of the missionaries, Charles Grant, wrote that "we cannot avoid recognizing in the people of Indostan a race of man lamentably degenerate and base, retaining but a feeble sense of moral obligation..." (71) This generally characterized the attitude by some missionaries towards African peoples with whom they worked.

For the most part, the missionaries set out to civilize Africans and change their ways to reflect more of the European ways. As Harding notes, the attitude of the missionaries and subsequently the colonizers reflected the following:

> Africans were defined as a combination of overgrown and witless children, lost heathen in need of salvation, and fearful, untrustworthy but fascinating and often desirable sensual savages whose African roots would soon wither away (ch. 2)

This change included changing their traditional religions, beliefs, practices, social and political structures-- the entire way of life. This view of the dual purpose of missionary work is reflected by Okot p'Bitek who argues that "the missionaries came to [Africa to] preach the gospel as well as to 'civilize' and their role as 'civilizers,' they were at one with the colonizing forces: indeed they were an important vehicle of Western imperialism, which readily lent to the Churches its wealth" (25).

Christianity did not always find an easy route into African societies; indeed, the spread of Christianity was often accompanied by recruitment of the leaders (chiefs, kings, and queens), sometimes in exchange for European goods. Bristol gives an example of the Christianization of one of the Kongo kingdoms, writing that "three missions sent to Ndongo, a Mbundu state in southeast of Luanda, met with failure in the seventeenth century. Ndongo finally accepted Roman Catholic missionaries in 1622 as a result of warfare with the Portuguese, and the queen, Ana Njinga, converted..." (70).

Christianity, modernity and Naming Conventions

Part of the conversion to Christianity was often reflected in name changes. Eventually, the lines between mission and colonization began to blur; the colonizers were Christians, and the

Christian missionaries collaborated with the colonizers. Christian missionaries did not only spread Christianity; they opened schools and apprenticeships which provided training and expanded economic opportunity for the individuals in the communities they worked.

Cohen notes that "it is not simply that the missions opened schools and made the acquisition of education possible. Christianity also provided values, norms and an ideology that subjectively predisposed pupils to achievement" (188). Further, Cohen notes that "it [Christianity] evolved into a way of life and an ideology – a body of norms and beliefs which the growing individual acquired through socialization in the home, at church, and later in school" (188).

This new process, as Cohen further postulates, begins with baptism; "in this ceremony, the child is given a Christian name, and is affiliated with the church", thus completing the transformation of the individual (188). Names, part of the transformational power of the colonizers, were also adopted for different reasons, a practice that goes on to date. Individuals would often adopt "Christian" names for ease in identification and pronunciation by the colonizers.

To some extent, the missionary enterprise succeeded: "Today, in Africa, due to the colonial mentality, African traditional religion is practiced by fewer than 30% of the population...today the traditional religion is perceived as paganism, devil-worship, barbaric, and backwards" (Nnam 196). The formalization of the colonial and post-colonial institutions further led to changes in names, property ownership, and formal systems. For instance, education, property ownership, bank accounts, and other formalized systems required "standardization" of names. This led to a decrease in what Mbiti describes as a propensity for Africans to "change names without any formalities about it, and a person [being] registered [for example in school, university and tax office] under one name today and another name 'tomorrow'"(115).

Today, there is a significant interaction of the past and the present with regard to naming conventions. Africans today often carry several different names; these can include Christian names, ethnic names and combinations thereof. There is no consensus regarding the process and changes that have occurred among many African societies with regard to naming. Ottenberg, for example, writes that among the Afikpo "the parents have considerable freedom to name their children, through the names, especially the first of the two, are generally sex-specific..." (18). This is also the case in the Kono community, in which more specific traditions (even in contemporary society) follow a more traditional route: girls' naming ceremonies happens on the third day and boys on the fourth, and names are derived and given by persons "honored" by the family (46).

Had the question of naming remained at the Christian conversion level, perhaps it would not have had such tragic consequences and outcomes in Africa. During most of the colonial period, colonized societies were generally separated (or subjected to divide-and-rule) to insure that colonial rule found fewer challenges. As it were, the import of ethnic identity was not as significant while the ethnic groups remained divided. When they later gained independence and the construction of the modern state became intrinsically interwoven with the ethnic identity, the importance of names and other destructive nomenclature effects began to show.

Political implications

The duality of names and the power relationships they entail do not only take prominence among individuals, but also among the larger societies, communities of choice and nations that individuals form. Name changes became more than "transition into modernity"; they altered the identity that previously characterized the individuals and societies during the pre-colonial period. The changes, as noted before, were wholesale and cultural. Coleman finds that conditions imposed by the missionaries and supported by colonial governments included "abandonment of such customs as initiation ceremonies...dancing…witch-doctoring, semi nudity, African names...." (97). He also observes that in addition, there was a perception of superiority of the European religion, and that "European values and institutions were considered superior to those of the African" (97). This perhaps demonstrates why the latter did not generally make it to the next phase of government and the modern nation.

Past the individuals and with the formation of the modern state, names and the broader concepts of identity have been leveraged and used as both uniting factors and objects of division especially amongst polities with weak democratic structures, where a name often means more, better or faster access to resources (education, scholarships, jobs, land title deeds) or other vignettes of modern social and economic progress. As missionaries, Christianity and the subsequent formalization of colonial rule took hold, leading to the modern nation-state, the method of containing dissent and uprising and thereby facilitating colonial rule (through, for example, divide-and-rule tactics) continued to use the ethnic division. Tragically and perhaps proverbially, it was easier to destroy than to build, to sow division than to unite. Majority of African countries were granted independence while deeply divided among the several ethnic groups constituting the state.

The majority of African states came into being buffeted by competing forces: those of leveraging nationalism and national identity to fight for independence, yet internally divided by their identities, arising from among others, the cultural importance and the pervasive group dynamics of their societies. As such, they often struggled with national identities and nationalism (unlike, for example, the Aryan German nation which "united" against the Jewish during the holocaust). It is perhaps important to review the concept of nationalism. Smith identifies five attributes and usages of the meaning of nationalism; these include (1) process of formation, or growth of nations, (2) a sentiment or consciousness of belonging to the nation; (3) a language and symbolism of the nation; (4) a social and political movement on behalf of the nation; (5) a doctrine and/or ideology of the nation, both general and particular (Smith 5-6).

Many African countries were quite successful in accomplishing the fourth attribute i.e. creating social and political movements leading to independence, but then they failed to achieve the rest of the meanings of nationalism (except, perhaps, within their divided communities). After independence, the states often quickly reverted to their constituent elements. Their new rulers moved quickly to appropriate and consolidate resources especially based on the particular communities, as politically prudent strategies to assure their support base and continued stay in power. This misappropriation of resources and unfair distribution of resources began the cycle of seeking support by elites from their "people," alleging marginalization and sometimes quickly reigniting old animosities.

Particularly in African countries, the local is national, and the national is often local. Most African countries often experience the schism between the local and the national, recognizing the importance of the local – which, unfortunately, often contributes to the complication of the national. National administrative structures often integrate – or frustrate – local structures, and the functionaries serve both national and local purposes. This is illustrated in the example given by Cohen:

> Authority is necessary to apply pressure to individuals to fulfil their obligations to the collective interests of the community and to maintain mechanisms for political communication, for formulation of problems, deliberation, decision-making and coordination of action... the Chief of Sabo acts as a Shari'a judge, regulating marriage, divorce, inheritance and custody over children... he also officiates in marriage and in naming ceremonies. (161-2)

It is evident then, that national administrators recognize the importance of the local administrators not only for that particular function, but also for the purposes of continuation of cultural aspects.

Integrating the communities' identities and the larger national identity that forms the state is not always easy, or successful. Countries – especially in Africa – have utilized a variety of approaches to integrate the communal and the national in order to give communities a sense of ownership, membership and decrease the perception of marginalization. Some countries have, for example, integrated local judicial mechanisms (*Sharia law*, traditional and tribal law), and have often turned their eye away from some practices that challenge national law (for example, the girl child education, early marriages or polygamy). Still, this has not provided for national cohesion in these countries; there are still schisms, which can often be traced to the ethnic conception of identity.

Names, nations, nationalism and globalization

Where then, does all this fit together-- names, identities, communities, nationalism and nations? So far names have been demonstrated as the basis of identity, not independent of communities and other vignettes of community such as naming ceremonies, kinship and identity. Individuals and communities are the basis for modern-day nations and states. The perceived differences (especially ethnic) between individuals have in the past been the cause of genocides, politicides and other crimes against members of one group over the other. In Africa, such perceived ethnic differences, elevated to the national level and the exercise of power, were primarily responsible for one of the worst genocides of the 20th Century.

Somewhat unfortunately, the modern nation facilitates the separation of one from the other (whether internal vs. external or internal vs. internal). Verdery conceives of the state as "a potent symbol and basis of classification within an international system of nation-states. It names the relation between states and their subjects and between states and other states; it is an ideological construct essential to assigning subject positions in the modern states..." (38). Verdery then outlines the relationship between the nation-state and the glue that binds it together, nationalism. Verdery writes that nationalism "is the political utilization of the symbol nation through discourse and political activity, as well as the sentiment that draws people into responding to this symbol's use" (38).

The unaddressed question, of course, is one of the roles of ethnic identity in the formation of nations-- especially by ethnic groups that are as divided as their names are distinct. According to Giddens, "those societies in which human beings have lived for all but a fraction of the existence of humankind--tribal societies--have been either destroyed or absorbed into larger entities" (qtd. in James 103). It is one thing to be absorbed; it is quite another to be successfully and *seamlessly* absorbed, if ongoing and recent conflicts are anything to go by. This is illustrated by the continuing agitation for separation of nations and peoples by their language and other ethnic attributes, even within developed societies. Billig illustrates this of Belgium, with the *Guardian* reporting that "the leaders of the main Flemish parties...had declared that Belgium should be split into a loose confederation of two independent states--Dutch-speaking Flanders and French-speaking Walonia" (13). Other countries, modern democracies such as Spain, continue to struggle with identity-based conflicts and threats to split (Basque separatism).

Of course, one can always refer back to the most widely acknowledged nation-state formation. Glover makes this observation:

> In Africa, there are more extreme cases of nation-states arising independently of any nationhood. Many state boundaries were lines drawn on maps by colonial governments and administrators, often cutting through the middle of territories inhabited by Africans who felt part of a single community and often putting together groups who had no sense of shared identity. (11-12)

Yet, this adhesion to culture and ethnicity is being challenged more by the rise of a global culture. According to Featherstone, such cultural globalization might decrease the sense of prominence attributed to the ethnic identity and more towards shared global norms. Featherstone writes that "we can point to cultural integration and cultural disintegration processes which transcend the state-society unit and can therefore be held to occur on a trans-national or trans-societal level" (1).

Ervin and Smith write that "as individuals, we are no longer isolated and unaffected by the actions of distant others. Human society is increasingly interconnected and interdependent" (8). Their definition of globalization mirrors that of Lechner which states that globalization "has at least these four elements: diffusion, interdependence, organization and culture or consciousness" (15). It is also defined as the "integration of political, economic and cultural activities of geographically and/or nationally separated peoples," "the increase of globalism," the "rapid movement toward international economic integration; consensus on political values, processes and principles and the revolution in information and communication technologies," and "the defining international system based on the inexorable integration of markets, nation-states and technologies" (Wells, Shuey & Kiely 38).

Globalization is often separated into its constituent components, mainly economic and cultural. It can be described briefly as diverse and distinct cultures now come into contact with cultural messages and norms that were once beyond their perception. Cultural interaction can have the effect of altering the beliefs and norms of others. Cultural interaction and the cultural change produced by it have created a situation of "cultural hybridization." '(Beynon and Dunkerley qtd. in Ervin & Smith 35)

Further, they differentiate the possible outcomes as "cultural globalization" that can lead to better understanding and cooperation, versus "cultural homogenization" that is a process of "cultural imperialism" (35).

Globalization is not seen to have affected all parts of the world equally. Schneider points out that "the benefits of global economic exchanges are unequal and reach mainly those who are already in a privileged position within society" (637). This reasoning can be successfully extended to the benefits of cultural globalization: it requires economic means and proper infrastructure to access, for example, television (such as cable programming), web content and other facets of modern cultural globalization. Perhaps governments facilitating access to information and thus impacting knowledge can assist individuals to become more active members of the global community, although part of this disconnect is due to socio-economic conditions that include poverty.

Can modern society, particularly African countries, overcome the challenges of ethnic identity? The previous discussions have shown that these ethnic and tribal-based identities have been utilized as means to further divide members of the same society, rather than leverage the differences to build robust nations. How can globalization, especially cultural globalization, positively impact groups, communities and societies to better understand each other and enjoin themselves in the global community, sharing the benefits of globalization and increased interconnectedness? It is not clear that ethnic identity and its attributes, including names, group and societal primary identities are much in retreat even with the anticipated and increasing globalization of societies, cultures and nation-states. Perhaps Africa is not unique; names and nomenclature in advanced industrial societies also offer insight into how diasporic communities have developed and conceived of their identities.

Names in the Diaspora: The Case of the African American

In the United States, the cultural experiences of the African American community have been quite the source of intellectual and cultural debate. For African Americans, long excised from their traditional and cultural roots in Africa, but equally marginalized and excluded as full members of the American nation until the civil rights era, the question of (formerly slave) African versus (White, Anglo-Saxon Protestant) American versus the emergent African American identity has led to the search of an acceptable/compromised African American identity grounded in both the geographic and ethnic origin, and the social, cultural, economic and post-slavery "black experience" in the United States.

Revisiting Burnard, it is clear how the African American community lost some of its collective identity. Burnard writes that "whites, slaves, and animals were differentiated in early Jamaica. In particular, the names given to blacks indicate that white Jamaicans thought Africans (whom they invariably denoted as "negroes" rather than slaves) to be people entirely different from themselves" (325-6). Burnard further argues that such patterns were not intended to continue the slaves' prior African culture. Indeed, Burnard notes that slaves were rarely allowed to name themselves; it is possible to construe--and characterize this--as part of the loss of identity, given that names were associated with identity. The irony of the naming conventions among members of the African American and diasporic community is evident in the adoption of names; Burnard states:

> When freedom afforded them the opportunity to name themselves, slave names became almost entirely extinct. Yet, at the same time that blacks rejected their slave heritage, they also

rejected their African heritage in order to mimic, incompletely, the European oppressors that they, ironically, aspired to become. (326)

To counter this loss of identity, often, programs that target African American (youth) are implemented to foster a cultural experience, often intermingled with the African experience. For example, Harvey and Hill chronicle a program targeting African American youth in Washington DC that partnered with a South African organization and sought to teach "Africentric values" (69). This program reflects the determination to establish connections between the African part with the American part of the African American community.

This gravitation towards a distinct, rooted cultural identity and place, however far removed from reality, is persistent and reflected not only in the African American community but also in many diasporic communities, often generations, removed from Africa. Expinoza writes of a "systematic almost total elimination of African cultures" (325) as a result of the slavery experience, with "Africa...identified as the mother country and blackness...seen as something of pride rather than a stigma of shame" (325). This attachment was subsequently followed by a "romanticization of the African identity, being that identity in black Africa is precisely ethnic identity" (326) that led to "rejecting a 'slave' name for an African name of one's own choosing [that] may well override the need to rigorously research one's tribal origins" (326). It is evident, therefore, that the need to find an identity supersedes the fact that there is not an "African" identity; rather, the "otherness" of African Americans drives the greater search for identification with that which appears more familiar.

Conclusions

There are several contestations in considering how names, naming and the entire nomenclature relates to identity at the community level, which in turn influences the way nations think of themselves and leverage their differences and common values to achieve national unity often from several disparate ethnic communities. While names are just one attribute of the constituent societies together with language, they are perhaps the most important identifiers of the differences between societies (and individuals). Modern nations are constituted from groups that retain ethnic identities and ethnic separation, and especially in the situation of African countries, this has historic and contemporary implications. African countries were constituted from ethnic groups, which were then co-opted into nation-states, often with little commonality. En route to nationhood, countries experienced Christianization, "civilization," colonization and divide and rule; upon independence, the divide-and-rule tactics often returned to haunt them, and they were unable to get over the schisms that divide(d) them.

Ethnic identities and their associated factors, including names, have brought destruction in the fabric of society, expressed in terms of ethnic conflict often leading to genocide and mass murders. Such outcomes are not necessarily specific to Africa; Europe, with its bloody history especially in the 20th Century, saw one of the worst massacres with the holocaust perpetrated by the Nazis. In the past quarter century, Europe has experienced similar disruptions with the breakup of Yugoslavia and the subsequent genocides, for example, against Serb Muslims. The recent invasion by Russia into Ukraine was ostensibly to protect Ukrainian-Russians. There are still many places in the world where the questions of life and death are still largely decided by such a simple combination of letters as names. This is mainly because they represent more than a name; they represent identity, often, of groups, of historic oppressors.

Given that names form part of an individual's core identity and that the African identity is tied to names and the ethnic group, it is unlikely that even globalization will have a diluting effect over how names continue to influence our conception of identity. Globalization, which has accelerated the transnational connections between individuals and groups all over the world, has not succeeded in diluting the importance that individuals and countries attach to identity. Contrary to popular hypotheses about the globalization of culture, it appears that there is globalization and diversification of the cultural experience, with individuals becoming diverse-identity persons rather than uni-identity individuals.

Therefore, globalization, while important in aggregating our cultural and other-world experiences, has not completely succeeded in eliminating our attachment to ethnic-based identity, and may continue to magnify the same.

It is evident then, that names, as part of individual and community identity, will continue to play a great role in individuals' lives, the affairs of the nation-state, and despite globalization and other larger concerns, nomenclature as one of the basic individual identifiers, remains at the crossroads of identity and the viability of the nation-state.

Works Cited

Amadiume, Ifi. *Male Daughters, Female Husbands: Gender and Sex in an African Society*. London: Zed Books, 1987. Print.

Billig, Michael. *Banal Nationalism*. London, UK: Sage Publications, 1995. Print.

Bristol, Joan Cameron. *Christians, Blasphemers, and Witches: Afro-Mexican Ritual Practice in the Seventeenth Century*. New Mexico, NM: U. of New Mexico P., 2007. Print.

Burnard, Trevor. "Slave Naming Patterns: Onomastics and the Taxonomy of Race in Eighteenth-Century Jamaica." *Journal of Interdisciplinary History*, xxxi: 3 (winter, 2001): 325–346.

Caldwell, JC and P Caldwell. "High fertility in Sub-Saharan Africa." *Scientific American*, 262, 5 (May 1990): 118 - 125. Print

Cohen, Abner. *Custom and Politics in Urban Africa: A Study of Hausa Migrants in Yoruba Towns*. London: Routledge, 1969. Print.

_ _ _ *The Politics of Elite Culture: Explorations in the Dramaturgy of Power in a Modern African Society*. Berkeley : U. of California P, 1981. Print.

Coleman, James S. Nigeria: *Background to Nationalism*. Los Angeles : U. of California P, 1958. Print.

D'Alisera, JoAnn. "Born in the USA: Naming Ceremonies of Infants Among Sierra Leoneans Living in the American Capital." *Anthropology Today* 14. 1 (Feb. 1998): 16-18Web. Accessed 03/15/2014

Dijksterhuis, Ap, Sander L. Koole, and Ad van Knippenberg. "What's in a Name: Implicit Self-Esteem and the Automatic Self." *Journal of Personality and Social Psychology* 80. 4 (2001): 669-685. Web. Accessed 3/16/2014

Droz, Yvan. "Conflicting Realities: the Kikuyu Childhood Ethos and the Ethic of the CRC." *Reconceptualizing Children's Rights in International Development: Living Rights, Social Justice, Translations.* Eds. Karl Hanson and Olga Nieuwenhuy. Cambridge: Cambridge UP, 2013. Print.

Expinoza, Stanley Crockett. "The Afro-Mexican: A History Relatively Untouched." , Eds. *Out of the Revolution: The Development of Africana Studies.* Eds. Delores P. Aldridge and Carlene Young. Lanham, MD: Lexington Books, 2000. Print.

Fearon, James D. and David D. Laitin. "Violence and the Social Construction of Ethnic Identity." *International Organization* 54.4 (Autumn 2000): 845-877. Web. Date accessed Featherstone, Mike. "Global Culture: An Introduction." *Global Culture: Nationalism, Globalization and Modernity.* Ed. Mike Featherstone. London: Sage, 1990. Print.

Gachuhi, J. Mugo. *African Youth and Family Planning Knowledge, Attitudes and Practices.* Discussion Paper 189. Institute for Development Studies, University of Nairobi. Web. Accessed 4/15/2014

Glover, Jonathan. "Nations, Identity and Conflict." In Robert McKim and Jeff McMahan, Eds. *The Morality of Nationalism.* New York: OUP, 1997. Print.

Hahn, Carl Hugo Linsingen, H. Vedder and L. Fourie. *The Native Tribes of South West Africa.* Oxford: Frank Cass, 1966. Print.

Harding, Vincent. *There Is a River: The Black Struggle for Freedom in America Paperback.* New York: Harcourt Brace, 1981. Print.

Harvey, Aminifu R. and Robert B. Hill. "Africentric Youth and Family Rites of Passage Program: Promoting Resilience among At-Risk African American Youths. *Social Work* 49.1 (2004): 65-74 Medium? Huntington, Samuel P. "The Clash of Civilizations?" *Foreign Affairs* 72. 3 (Summer, 1993): 22 – 49. Medium James, Paul. *Globalism, Nationalism, Tribalism: Bringing Theory Back in.* London: Sage, 2006. Print.

Jeismann, Michael. "Nation, Identity and Enmity: Towards a Theory of Political Identification." . *What Is a Nation? : Europe 1789-1914: Europe 1789-1914*. Eds. Timothy Baycroft and Mark Hewitson, Oxford: OUP, 2006. Print.

Jespersen, Otto. *Mankind, Nation and Individual: From a Linguistic Point of View*. Bloomington: Indiana UP, 1964. Print.

Johnson, Paul. *History of Christianity*. New York: Simon & Schuster, 1976. Print.

Kalu, Ogbu U. "Gods as Policemen: Religion and Social Control in Igboland." . *Religious Plurality in Africa: Essays in Honour of John S. Mbiti*. Eds. Jacob K. Olupona and Sulayman S. Nyang. New York: De Gruyter, 1993. Print.

Lechner, Frank J. *Globalization: The Making of World Society*. Malden, MA: Wiley-Blackwell, 2009. Print.

Martin, Ben L. "From Negro to Black to African American: The Power of Names and Naming." *Political Science Quarterly* 106.1 (Spring, 1991): 83-107. Web, July 2014

Mbiti, John S. *African Religions and Philosophy*. 2nd Ed. Oxford: Heinemann, 1969. Print.

Newell, Stephanie. *The Power to Name: A History of Anonymity in Colonial West Africa*. Athens, OH: Ohio UP., 2013. Print.

Nnam, Nkuzi Michael. *Colonial Mentality in Africa*. Lanham, MD: Forbes Books, 2007. Print.

Nyanzi, Stella, HawahManneh and GijsWalraven. "Traditional Birth Attendants in Rural Gambia: Beyond Health to Social Cohesion." *African Journal of Reproductive Health,* 11. 1 (Apr. 2007): 43-56. Electronic. Accessed 07/20/2014

Ottenberg, Simon. *Boyhood Rituals in an African Society: An Interpretation*. U. of Washington P, 1989. Print.

Renan, Ernst. "What is a nation?" http://ig.cs.tu-berlin.de/oldstatic/w2001/eu1/dokumente/Basistexte/Renan1882EN-Nation.pdf Web. Accessed 22 July 2014

Parsons, Robert T. *Religion in African society*. The Hague: E. J. Brill, 1964. Print.

p'Bitek, Okot. "Chapter six." *Critiques of Christianity in African Literature*. Ed. Jesse Ndwiga Kanyua Mugambi. Nairobi: East African Educational Publishers, 1992. Print.

Schneider, Gerald. "War in the Era of Economic Globalization." *The Blackwell Companion to Globalization.* Ed. George Ritzer. Malden, MA: Blackwell Publishing, 2007. Print.

Smith, Anthony D. *Nationalism.* Malden, MA: Polity Press, 2010. Print.

Verdery, Katherine. "Whither "Nation" and "Nationalism"? *Daedalus*, 122, No. 3, Reconstructing Nations and States (summer, 1993): 37-46. Accessed 5/14/2014

Wells, Gary J. Robert Shuey and Ray Kiely. *Globalization.* Huntington, NY: Novinka Books, 2001. Print.

Wojcicki, J. M. "Traditional Behavioural practices, the Exchange of Saliva and HHV-8 Transmission in Sub-Saharan African Populations." *British Journal of Cancer* 89 (2003): 2016–2017. Accessed 4/15/2014

Chapter Seven

The Global Reader and Names in Literary Works by Peter W. Vakunta, Bill F. Ndi and Emmanuel Fru Doh

By
Bill F. Ndi

Names and naming are an important ingredient in the creative tradition of the new and emerging literature of the Cameroons and have found sanctuary in the literary landscape of authors from the English speaking Cameroons specifically. To serve the purpose of this investigation, Emmanuel Fru Doh's (EFD) *The Fire Within* (2009) will be critically examined. Also under analysis will be Peter Wuteh Vakunta's "Rap on Nomenclature" (2008) (Rap) and a number of poems by Bill F. Ndi viz. "Bangolan Question" (2009) and "Epigram 53" (2010). Analyzing these creative works would highlight the importance of names from a microcosmic perspective within the modern context of globalization. In this context some cultures are dominating while others are being dominated. The dominated cultures seem to be receding or giving way to the dominant and hegemonic ones with unprecedented outcomes. It is the claim of this study to highlight the uncontested significance of the need for the global reader to have a good grasp of the poetization of names in the Anglophone Cameroonian Literature (ACL) for a better appreciation and understanding of any work from this locale in question. This emerging literature offers the possibility for the global reader to fully appreciate the depth and breadth of the ACL writers' creativity. Elucidating names clarifies critical understanding of the works and makes sense. Character and name are more often than not indissociable. This accounts for why Soyinka affirms that "names have meaning, and – as they would have us believe, names push their bearers to actualize their encoded meanings." (Web September 4, 2013). Names within this literary framework would help to substantiate the ways in which ACL authors conceive the idea that both names and naming are architects of a people's life, thoughts and thinking in general and most specifically the writers'. In short, Soyinka asserts, "Child naming, on this continent, is itself a creative act" (Web September 4, 2013). Is it therefore possible to follow a similar logic and intimate that this cultural creative act has been translated into the works by writers from the African continent in general and most specifically those from the English speaking Cameroons?

If so, then some critical questions need to be addressed in this study. These include: what place do names from this microcosm hold within the modern globalized and globalizing cultural context? Can names from this receding ACL culture stand the heat of the dominant hegemonic cultures? Are names just primary markers of identity or literary and semiotic as well as semantic signs adding to and shaping the understanding of these works of literature? Are there any rules governing character names in ACL or are they just arbitrary? Do ACL writers in poetizing names follow any convention be it informally or internationally agreed upon? How and why do these writers use the names they give to their characters? Are they just abiding by what Bourdieu considers to be an imposition of boundaries on the individual that dictates 'what he is and what he must be' (120-1)? Could it be for reasons of perpetuating a patrilineage or a dying linguistic code in a globalizing world?

As stated prior, this analysis of names within a literary framework would help substantiate the ways in which names and naming shape and influence the lives, thoughts and thinking of a people. Ndi's "Bangolan Question" (2009), exposes names as a guiding philosophy for a people within a culture. Therein, names are also viewed as a probe into a people's history and their place in a globalizing world. Ndi's "Epigram 53" (2010) just as EFD's work pits the name as a burden. And in Vakunta's "Rap on Nomenclature" name change become a transforming process of making others "human counterfeits". Over and above, in EFD's *The Fire Within* (2008), a name becomes the embodiment of human suffering from life to death, human thoughts and appreciation, etc. It is therefore evident from this preview, that character names from ACL writers in particular and African in general have the potential to provide hitherto and otherwise unavailable insight into intercultural blending and understanding within the venture of literary analysis and the understanding of the various cultural processes far removed from those or that with which one is familiar. This strongly refutes Derrida's claim that names do not fix identities and that characters can break free from their received names (12-13). If one were to subscribe to Derrida's assertion, then highlighting the consequence of a name change will come into play. The name thus transcends its primary role/function as a character identity marker to become an embodiment of the character's wellbeing or malaise; in short his or her entire existence. Pursuant to the aforesaid, how do ACL writers conceptualize names in their oeuvres?

A judicious point to begin examining how these writers conceive names would be a critical look at the poem "Bangolan Question". The poem draws on names as an attitude towards life. It is clear as one reads along that the poet is addressing philosophizing on a name. He asks a key question which, in the poem, is used as a name that for centuries has served as a drive or a leitmotif for the Bangolan people. He follows methodically the historical infringement on Bangolan culture by a foreign one which disparages it as barbaric whereas the people of Bangolan who lived the culture were, as he writes:

…happy
Not without their own philosophy (Stanza1 L. 9-10)

This, for the writer, is an indication that the name is the culminating point of the thinking of the Bangolan people or as Soyinka would posit, "for African societies, 'the name is father to the child'." (Web September 4, 2013). "Bangolan Question" points out things that preceded colonization which came along with a condescending look upon the lifestyle the people had lived hitherto. It could be that the persona is questioning the essence of contemporary globalization with a look cast at the African pre-colonial and colonial past. The colonialist considered the Bangolan people no better than "wild beast", without a philosophy, who would need to learn everything. They were reduced to what those colonists pleased. But the most essential thing for the persona is when he goes on to spell out the issue of naming in the following lines:

> As my father told me of his father
> Who named my late uncle *Mundaka*?
> A question in Bangolan (Stanza 1 L. 11-13)

In his consciousness, this persona carefully examines names and naming within this pre and postcolonial cultural setting which Wole Soyinka also does in "A Name is More than the Tyranny of Taste." (Web September 4, 2013). The poem indicates the usefulness of names such as the Bangolan Question which serves as a scan "to rid the country of its thorns" and provide something concrete and meaningful not illusive or utopian solutions to the problems that the people face. The poem reads:

> That for years did serve as scan
> To rid the country of its thorns
> And provide the nation with corns
> With ucopia
> Not utopia. (Stanza 1 L. 14-18)

The poet is here at his best playing with both words and ideas drawing attention to the psychological and material fulfillment a name can give by providing a "nation with corns". The last two verses here play on the idea of Cornucopia, a horn of abundance, and the idea of corn (the staple food of this people) that is utopian in nature. So to the poet, through punning, this Bangolan question is a name at its best. This is comforted by Kumar, Pattanayak and Johnson in the introduction to their work *Framing my Name: Extending Educational Boundaries*, when they write: "The process of naming follows several pathways. Some are given a formal name at birth. Other individuals are named according to social relations" (4). The Bangolan question, "Mundaka?" as a name is not limited to social relations but extends to international relations and invites the global reader to perceive the name from this part of the world from the perspective of International History and the relations amongst individuals as well as that amongst the nations of the world. It is only from this perspective that the global reader can fully apprehend the relationship of the dominating-dominated. That is certainly why Ndũngi wa Mũngai (2010) claims that,

> [A] name tells a lot about you and acts as a window for others to peep in, as they attempt to know you. In some cases, the name can determine whether you live or die depending on who is peeping and what their intentions are (102).

It is also along similar lines that Vakunta's poem highlight names as the most valued gift that one can't be permitted to mess around with. He writes:

> People's names are their most
> Valued gifts from birth.
> Let's steer clear of trifling with them.
> The sweetest music to any one's ear
> Is certainly his/her name!
> We have no carte blanche to
> Mess with those names!
> Vakunta (2009) (Stanza 4 L. 1-7)

The persona here strikes a chord on names as being people's "… most/Valued gift from birth." Not only is a name the most valued, it is a rarity that a person or a character cannot procure one for him/herself. And though it is given by others who have the mandate to do so, even the giver once he or she has so done has no right to tamper with it.

This is the same trend of argument that emerges from the second stanza of the poem "Bangolan Question". It drives home the issues of misnaming. In explaining what the question stands for the persona emphasises on its nature and compares it to the deformed name which he considers flat in the West, the infringing and interfering culture.

> Mundaka translates "What have I done?"
> Not the flat western "What have I done?"

(Stanza 2, L. 1-2)

Debi Prasanna Pattanayak in the chapter "Establishing the space of naming" of *Framing my Name* makes a curious analogy to this phenomenon where the words all mean the same but for reasons of fanaticism, religious transgressions and religious intolerance no one is allowed to mess around with certain names across languages. It is against this backdrop that we read: "In spite of the sameness of meaning, the words refer to different languages and religions… Religious fanatics do not permit transgression of names across languages" (70).

Therefore, in framing the questions in L1 & L2 stanza 2 of "Bangolan Question, what is remarkable is the fact that the wording of the questions are the same but for the fact that the persona is careful to specify one as being flat as well as specifying its origin: the West. In line with this reading of the poem, mispronouncing a name thwarts and flattens the desires, hopes and aspirations of the name bearers, their parents, and their society. The persona, here, seems to transpose an idea from Alexander Pope who in discussing poetry, suggests that,

> it is not enough that nothing offends the ear, but a good poet will adapt the very sounds as well as words (i.e. names), to the thing (i.e. persons/character or place) he treats of. …The onomatopoeic qualities of a word {name} are as important as its meaning especially in poetry (Audra & Williams 281).

A name thus becomes a unit of sounds (phoneme) as well as a unit of sense (sememe). And though Pope above underlines its importance especially in poetry, the global reader needs to pay attention to the onomatopoeic qualities of name originating from across cultures. In the two verses cited above, the persona qualifies the second as /flat western, "what have I done?"/. This is as if the persona wishes to inform the reader of his opposition to the globalizing infringement on local names. Having the name right makes it meaningful and worthwhile to the name bearer. It also promotes better understanding. This idea is spelled out in Vakunta's "Rap" (2009). In this light, it is evident that meaning in general might be gleaned by the global reader from his giving names their rightful attribution and failure of which will have the effect Vakunta spells out in these terms:

> We make others feel
> Like human counterfeits!
> (Vakunta 2009)

Furthermore, the persona in "Bangolan Question" also points out how in the global world, naming takes on a political agenda. The last lines of the poem seem to toll the death-knell on the drift from traditional naming system to a global system which to the poet is expressed through the rhymes Village (the idea of collectivity or community togetherness)/pillage (Chaos, dispersion and volatility). This rhyme underscores where the "right dose" is "…that primitive village and on what scale pillage, "the global" is practised. In using a name in this poem the writer seems to drive home his scorn for the trend of globalization which is looting from weaker cultures structured in and around the notion of a village. However, it is striking that the same globalization to effectively pillage conceives its mission in term of a village. This is an irony to which the persona in Ndi's poem draws attention. In the last line he/she hints at the global village rhyming/resounding with pillage rather with village as he/she knows it.

> As they their agenda make political
> We of our agenda do make ethical
> Ours and theirs might not be close
> But fairness by the right dose
> Forebears had in that primitive village
> Not the global resounding with pillage.
> (Stanza 2, L. 13-18)

Here the poet raises ethical concerns as opposed to political concerns. Just like in practical ethics it is presumed that no society can survive if it allows its members to kill one another without restriction, so much could be said of naming and reading names and their rightful attributions. Anyone that allows the distortion of the attribution of names, identity and cultures (under whatever pretext) without restrictions kills both the naming institution and its *raison d'être*. It is for this reason that Debi Prasanna Pattanayak stresses that, "Names are carriers of caste, religious or cultural significance." (70) And better still Ndũngi wa Mũngai asserts that "Immortality is in your name" (101).

The above assertion cannot be contested in the case of character names in the works of ACL writers. A quick look at the poem *Epigram 53* by Ndi, would readily hammer home the idea of caste/class, religious and or cultural significance. The dramatic opening of this aphorism projects a name as a burden, "the load." The mention of name comes right on the third line as if to portray that the name as a load is not so apparent whereas for the bearer it is a big, big load because to bear his name and be happy priding himself as one with such a name, the bearer has to work within the confines or restrictions laid by his/her name, (Bourdieu 120-1) This view is reiterated by Soyinka in his keynote address at FESPACO 2013 in which he states that : "We all share – with variations – a basic culture, and that culture places a heavy premium on – for instance – child naming. 'The child is father of the man', as the poet William Wordsworth reminds us." (Web September 4, 2013). Epigram 53 encrypts the name thus:

> Viz.   Nobility,
>   Dignity,
> And   Integrity!

The above epigram like the rest in the collection is what forces the global reader to reconsider the world ostensibly transformed into a canvas, a painting, and events with varied shades that facilitate or complicate emerging renditions as a result of a gift, a name the bearer as well as he/she who uses it is trapped in. It is in this regards that the reviewer of this collection of *Epigrams* stresses in the blurb that, "in the end, the reader is left richer as he begins to wonder afresh at so much that had been taken for granted" (Doh 2010). Nonetheless, the resultant ambivalent nomenclature from christening as the above analysis contends points to opposing forces responsible for the travail of the protagonist.

The protagonist of EFD's *The Fire Within* is an epitome of how this ACL writer skillfully picks a name to have the global reader gasping if the outcome of her actions is the result of her name or if her name is just a nomenclatural accident. She fits her own name very well. For a start, the name *Mungeu'* needs being defined. It is an encryption. Should the global reader not know what it means, it suffices for him/her to follow the protagonist through her travails, trials and tribulation to know exactly what this word means in the *Ngemba language* spoken in the Grassfields of the Cameroons. This language belongs to the Grassfields Bantu languages of the western grasslands of Cameroon. Relevant to this study of the name and the global reader is the fact that the very first mention of Mungeu' reveals her suffering through pregnancy. It is this suffering that leaves her step-sister, Mabel counting sheep and having sleepless nights. This suffering is given complete form in the Narrator's vivid description of Mungeu' at the beginning of the novel when her elder step-sister sees her staggering back from the bathroom and enquires, "what's happening? (6). Here, the Narrator seizes this opportunity to tell of Mungeu's reaction as well as her appearance. He says: "Mungeu' could only stare weakly. Her uncombed hair completed the picture of misery she painted" (6). This, in a way, is a route for EFD who avoids translating or transliterating this character's name into language he writes in. He however does by allowing the fate that befalls Mungeu' from start to finish define the *Ngemba* expression here used as a character name. In this guise, EFD does what Joseph Lo Bianco in *Framing My Name* points out when discussing "ways of regulating knowledge of strangers' personal names, mostly by restricting who has access to such names" (x). Therefore EFD's use of this name is not gratis.

Contrary to McIntosh's assertion that "[individuals] will often use a Christian name such as John and Ruth to an outsider' and not disclose names that carry a cultural significance" (150), EFD resorts to the reverse. The protagonist's name carries with it its cultural significance and complication. In most of the Bantu Languages spoken in the Grassfields of the Cameroons from where EFD hails, *Mungeu'* translated into English means, "Suffering Child" or if transliterated, *Mu* = Child, *ngeu'* = *suffer, suffering*. Is it then a coincidence that from start to finish Mungeu's travails, trials and tribulations should only compound till her death? Is this poetization of name not reminiscent of a political statement? Mungeu' suffers enormously in the hands of the very ones who should be her keepers like the bulk of English speaking people from West Caramenju suffering in the hands of their French speaking brothers and sisters from East Caramenju. This dereliction of duties by the keepers leaves Mungeu' as well as the English speaking Caramenjuans in a pool of suffering even when some respite is expected. Is there as such any correlation between a name bearer and his or her actualization of the embedded meaning of his or her name?

In this guise EFD also has one of his most repulsive characters, Angwi (a name just one letter removed from being pronounced "angry") in one of her effusive outburst tell Mungeu' what she has always thought of her: "I knew there was nothing but the shadow of ill luck over you and now you've transferred it to my daughter" (31). This also captures (at a certain level) "the cognitive significance of an indexical expression for those competent in the language. As with Frege's notion, there is a connection between character and definite descriptions" (Web. 7/15/2013). As such it is no surprise that even when Mabel after her ordeal comes back to find out that Mungeu' is absent she cannot help but wonder "what grief is this?" (58). Mabel's further questioning and frustrations clearly highlight the authors concern for this character he has created to replicate the suffering of his people. She questions: "How can a girl go on suffering all through her life and yet one cannot find what she has done wrong? Things just keep going wrong for her all the time?" (58-59). Upon asking these questions the Narrator apprehends the essence of Mabel's mood and states that she "stared at the dismal sky as if questioning nature why Mungeu' had to suffer so much" (59). This is in line with what Soyinka in "A Name is more than a Tyranny of Taste" underscores when he states that "some images become eventually attached to words with such intimacy that they can no longer be prised apart" (Web September 4, 2013). And further claims, "no parent [gives] to their babies names that embed evil meanings". So why would the writer?

Along similar lines, one cannot help but quest the essence of EFD giving Mungeu's stepsister a Latin sounding name. Could EFD's choice of a Western name for Mungeu's stepsister be translated to Ndũngi wa Mũngai's (2010) assertion that: "The [given] acquired European name [is] was a symbolic ticket to a heaven where one would be made 'white as snow'." (104)? Or again could it be as Soyinka points out that, "it can prove a curse or a blessing" which in Mabel's case as opposed to her stepsister's is indeed a blessing? (Web September 4, 2013).

Mungeu' embodies the suffering of her people and one could wonder why the author allows this girl from birth to death to shoulder the burden of her people like Christ humankind's. Why should the author choose a woman to embody such? At her death, this becomes a titillating subtext in EFD's world. It is when her family has a sense of coming together and unity. Could this note of hope, identical to that of Christ dying to safe mankind, be EFD's way of telling the global reader that the fate of his people is in the hands of women who already by virtue of their *womanness,* and in the corrupt Republic of Caramenju, are suffering yet, struggling to keep faith in those who have disappointed mankind?

The central thematic concern of EFD's *The Fire Within* is semantically interchangeable with the sememe of the protagonist's name, *Mungeu'*. When Lo Bianco talks of ways of regulating knowledge of names, he also spells out that,

> Another [way] is to offer a distanced or public version of a name, often supplemented by grammatical and lexical politeness rules that allow conversation to proceed while keeping personal distances intact. A common method is to surround our name with other names, so that layers of naming correspond to layers of intimacy, in ever declining circles (x).

It must however be noted in EFD's case that he does not surround the name with other names (i.e. surnames, first name) as if to acknowledge that everyone in the Savannah Province of Caramenju is intimately acquainted with the protagonist's plight. The suffering of the English speaking Caramenjuan is compounded in the protagonist's single name. And as a global reader, one cannot but wonder if EFD picked this name for his character as a result of pure chance and coincidence. Surmising upon the consideration that in the world of creativity, chance and coincidence, more often than not, yield way to design would clarify any lingering doubts.

However questions still persist as to why the writer proceeded thus. Could his storyline have its effectiveness if the protagonist was named Rose, Martha, Lily, etc.? Further still, the name choice attributed to a female character instead of a male character, to embody the suffering of a people could be a subtle reinforcement of the idea that women, not only in the poetic scape but in the world as we know it, are put through unnamable travails, trials and tribulations. Again the reader need not confound what Lo Bianco considers as a conscious act of not surrounding the protagonist's name to create layers of intimacy (qtd. in Kumar, Pattanayak and Johnson x) with the writer's rejection or ignorance of this aspect of naming. We come across in the novel, the protagonist's elder stepsister, Mabel invariably addressed by her last name, Miss Anye or again in the case when the protagonist addresses Mabel's mother "Ma Bih, …" (45). The Narrator tells us she uses, "…Mabel's surname to address Angwi as a sign of respect" (45). In this instance, by EFD resorting to allowing the reader access to Mungeu's middle alone, the writer seems to be making a statement. In a prior book chapter, "Names, the Envelope of Destiny in the Grassfields of Cameroon" in *Framing my Name,* Ndi (2010) asserts that "People are easily identified with their first names, but having knowledge of someone's middle name becomes a privilege reserved for a select few" (21). In EFD's case here it is as if the author is making plain that his primary reader has intimate knowledge not just of the character but of the character's travail.

The structure of any novel or literary piece, more often than not is not left to chance and coincidence. Literary creativity entails design as aforementioned. Character names in works of fiction generally fall under this category discarding chance, coincidence and arbitrariness. Just as in real life a parent or parents would put in careful thought in the choice of name for the offspring, so does an author for his or her fictional characters. These characters are the ones to embody the author's ideals or his/her aversions. Besides this careful consideration in naming characters, EFD makes of names the vehicle that moves the plot or foretells events to come. It is in this light that, at a pivotal moment in the story when the elders are gathered to compel Mungeu' to give them the name of he who got her pregnant, Pa Anye lashes out, "how you have grown or tumbled up is not important here today. What is important is the name of your bastard's father. We must have his name" (41). The emphasis on names in this episode foreshadows, should they have his name, the horrors awaiting him to "determine whether [he] live[s] or die" (Ndũngi wa Mũngai 102). This instance is even tantamount to hinting that possessing an individual's name is already having the person at one's own mercy.

The centrality of names in EFD's work like those by Vakunta and Ndi spell most of the characters' attitude and their becoming. When we meet the driver who comes to pick up Mungeu' from Batemba to Nju'nki, the Narrator does not name him until they have gone halfway the journey. He is the unnamed source from which the protagonist would find some respite. The Narrator introduces him through Mungeu's thoughts as "an embodiment of humour [sic] and understanding…" (51). Also when the reader first sees him introduced, the Narrator uses such expressions as, "he jumped out of the bus playfully", "the driver joked along" and the driver like a diplomatic orderly, jokingly ushered Mungeu'…" (50). It is still along playful and joking lines that the driver anchors on the central concern for names. At halfway the journey, he engages Mungeu' in a conversation in which he claims to be working his punishment for having delayed Mungeu' from leaving Batemba earlier. He requests a compensation which would be his name given to the child Mungeu' is pregnant with. This request might leave the global reader wondering why an unknown stranger would ask another to name their unborn child after them. However, it is synonymous to what Ndũngi wa Mũngai in "Immortality is in your name" strives at while asserting that naming the child guarantees immortality as the name is perpetuated for, he writes "the person whose name is given to a baby also takes pride in being 'born' and has special responsibilities in nurturing that child" (103). This request is for Ndomnjie a means of attaining immortality.

It is only after this request by Ndomnjie that he introduces himself and we get to know his name. "I'm Ndomnjie"(51) he says.

Interestingly enough, Ndomnjie plays a symbolic role of being available for his passengers. He is the guide that leads people from one place to their destinations and so does without selecting. He satisfies all. He is the one who initiates the discussion on the thorny questions and doubts that Mungeu' has been nursing all along the journey. With this overture, Mungeu' feels a little freer to open up when he asks, "So what are you going to do in Nju'nki?" (51). In spite of Ndomnjie's suspicion that Mungeu' might be a wife running away from a husband with whom she has quarreled, he still offers to help her. Were one to conjecture what Ndomnjie stands for through the deeds and actions of this engaging driver who from pick up to drop off of his passengers, plays the role of a guide, an enlivener who makes himself available like a road or pathway to all users, and coupled with his profession as one who is constantly on the road, it would be safe to conceive the word *Ndomnjie* as a thoroughfare or a way. *Ndomnjie* is the Ngemba word for the main road. He symbolizes for EFD the main road which is there at the service of all. He is not selective in the choice of people he supports; not even Mungeu's father who had so wrong his own daughter. His name, thus, becomes for EFD what Derrida calls "an agency to which the recognition of the subject is confided" (qtd. *in* Margaret Kumar and Supriya Pattanayak 4).

In choosing a name for the sole psychiatric facility in the entire country, Caramenju, EFD resorts to an historical analepse. He alludes to one of the feverish peak of insanity in the History of the Western world; in short of the world. Though Napoleon Bonaparte may be celebrated as a hero with numerous accomplishments in some circles, he, nonetheless, stirred trouble almost everywhere in Europe and beyond. We must not forget he has been characterized by historians as the tyrant "who bit more than he could chew." This description strangely enough replicates that of this single center striving to handle all psychiatric cases that it simply cannot. Besides EFD tellingly sets his novel in a bilingual Caramenju in which the majority is French speaking and seem to operate in an arbitrary manner that leaves their English speaking counterparts confused, depressed and worried. This is EFD evocatively reminding the global reader of the confusion that Napoleon Bonaparte threw all of Europe in, in the wake of what has come to be known as the

Napoleonic Wars. Dr. Wirghan's questioning in disbelief is EFD's way to highlight that any association with Bonaparte is incomprehensible and even inexplicable. Unable to understand and explain this, Dr. Wirghan asks, "[a]nd they've not been able to help this young man? (3). Moreover, at the *Centre Bonaparte* named after the French Emperor, it comes as no surprise that no one there speaks English. The Emperor's name rekindles the arch-rivalry once lived between the French and the English which is now being played in another theater, Caramenju. EFD's suggestive use of Bonaparte's name here transcends mere suggestion. And like Soyinka, in his keynote address to FESPACO 2013, contends, the name as a word "can distort the palpable reality that your own senses have already determined" (Web September 4, 2013).

The plethora of names in *The Fire Within* besides the exploration we have seen thus far, also serve a variety of literary function. They indicate the profession of the Character, e.g. Nemo-Aku. They serve as pointers to the rich cultural diversity of the Cosmopolis that is the setting of the story: Batemba as well as that of Caramenju/Cameroon. EFD's poetization of names is a gesture to show the global reader that in Batemba one can find people from many other regions of the country as well as other parts of the world. This lends EFD's novel its universality and timelessness. Some names mark the religion of the characters and others serve to indicate the polyphonous nature of Caramenju, the setting. Therefore, it is no surprise that the reader comes across character names such as Jane-Frances, Agbor, Mabel, Tita, Mambo, Ndolo, Pa Ebot, Ebot Tanyi Ebot, Pendergreen, André, Acongne, Wumburo, Mbela and Musa, certainly a Muslim. Over and above, naming is not an act done without due consideration be it by parents our by a creative writer. To give the name "the power of secret signs requiring reverence from those who have the names as well as those who use the names" (Ndi qtd. in Kumar, Pattanayak and Johnson 19-30) it becomes imperative to consider what the heart desires the most. With the extraneous factors against which this character is helpless, does she or her society simply forfeit the belief system?

The above question brings to mind the evocation in the introduction of the processes of naming and names as the custodian of hopes, aspiration of a people and a political statement by such an individual or a group. This consolidates why Mungeu' chooses to make it an expression of love and affection as well as gratitude for help and love received. When the child who at the beginning of the novel spells doom for the protagonist is born, the Narrator tells the reader the choice she has made to name her child and why. She chooses Ndolo after the wife of her benefactor, and Mabel after her stepsister she loves dearly. In naming her child thus, Mungeu' wishes to replicate the parental love she has received from her stepsister Mabel and from her benefactors, the Ndomnjies. She also wishes that the kind of education she never had the opportunity to have, which her stepsister Mabel had, be that which Ndolo-Mabel receives. It is pursuant to this that the Narrator brings to the forefront that, "as a way of showing her gratitude to Ndomnjie's family and her stepsister, Mabel" (55). Also, in naming this child, EFD seems to have Mungeu' go for a traditional as well as a western value she craves the most. The child's name is a binomial consisting of *Ndolo* Cameroonian Douala for "Love" and *Mabel* from Latin meaning 'beautiful, loving, lovable.' It is plausible to read in this fusion of traditional and western value of love by this writer as a means of pointing out the good aspects of both value systems that needs immortalization. Yet for immortalization to be the sufferer would pay the price. Certainly, this is a hopeful note for the global reader that the despair in which the Anglophone Cameroonian is trapped will not survive eternally thanks to love.

Looking at the works of these ACL writers, it is clear that names and naming are of such relevance in their context that they become the driving and inspirational force of their literary creativity. The global reader perceives this through the central thematic concerns of the works, through the characters' actions in abetting or disrupting the action of the novel. They are far removed from simply primary markers of identity to becoming literary, semantic, and semiotic signs consciously used by the creative writers to add to and to shape the understanding of their works of literature. Elucidating names in these works have helped to clarify understanding of the works and makes sense as the authors conceptualize and jostle with character and name as indissociable accomplices. Important to EFD's naming process is that he chooses to have his protagonist embody the political stalemate which reduces his people, especially the Anglophone Cameroonians, to sufferers. Vakunta's take is that it makes them counterfeit and Ndi seem to intimate a loss of cultural value system in names and naming which at some distant past made the Lords/leaders, i.e. Ndi, worth the weight of their names. As a consequence, names in the works of these authors become, for the global reader, the drink with which to wash down the literary caviar prepared by ACL writers. The name, thus, has in the works of these authors the ability to expand rather than to shrink the scope of the global reader's imagination as well as the overall literary analysis he or she, as a critic, undertakes.

Works Cited

- Bill F. Ndi. "Bangolan Question" in *Musings on Ars Poetica: Poetic Reflections on the Poet and Poetry in Verse,* Mankon-Bamenda, Langaa RPCIG, 2009. Print.
- _____, "Epigram 53" in *Epigrams …!* , Mankon-Bamenda, Langaa RPCIG, 2012. Print.
- Bourdieu, P., *Language and Symbolic Power,* Polity Press, Cambridge1991. Print.
- Debi Prasanna Pattanayak "Establishing the space of naming" in *Framing my Name: Extending Educational Boundaries,* Altona, Victoria, Australia, 2010. Print
- Derrida, J., *On the name/ Jacques Derrida*; edited by Thomas Dutoit, Stanford University Press, Stanford, Calif. 1995. Print.
- Audra, E. & Aubrey L. Williams –*Pastoral Poetry: An Essay on Criticism,* Yale, Yale U.P.1961. Print
- Emmanuel Fru Doh's *The Fire Within* Mankon-Bamenda, Langaa RPCIG, 2009. Print.
- Margaret Kumar, Supriya Pattanayak and Richard Johnson. *Framing my Name: Extending Educational Boundaries,* Altona, Victoria, Australia 2010. Print

- McIntosh, Ian S., 'Personal names and the negotiation of change: reconsidering Arnhem Land's adjustment movement', Anthropological Forum, 14:2, (141-162). 2004. Print
- Ndũngi wa Mũngai "Immortality is in your name" in *Framing My Name: Extending Educational Boundaries,* Altona, Victoria, Australia in 2010. Print
- Peter Wuteh Vakunta "Rap on Nomenclature" 2008. Print.
- Webpage http://philpapers.org/sep/names/ access 07/15/2013
- http://plato.stanford.edu/entries/names/#1 access 07/15/2013
- http://www.thebritishblacklist.com/read-legendary-author-wole-soyinkas-epic-keynote-address-speech-fespaco-2013/ access 09/ 4/2013

Annex: Corpus

Bangolan Question

Before they brought us their school
Ghana had the Golden Stool
In their school they pointed towards Greece
Reducing us to what they did please
Telling us of the wild beasts,
Our ancestors with the least
Worry being the love for wisdom
Waiting to hear of a Greek kingdom
They never in mind had but were happy
Not without their own philosophy
As my father told me of his father
Who named my late uncle *Mundaka*?
A question in Bangolan
That for years did serve as scan
To rid the country of its thorns
And provide the nation with corns
With ucopia
Not utopia.

Mundaka translates "What have I done?"
Not the flat western "What have I done?"
But that which seeks to answer why
Spears, arrows and thorns seek not the sky
But fly after human hearts
In need of shields against darts
From nature and from our headmen
Worse than the goads of herdsmen
On the cows falling herding them down stream
As our headmen would rather hear us scream
With their new song of Globalisation
Forgetting we would ours on compassion
As they their agenda make political
We of our agenda do make ethical
Ours and theirs might not be close
But fairness by the right dose
Forebears had in that primitive village
Not the global resounding with pillage.

Curled from *Musings on Ars Poetica: Poetic Reflections on the Poet and Poetry in Verse,* by Bill F. NDI, Mankon, Bamenda, African Books Collective/Langaa Publishers, 2009

(Epigram 53)

The load,
The load on my shoulder
Is that of a name's
Attributes,
Viz.   Nobility,
    Dignity,
And   Integrity!
And one must have these
To happily and proudly pride himself as one!

Curled from *Epigrams ...!*, by Bill F. NDI, Mankon, Bamenda, African Books Collective/Langaa Publishers, 2012

Rap On Nomemclature

What's in a name?
There's nothing more important
Than a person's name.
The problem is we toy
Around too often with names,
Oftentimes for flimsy reasons.
People are no longer happy
With their real names!
They take liberties with nomenclature:
Adorning names devoid of signification!

Elizabeth has become Beth;
Susan has metamorphosed into Sue;
Patricia has been reborn as Pat alias Patty;
Christopher has been transformed into Chris;
Peter is now Pete;
Michael is Mike;
Charles is Chuck,
Anasthasia has been truncated into Ana;
William has become Bill.
And the list continues.
Why are we doing this?
We make others feel
Like human counterfeits!

The art of naming
Is of such crucial importance
That linguistic gurus have coined
A term for it—*onomastics*
Do you know what's done
To people who have tongue-twisting names?
Like *Shokolokobangoshia*?
We ignore them altogether?
Isn't that smart!

People's names are their most

Valued gifts from birth.
Let's steer clear of trifling with them.
The sweetest music to any one's ear
Is certainly his/her name!
We have no carte blanche to
Mess with those names!

©Vakunta 2009

Chapter Eight

All in a Name: Nomenclature in Francis B. Nyamnjoh's *The Travail of Dieudonné* and Bill F. Ndi's *Gods in the Ivory Towers*

By
Adaku T. Ankumah

Names speak. They offer a wide range of deep-level communications that reveal not only identity but shared languages, histories, behavioral expectations, resistance, creativity, and personal accountabilities (King ix).

Names, indeed, do speak, as Debra Walker King notes in her book *Deep Talk,* and they have meaning and relevance in Africa and African writing, most especially in Anglophone Cameroonian writing. Wole Soyinka, Nobel laureate and keynote speaker at the CODESRIA-Guild of African Filmmakers-FESPACO Workshop underscores the significance of naming when he modifies William Wordsworth's famous line, "The child is father of the man" to state the significance of naming in Africa: "[T]he name is father to the child." He notes the "careful thought" that goes into the process, even a "sense of history, hopes and expectations" which accompany the process. His conclusion is that "[c]hild naming, on this continent, is itself a creative act" ("A Name").

Naming in literature is not a random or erratic process; authors spend much time thinking through the process of naming characters because of the impact names can have on a text. They can relay important information about literary elements such as plot, character or theme to the reader. This chapter examines the use of names in *The Travail of Dieudonné*, a novel by Francis Nyamnjoh, and also in a one act play by Bill F. Ndi entitled *Gods in the Ivory Towers*. Both authors capitalize on naming as the cornerstone with which to lay the foundation of their works. To appreciate the richness of the theme, plot, and characterization, the international reader must understand names in the context of the authors' writings and the power they hold to make deciphering these texts a less daunting task. The context and background around which these authors write is unique in the sense that they hail from a nation with well over 240 languages and nomenclatural traditions, making the polyphonous nature of their character names contribute to the work a whole creative venture in itself.

Onomastics plays an important role in the novels of Francis B. Nyamnjoh and in Bill F. Ndi's one-act play *Gods in the Ivory Towers* in three major areas: names of places (toponyms), the names of businesses and business products and names of characters (charactonyms/aptonyms). A reading of these names in both the novel and the play reveals the inordinate attention Nyamnjoh and Ndi seem to give and the joy they seem to derive in creating these names. In his novel *The Travail of Dieudonné*, Francis B. Nyamnjoh chronicles the latter end of the life of his protagonist Dieudonné, a man whose marginalized position in society has brought him serious problems, including his struggles to survive. Tossed from one white employer to the next, he receives his walking papers from the last white couple, the Toubaabys. Eventually, he gathers at a local bar with a student of his boss and a motley group of citizens to listen to his story. Nyamnjoh is focused on the disenchantment of the marginalized like Dieudonné and the others gathered in the bar, those for whom independence has brought disillusionment in their socio-economic status. They find themselves at the fringe of society, looking in as their national leaders amass wealth and deprive them of a decent livelihood. Instead of succumbing to their oppressive conditions, these men and women appropriate the power to articulate their problems and express hope about the future. Bill F. Ndi's *Gods in the Ivory Towers* is centered on a protagonist from the Anglophone side of a bilingual English/French speaking country. He attempts to progress in a Francophone university, a place that is discouraging and hard for non Francophones to succeed at. Ndi's play chronicles the challenges the protagonist, who is named after the mountains that pose as a threat to his people, faces to overcome the status quo and succeed. In the fictional world of both texts, names become extensions of the dreams and ambitions of a people who are resilient and refuse to resign under their oppressive conditions.

Authors may choose to use real place names in their fictional texts; thus city names like Lagos, Yaoundé or New York appear in novels, though some may argue whether the real names are presented through a fictional filter as Frederick Kroon maintains in his article on "Make-Believe and Fictional Reality"(qtd. in Hedger). However writers may also choose to fictionalize the names of places and as Hedger notes, the writer may choose this fictional approach mainly to emphasize some aspects of the location. "The artist or creator of a given fiction,"notes Hedger, "can create a lens which changes or modifies reality however she sees fit: ("New York"). Thus though the reader notices the similarities between actual Cameroon and the setting of the story, the author discards Cameroon for Mimboland to draw attention to some aspect of the real Cameroon. *Mimbo* in Cameroonian pidgin refers to alcohol be it beer, wine, hard liquor; thus for the author to name the country Mimboland underscores his view of Cameroon as a land of alcoholics and alcohol as the national pastime. Indeed, alcohol plays a major role in the novel as it is used by both poor and rich, the ruled and the ruling class for various purposes. For the poor and marginalized gathered at Le Grand Canari, alcohol loosens their tongue and helps them to escape their woes momentarily. Dieudonné, who calls himself a "committed drinker,"finds a friend in a bottle of beer. The ruling class strongly encourages drinking to numb the people, to have them forget their financial and domestic woes and thus avoid suicides and political violence. In fact, the scholar-activist Dieumerci informs the reader that it is easier to obtain a permit to open up drinking bars than to get these permits for other businesses. Moreover, higher-ups, including the president, own the most prosperous breweries and therefore profit from the woes of the people.

In urban lingo, *mimbo* is the masculine form of the feminine *bimbo*, a term used to describe a woman who has an exaggerated view of herself and her sexual appeal or one who is an airhead, a person who is inept or foolish. Using this definition, Mimbolanders, then, are clueless as to how to deal with their mounting problem; they lack the perception and the understanding to arrive at a solution to their problems, with drinking being their major way of dealing temporarily with these.

Toponyms also help to reinforce the novel's focus on the socio-economic gap between the elite and the poor. The first area described by the narrator, Beverly Hills, is reserved for the affluent like the last couple Dieudonné works for, the Toubaabys. Named after the Californian city made up of wealthy, mostly white people, Beverly Hills in Mimboland is the envy of the poor who go in there only to work as houseboys, cooks and maids. The narrator describes the area as seen by the poor:

> [Beverly Hills is] the exclusive exuberance of Nyamandem, where . . . the stolen wealth that failed to make its way out of the country tended to be buried in extravagant luxuries that were simply out of this world. At Beverly Hills, passers-by were never tired of feeding their eyes with sights of wonderful white houses that looked like wedding cakes. (3)

This ostentatious display of wealth appears incongruous with the name of the capital city Nyamadem, a city unlike Yaoundé; one gets the word *nyama* which means meat or animal. Thus defined in animalistic terms, the city's rich as carnivorous people who prey on the poor and their services are highlighted by the author. For the rich, their segregated location affords them the opportunity to take "refuge from the contagion of the nouveau pauvre" (3). The imagery used implies that the poor are harmful or undesirable and that contact with them, unless to serve them, is bound to leave the rich with some negative consequences. Thus they take shelter in their sanitized environments to escape the contamination. No wonder the poor describe Beverly Hills as "the poor man's idea of paradise" (3), a place of supreme beauty and perfection, the ultimate dwelling place with all kinds of material comfort, which, unfortunately, is unattainable to them. Dieumerci, the student of Monsieur Toubaaby, discovers that this "sumptuous residential paradise" is mainly inhabited by foreigners and "a handful of distinguished nationals" (20). Even though Mimboland is a postcolonial country, the organization of the country follows the organization of a colonial settlement: the colonial masters live in this residential paradise, with a handful of distinguished nationals qualified to dwell with them. When an unnamed "nosy journalist" did an investigative report about the residents of this neighborhood who drive "big tough Mercedes and sports cars," he was jailed for his "daring pieces" and for refusing to be silenced by bribes (20). The author may have refused to name this journalist because bearing a name is risky in a country whose leadership does not tolerate criticism.

In contrast to the dwelling place of the rich, the dwelling places of the poor do not bear such lofty names. On the contrary, the names are associated with animals. "Swine Quarter," the name given to the area where the poor live, underscore the physical and economic conditions of its residents. A synonym for a pig, an animal detested for being unclean, wallowing in filth, the name Swine Quarter suggests a less than salubrious place to live, a pigsty, as the narrator reveals:

> The general level of hygiene in this part of Nyamandem was below zero and Dieumerci's appetite fled because of the nasty sights he saw. He didn't know whom to blame for the indiscriminate disposal of human excrement, dog shit, and the colony of flies that exploited the situation, or the multitudes of rats and cockroaches that celebrated impunity. (149)

Dieumerci is convinced that these pests are in the wrong location, stuck to destitution; they will be better off migrating to Beverly Hills where food is in abundance. These insects and animals know, however, of the " 'raticides' and insecticides [employed] to deny them visas and a right to life" while "stray cats and homeless dogs" have parties organized for them (150).

Ndi also uses nomenclature to express his perception of life for the real Cameroon, fictionalized as Ngoa. To underscore the forbidding nature of the place and the challenges to success, Ndi employs names to suggest the way out of the predicament of the villagers. Through the use of toponyms, Ndi addresses their landscape, exposes their psychological state and challenges the people to overcome their circumstances. This one-act play is set in the village of Ngoa, a village whose name is phonetically identical to the name of the protagonist, Ngwa. This close identification is not co-incidental. While Ngoa is reluctant to accept change, its homophone Ngwa, spelled with a "w" is doubly reluctant to allow anything that is synonymous with oppression and bastardization of academics to stand in his way. The alteration in spelling could be the author's way of using a name to call for the much desired change he wishes to see in his home country.

The Narrator informs the audience that the village is a moor land and it has greenery, but the name does not come from this plush landscape. Instead, the village is named after a hill that scares the villagers so much that nobody likes to mention its name as they pass through the village; it is the unmentionable for fear of attracting more evil. Thus a luscious environment, fertile and productive land has become a wasteland for its citizens. The author seems to suggest that there is nothing wrong with the landscape; indeed, it should work in the favor of the people. However, the older people are unable to function, and the Narrator cries for "wasted youth" (4), young, energetic people who should take advantage of this landscape to progress, but they are also hindered by this indomitable hill.

The condition of the villagers is depressing since they have succumbed to their fears about the hill and are paralyzed by this daunting landscape in their midst. Though they choose to avoid it or ignore it, their lives are shaped by it. This brings to mind Tennessee Williams' claim of "a structure whose name is a touch of accidental poetic truth. . . burning with the slow and implacable fires of human desperation" (971). The only one in the village who refuses to acquiesce to this hill is Pa Mbeh, whom the villagers call a "lunatic" because he acts contrary to the rest of them. Though there are people with mental illnesses who bear the name of lunatic, in most communities, the name is also given to those who defy the status quo, who challenge existing thinking. Mbeh's name, which originates from the Grassfields of Cameroon, suggests nobility since it is the response people give to a king when he addresses them (Ndi). Thus Mbeh is a man who hopes to inspire his people to nobility and excellence with a novel way of naming. Pa Mbeh decides to name his child after this same hill that poses a threat to the village, and the Narrator explains his reasoning: "[H]e was imbuing this child with the strength which will permit him untie the fate the gods have tied and dropped in front of his fellow villagers"(4-5). In so doing, as a visionary, dreamer and madman, Mbeh declares his son to be a child of destiny, one who has the potential to deliver villagers who have retreated from life's challenges.

The next category of naming, found more in Nyamnjoh's work, is associated with the names of businesses and commercial products. The names of their bars and beers provide an ironic commentary on their wretched living conditions. There is a discrepancy between the names of these places and the actual living conditions. As human beings, they also long for an escape from their misery. They dream of better places instead of "dilapidated shacks" (42), and their resilience comes through the names of these bars. Such names as "Eldorado" and "Rêve-d'or" [French for Golden Dream] divulge their longings to attain that place of wealth and opportunity. In the same way, names like "Maison Blanche" [French for White House] display their desire to move "from the outhouse to the White House," in the words of Jesse Jackson, talking about the hopes and aspirations of African Americans. Dieudonné's favorite bar, though, is Le Grand Canari (The Big Canary) which is located at "le Carrefour de la joie of Swine Quarter" [the crossroad of joy]. *Joy* and *Swine Quarter* appear oxymoronic, but this seemingly contradictory juxtaposition reveals the indomitable spirit of the residents. They may be invisible to the rich, barely have enough to survive, but they will not be subdued by their circumstances. They choose to embrace life instead of succumb to death.

One cannot conclude this discussion on business names without a reference to the names of commercial products, such as beer, the favored drink for the national pastime of the people of Mimboland. Nuessel notes that naming both alcoholic and non-alcoholic beverages requires "creativity and imagination" so the names can conjure up a "mood of relaxation, escape, and amusement" (123-4). There is no shortage of all three in Nyamnjoh's work. Mimboland's favorite beer, according to the narrator, is King Size, "a premium quality beer, genuinely fresh with rich smooth, deeply, [sic] satisfying taste with a million of sparkling bubbles . . . a beer with which there is never a dull moment." Dieudonné compares it to the River Nile: "Once you have drunk from it, you will return to drink again and again" (44). The people gathered at the Grand Canari drink to escape their troubles. The beer names also "conjure up visions of strength, exotic places, special events, and sensuality," notes Nuessel (124). The sensual is definitely a big part of the names. For example, the civil servant Chopngomna prefers Gold Harp which he uses like an acronym: **g**et **o**ne **l**ady **d**aily, **h**ave **a**nother **r**eserved **p**ermanently (48). His mistress likes drinking Amstel which Chopngomna prefers to stand for "aime-moisitueslibre" [love me if you're free, unhitched—my translation] (50). For those assembled at Le Grand Canari, the combination of escape, amusement and sensuality informs their behavior at the bar.

The area of onomastics that has the greatest bearing on crucial literary aspects of plot and theme has to be proper names. From the names of the rich, sometimes used satirically, to the names of the poor, which offer resistance and hope, names reveal a whole lot. In *The Travail of Dieudonné*, the author reveals that in a multicultural, multi-religious culture, names are at times a means of survival for the disadvantaged, as Dieudonné discovers. The protagonist, Dieudonné, is first named Alla-Go'onga by his parents, a name which means God Almighty and expresses the religious fervor of his parents. In his struggle to get a job, Alla-Go'onga is introduced to a "staunch Catholic who would only hire [him] if [he] changed [his] pagan name to something more Christian" (75). Thus Alla-Go'onga is unnamed and rechristened Dieudonné, just to assist him in getting a job with this foreign woman who remains oblivious to the religious nature of the first name she rejected. Dieudonné also is desperate for a job. Like Shakespeare's Juliet, he questions himself, "What's in a name?" He has arrived at the point where getting a job is more important than the names he is called. However, as Dieudonné informs us, this thoughtless act of rejecting his original name and arbitrarily assuming another destroys "whatever sense of self" he has been trying to cultivate (75). Dieudonné is cognizant of what Debra King notes regarding renaming and unnaming: they lead to fragmentation and at times contradicting characterization (84-5). Allah-Go'onga, a Moslem, has become Dieudonné, a Catholic who is not supposed to eat meat on Fridays; however, on one of the holy days of Christians, the priest catches Dieudonné eating meat. In an ironic twist, Dieudonné justifies his "un-Catholic" behavior with the unnaming process he had to go through to become Dieudonné:

> Upon her ladyship's insistence, you took a bowl of water and sprinkled it on me and pronounced me Dieudonné. Similarly, I took meat, sprinkled some water on it, and pronounced the meat fish. If it worked for you as a priest, it should work for your disciples.' The priest left tongue-tied. (75)

Dieudonné's new name does not come with a corresponding change in him; instead it continues his downward spiral, including losing his job for which he sacrificed his name. This unfortunate turn of affairs must have led Peter Vakunta to ponder the ambivalence in the name Dieudonné. The French name translates to *God given*, which raises several issues for the critic: "Are Dieudonné's travails attributable to Providence—a force he believes in—or to extraneous factors against which he is powerless?" ("Triple Estrangement"). Definitely, the novel seems to support these positions, for the characters assembled at Le Grand Canari know from their experiences that there is "really little one could do to influence the stubborn humiliations of life" (54). By imbuing Dieudonné's name with ambiguity, however, the author opens up several possibilities to unlocking the text. The marginalized who are living in a dysfunctional post-colonial country may find themselves powerless; that is their "God-given" situation. However, their conspiracy of silence in the face of these difficulties, their inaction and acquiescence by not challenging the status quo, is not providential but human.

Character names do not come from the religious realm alone but also from race. Thus the white academic couple Dieudonné works for is identified by their race in their name which means "whites"or someone from Europe. Toubab, a Central and West African name for a European, is also considered a mispronunciation of the Arabic tabib, meaning a doctor ("Toubabs") or again French colloquialism (toubabou) for a white or westerner. Both meanings apply to the Toubaabys who are Europeans with PhDs in Sociology, reinforcing the idea of the colonial mindset, the imperialistic disposition that the colonizer holds the solution—physically, materially and spiritually-- to the problems of the colonized. Given this binary position of superior/inferior, these westerners treat their animals better than the local people, as Dieudonné informs his captive audience that the "darling children" of the Toubaabys, one dog and eight cats, are flown to Europe for medical attention, yet sick human beings don't have medical care. The crowd gathered at Le Grand Canari finds this information difficult to digest. The inhumanity of the Toubaabys is further highlighted in the amount of money they are willing to spend on animals (MIM100,000) as opposed to the meager MIM 6,000 they spend on Dieudonné. When Dieudonné drinks an expensive wine trying to survive a three-day lock-in after an attempted coup at a time the Toubaaby's are in their country, Madame is infuriated with him, more interested in her animals and their survival than in the survival of a human being. Even Dieumerci, Monsieur's student, is shocked that the two can sit down and eat lunch without inviting him. The Toubaabys thus live the smugness and arrogance embedded in their name.

"Names," as Soyinka notes in his FESPACO address, "push their bearers to actualize their encoded meanings" ("A Name"). The characters in *The Travail of Dieudonné* live out their names, helping to advance the plot and themes of the novel. In his review of Nyamnjoh's novel, Peter W. Vakunta notes the symbolism and significance attached to the names of the characters such as Chopngomna, a tall, dark man who works as a cashier at the state treasury ("Triple Estrangement"). In addition to his given name, he has other sobriquets that reveal his character, for as Alastair Fowler notes, "nicknames reflect a salient aspect of appearance, personality or achievement"(149). Chopngomna's names certainly expose the weaknesses in his character, from excessive drinking, womanizing to a corrupt public official. In beer circles, he is "Bonbon Alcoolisé" candy with alcohol in it, emphasizing his love for alcohol, without the alcohol getting the better part of him or Le Bao, the short form of "Baobab indéracinable" or the baobab that cannot be uprooted or totally destroyed. The baobab is a tree with a short, thick swollen trunk that stores water; in the same way, this Bao can imbibe alcohol without admitting to getting drunk (45). To the "aspiring girls of a nearby high school," he is Joli Bébé i.e. handsome baby. His admirers call him "Moni Man Chop Fine Ting," [the wealthy man who enjoys the good things], alluding to his acquired wealth, including owning the most expensive cell phones with the fanciest ring tones in town. Men who feel dwarfed in his presence call him "Cow with Four Stomachs" (43-44). All these names unpack a whole lot about this character to the reader, revealing a womanizer who has to "get one lady daily and have another reserved permanently"(48), loves the bottle and throws his weight around.

Apart from his traditional given name, Chopngomna has multiple sobriquets. Unlike names which are given by parents, nicknames are given by people around who express their knowledge of another in the names they bestow on them. Thus to those who frequent the Grand Canari, Chopngomna is identified as "the man with the bleeding wallet," a civil servant who lives by what he refers to as "a proud tradition of the civil service . . . [that] a goat is meant to eat where it is tethered"(73). To him, accepting bribes, therefore, is part of the job description of being in the civil service. The "Chop"in his name most likely comes from the West African pidgin word meaning *to eat*, and Vakunta considers his name as a "metonym for the endemic corruption that has become widespread in Mimboland" ("Triple Estrangement"). The last part of his name, *ngomna* is the pidgin word for government; thus put together, this man milks the government to earn his living. In contrast to the words of John F. Kennedy, this man is not asking what he can do for his country but what his country can do for him. Ironically, Chopngomna's name seems to contradict the man's actions since he is the "cheerful giver of the group" (47). His favorite saying, "Action speaks louder than words," explains this seeming contradiction of the generosity of a man who milks the government. His actions are no different from the government's actions, for the ruling elite makes false promises to their people that things will improve, buy their votes and embezzle the bulk of the people's resources. The crumbs that they throw at their people are in reality not due to their generosity; they are just giving back what they took by force. With the multiplicity of nicknames and his carefully woven given name, Chopngomna provides the bird's eye view serving as a determinant to all that which characterize this fictional character.

This negative characterization of civil servants is magnified several times in the presentation of the chief civil servant of Mimboland, His Excellency President Longstay. The author's attitude towards the president of Mimboland is reflected in the name he chooses for him, which aptly fits him. His name Longstay sums up the people's thinking about his presidency: he has stayed too long. In a picture of his on the wall of Grand Canari are these words "inscribed in bold-blood red letters: 'L'homme lion, l'homme des grandes ambitions'" (3) [the lion man, the man of great ambitions]. This is indicative of the political ambitions of this man. He does not just want to be a president for life but also to remove opposition from his ambitions. The lion has blood on his hands as he has annihilated those who oppose his long reign. In addition to his name Longstay, the president is sarcastically named "Le Guide Eclairé, The Enlightened Guide of Mimboland" (3). The irony in this name follows immediately when the narrator gives another name: "someone whom God rejected as the records of the seminary where he trained would bear out" (3). How can a man rejected by God be an "Enlightened Guide" of a country? Rather, a country ruled by a man rejected by God is doomed. "A disillusioned civil servant" half drunk at Le Grand Canari, and who has taken up farming now just to survive the economic hardships, speaks on behalf of the people who had high expectations for Longstay's presidency. They were told "things were going to change"; now they "live a world of words not of miracles" (30). This man is indeed an "enemy of the people," but his ruthlessness and longevity may explain the people's predicament in dealing with this tyrant.

Naming does not elude gender issues in The Travail of *Dieudonné*. Nyamnjoh's female characters also bear names which reveal their aspirations and cultural inclinations. The character whose name most resembles the name of a Western female is Margarita, a dark woman who is one of Chopngomna's regular girlfriends, and whose name is the Spanish form of Margaret and is also the name of a cocktail made with tequila, which is an orange-flavored liqueur, and lemon or lime juice. In urban terminology, a Margarita is a "hot," sexy woman that guys want to date. Unlike

Precious who is associated with the natural style—"No Wig, no bleaching creams, no screaming perfumes, no red-hot lipstick, nothing. Just her immaculate ebony dark, composed self" (158)— Margarita can be defined by these words: affected, artificial, unnatural. Well dressed and coiffed with faux hair, Margarita lives up to the sensuous meaning of her name and her love for western consumerism. The effect she has on her boyfriend is certainly not the same as one gets from drinking a margarita, leaving her boyfriend worried about her cultural attachments:

> The fact that Margarita was aggressively buying into Muzungulander cultural values, especially the new consumer dimensions of being Muzungulander, worried him at times— not so much because of the extra demands on his wallet but because of the mimicry it brought about, making his otherwise beautiful, elegant and dignified Margarita appear ludicrously devalued and idiotic in her imitativeness. Sometimes he wondered, in amusement, of course, what would be left of Margarita if she were to strip to only what God had endowed her with at birth, as even her hair, finger and toe nails would have to come off, given that these were all additives, externally grafted beautifiers from dead Muzungulander women. (113)

Margarita's indiscriminate appetite for all things Muzungulandish is not limited to Western consumerism. The character that mimics western women and their feminist ideals, she delivers the feminist position in a group dominated by men. The men at the bar, especially Chopngomna, construe of women as parasites who feed off men by gutting them to pay for things they buy, from clothing to drinks. "'Why should you think I should always be the one to pay?' inquired Chopngomna rather light-heartedly" (88). When Margarita questions him about the validity of that statement, he gives a more serious response: "Because you women think it is your birthright to receive from men, and that it's our duty to keep giving" (89). She insists on paying for drinks for Dieudonné, and challenges Chopngomna's argument that women think it is their "birthright" to get things from men. She immediately refutes her boyfriend's assertion, calling men "braggarts." To the applause of the other women, she delivers a closing comment that feminists would cheer, even with her faulty grammar of double negatives: "We don't want nobody to give us nothing. Open up the door and we'll get it ourselves. As women, we are what you shall never be: **W**ell **o**rganized **men**" [emphasis mine] (89).

Names can also be used for satiric purposes, and as Alastair Fowler notes, the names used for this purpose tend to be grotesque (41). Madame Gazellia Mamelle, proprietress of the Grand Canari, "a veuvejoyeuse ("a happy widow"—my translation) and lioness" (3) is one such woman whose grotesque name becomes a source of humor in the novel as the author exposes her greedy nature. The name Gazellia, which echoes *gazillion*, suggests huge, or an extremely large or unspecified number, placed before Mamelle, French for breasts, emphasizes her prodigious size, her voluptuous nature and greed as she milks Precious and her clients, "laughing all the way to the bank" (156) with her gains. She is one of the "enabled" who has a keen grasp of the deplorable situation of the masses; she is aware of their daily struggles. With this knowledge, she has become one of the "opportunists" who want to keep things as they are so she can "[cash] in on mass misery big time" (154). Thus she sets up a "permanent all-purpose, all-night, all-day band" (154) to make sure the cash registers don't stop ringing. Madame Gazellia Mamelle lives up to the sensuous part of her name as she solicits younger men with "enticements of cash, car and mobile phone" and rumor adds that she has a horsewhip to "exact compliance in her bedroom" (161).

Finally, the name Precious, given to the slim "provocative singer" and waitress (155) who is also nicknamed SIDA, from a French acronym (**S**alaire **I**nsuffisant **D**ifficilement **A**cquis) that underscores the fact that she is overworked and underpaid (159), but which ironically is also the acronym for AIDS in French (**S**yndrôme d'**I**mmuno-**D**éficitaire **A**cquis). The reality of some of these marginalized groups, especially in Africa, is the probability of living with AIDS greatly increases. Given their uncertain economic situation, some are ready to engage in sexual activities just to get financial benefits to survive their harsh conditions. Such may be the case of the two "beautiful plump ladies"(47) who find themselves surrounding an albino gentleman, Bonblanc Mukula Ni-Ni, competing for his attention. The AIDS association becomes more pertinent as she is frustrated with her boyfriend Dieumerci's reluctance to engage in "full contact" but rather asks these questions: "Do you know the ex-boyfriend of your ex-boyfriend's ex-girlfriend" and as she sings a song based on a young woman's letter in which she shares her frustration with the "challenges of safe sex" with her male friend who is called Mr. Kondom (161), a not-so-subtle reference to condoms and their supposed role in safe sex.

Precious is highly esteemed by the clientele and community, including Dieumerci, who is attracted to her, having risen to "ghetto stardom" with her lyrics which show her identification with them:

Some days we have work, some days we don't; but the price of bread must always be met," she sings, and they know that she knows where the shoe of life's uncertainties pinches them the most. Like all ordinary Mimbolanders in bleeding ghettoes like Swine Quarter, her fans have refused to give the powerful the pleasure of leading them away in handcuffs. (160)

Her ability to articulate the sufferings of the downtrodden and express their pain in music has earned her the name of "a dangerous girl to follow closely" [my translation of "une fille dangereuse à suivre de près"] (160). Yet what endears her to her ghetto friends makes her a threat to the governing authorities who have banned her lead song from her debut album, Swine Quarter. Ironically, they love the music—not the words—and in their private quarters, the "high and mighty of Beverly Hills" use her music at their parties and fitness clubs. Some of the elite men are having "wild fantasies" about her that she does not answer her own mobile phone (160). Thus Precious is greatly loved and treasured by people from all segments of life for various reasons: the poor because she is one of them and her lyrics resonate with them; the rich for her titillating tunes which aid their love life.

Names in the novel are not used merely to outline the alienated status of the characters gathered at Le Grand Canari Bar. Names also reveal the resistance and resilience of these citizens. Perhaps no name captures that more than that of the student Dieumerci [*Thank*

God], whose name, like Dieudonné's, begins with God. He is a student who is preparing his mini-dissertation for an honors degree in Social History. His mandate from his academic advisor Monsieur Toubaaby is to take nothing for granted but to "[create] something new through constant and critical interrogation of received wisdom" (24). His acquaintance with Dieudonné in the Toubaabys' home as he goes to utilize the resources of their vast library introduces hope into the novel. The Toubaabys, especially Madame, sees Dieudonné as nothing more than a "silly fool" with a "thick skull" (25), an old man to tolerate since he cares for their "darling children," a dog and cats. Dieumerci's gaze into the old man's eyes reveals a total assessment of the old man. He may be weak, but he's a harmless man (26). In their short conversation, Dieumerci admits the old man is "a most exciting old man" who will liven his library hours at the Toubaabys with his exciting sense of humor. The feeling is mutual, as Dieudonné thanks "Papa God" (*Dieumerci*) for his new-found friend (29). Both are witty, using words to articulate what they consider to be their country's problems. Dieumerci laments the government's neglect of the people: "Because the only time government remembers my people is when there are false promises to make, taxes to collect, or electoral votes to collect" (30).

Without Dieumerci's interest in hearing Dieudonné's story and using the untold story of the down-and-out people like Dieudonné, the gathering at the Grand Canari will not have been possible. Certainly, Dieumerci has his own agenda: to fill in the gaps in his research with additional information from Dieudonné. However, his interests go beyond research and personal interest (35). Dieumerci becomes the son that Dieudonné always wanted but does not have (26). When Dieudonné breaks down, weeping inconsolably for ten minutes, Dieumerci assumes responsibility for him and takes him to bed. After the Toubaabys fire him, Dieumerci thinks of ways to support him, showing him the same love and respect he shows his own father (129). He decides not to keep the money he earns as substitute servant at the Toubaabys' but to give it to Dieudonné. He also decides to give him two of his own shirts. He even considers putting money aside to allow Dieudonné to go back to his native Warzone to see what remains of his family.

Indeed, Dieudonné can thank God for this God-sent son who treats him better than some biological children treat their parents. The morning after Dieudonné is fired, Dieumerci goes to visit Dieudonné with two loaves of bread for his older friend. Dieudonné, who has known abandonment all his life, is taken by surprise for this kindness shown by a young man he barely knows. His appreciation is shown in his countenance and words: "Dieudonné's eyes brightened and his countenance changed to accommodate the *window of hope* (italics added) Dieumerci had opened. With his eyes he smiled 'Ahsante sana' and thanked Allah the Almighty even before a loaf of bread was offered" (151). Living up to his name, Dieumerci is also thankful "that he hadn't come a minute too late" (151).

Dieumerci brings hope to Dieudonné as he procures employment for him with the African version of the Toubaabys—the Mohammeds—and presents him with money. Because of his support, Dieudonné does not give up on life. Yes, at times he is crushed by the vicissitudes of life, but he is "doggedly devoted" (164) to not succumbing to these pressures. In the company of Dieumerci, he defies the invisible forces pursuing him, for Dieumerci "gives him reason to keep hope alive" (164). It is not accidental that Dieumerci has the final words in the novel: "Those who say little things don't matter [. . .] should know how the lion feels when a fly enters its nostrils" (164). Engaged in academic pursuits so that one day he will become a "dispenser of Knowledge" like Monsieur Toubaaby, Dieumerci refuses to be thrown under the foot by academics and elites. His learning does not isolate him in an ivory tower as it has the Toubaabys who fail to see humanity in Dieudonné and would rather treat animals humanely than treat a human being kindly His personal touch and involvement make Dieudonné wish his young friend would never grow older to maintain that freshness that is missing from the Toubaabys.

In *Gods in the Ivory Towers*, Ngwa embodies in his name the aspirations of his father who names him, but at the same time his name evokes for the villagers, their struggles, and frustrations with life in their village. How do they respond to him, for they responded to his father by calling him mad. His friend Mballa summarizes the villagers' response as he bursts out laughing in front of Ngwa who is at a loss as to the cause of this in-your-face laughter:

> Mballa: (*Stands up from his sitting position. Scratches his forehead.*) I just don't know how to put it. But I will be plain and direct! Do you think your father did justice in choosing your name? (*Looks up at Ngwa in the face and does not wait for an answer.*) Just look at where they are; tell me whether you admire such a life! I doubt even if you like to live. Aren't we supposed to aim at a better life. . . ? Alas! The name of this village and hill at the foot of which we stand is like God never wanted us to live . . . (*Serious*) And I ask why He painstakingly created us and lead us to this place! Is this a transition camp to go to paradise? Maybe this is purgatory! (*Sarcastic laugh*) Ha! Ha! (6)

It is clear from this statement that the people find Mbeh's goals laughable, ridiculous, impossible, for they have accepted the hopelessness of their condition and attribute their failures to divine will; thus they are not responsible for any betterment of themselves. Mballa, a name that is limited to a region of the country, reflects the prevailing mindset of the people; they have acquiesced to their corrupt environment, and they intend to remain that way. A characternym like Ngwa's holds no excitement for their future in their earthly purgatory. They will continue to live defeatist lives until the bitter end. Nothing good will come to them in their God-forsaken Ngoa. Nonetheless, Ngwa, inspired by and conscious of the power in the name he bears, asserts the name which goads his bravery and brazenness to attempt to flex his muscles at the institutions of Ngoa. He sees himself destined to play a very significant role in the liberation of his country, as he reveals to Mballa:

Look at. . . my friend, I laugh not because I am stupid. Maybe because I am blind to seeing the plagues around us and have for eyes just the mind. And far beyond the ordinary, and maybe the naming! (*Toning higher*)Yes! My name! Yes, it was justice! I mean justice done! Done to me and to entire people of Ngoa! Mbeh shall not live to reap the product of his imagination; the iron with which he moulded me, now mustering like troops on hills, shall crack down this small hillock. (7).

Ngwa, a typical malcontent whose attitude and behavior are shaped by the consciousness of the intent at the origin of his name, is very much aware that he is a child of destiny, with a powerful name whose impact goes beyond himself to the whole village. So confident is Ngwa in the power of his name that at his lowest point in the play when he is forcefully ejected from Ngoa, he does not retreat but is confident about his future: "We shall meet again when I shall rise to face Ngoa anew" (45). His enemies do not have the last word. In short, his name accounts for his resolve to fulfill his father's dream, vision, and even folly, all caged in the name. It is this name that stirs the course and outcome of this play.

Though Ngwa's name holds promise for the future, the names of other characters do not hold such promise. As evidenced in the opening quotation from Debra King, names at times are linked to resistance and personal accountability, and the names of the two antagonists in this play fall into these categories. In the case of the despicable HOD, the author provides two names: the initials used which identify his function, not his name and his name Professor Guignol, the French for "puppet." Ndi seems to focus on his function as a representative of the Francophone side of the country who is at the university to maintain the status quo for the majority. Thus he is a pawn of the government, controlled by others who are more powerful but giving the appearance that he is in charge. Is there an attempt here to deny his humanity since of all the characters, he appears to be the least humane towards the protagonist? The moment HOD lays eyes on Ngwa, his demeanor changes from a flirtatious mood with his mistress Nnomo to an angry scowl or "spite" as the stage directions put it, at the young man whose presence has stalled his sexual moves and who happens to come from the wrong side of the village. His next question is even more ridiculous in a bilingual country: "But may I ask if he is from our part of the . . . . Er! I mean, is he Francophone?" His hesitation indicates that he is aware of the inappropriateness of the question, but like his Francophone counterparts who want to stall the progress of the Anglophones, he must know.

Ngwa's response that he is a polyglot does not change the focus of the discussions; HOD's linguistic discrimination becomes more obvious as he tells Ngwa that he is taking the seat of a francophone student. This incident is not a contrived one since the playwright faced a similar situation as a student at the University of Yaoundé when "some narrow-minded examiners" denied Ndi the opportunity to defend his dissertation in French "because he wanted to take the place of Francophones" (Doh 4). In frustration, Ndi had to give up after all the years he had put into his studies. Ngwa fares slightly better, for HOD eventually agrees to allow Nnomo to supervise Ngwa's work, though he insists on closely monitoring them so Ngwa will not develop an amorous relationship with his mistress. After HOD's acceptance of the pair working together, Nnomo tries to mollify Ngwa by suggesting that HOD is not evil after all:

Nnomo: "You see what I told you? He has accepted! He is such a good person!
Ngwa: Good, really indeed, a good person I reckon!" (27).

It is clear that Ngwa's assessment of the same man is totally different. HOD ejects Ngwa from the academy not based on any evidence of evildoing on his part but because his mistress says so, and Ngwa comes from the wrong side of the country. Thus he is a "primitive non-native" who does not deserve to be in a place for "smart civilised [sic] people!"(44). Ngwa reveals his shock that such a person could be an intellectual: "How did you ever become a professor if objectivity was not anywhere in your lexicon? . . . Your professorship, I believe, was from the gutter picked like that of most of your colleagues in this village college!"(44). Professor Guignol clearly emerges as the villain in the play, and the author's naming techniques serve his purpose of revealing a man manipulated by others and using his viciousness and inhumanity to deny Anglophones an opportunity to improve themselves. The acts of intimidation and violence aimed at frustrating the efforts of the Anglophones who attempt to progress and do so in an honest manner constitute in this play and for the playwright a way of exposing the weakness and unscrupulousness of institutions which should aim at encompassing the "universe" in the University.

HOD's mistress and accomplice, Nnomo, seems determined to frustrate Ngwa's academic ambitions by offering her body. After Nnomo's failed attempt to seduce Ngwa, she reports him to HOD as the guilty party, and he becomes the lashing rod for Ngwa, pouncing on him calling him a primitive, uncivilized person. In the end, with the help of Nnomo, he throws Ngwa down the abyss and go to celebrate their relief at the bar. Her name, Nnomo, which appears like a homophone of "no more" may be Ngwa's way of resisting the frustration that Nnomo, her lover, and those on the same linguistic side put in the way of the Anglophone citizens. Ngwa's refusal of Nnomo's advances is a symbolic and yet ironic way that the playwright uses a name to subvert it while letting its bearer understand that her abuses of power shall "no more" be tolerated.

However, Nnomo ("no more") may also refer to the character's frustrations or failures in her personal life as she confesses to Ngwa before seducing him: "O, I am rich and have everything a woman should. But, is it really worth the while having the world's gold with just no comfort and being so lonely? . . . Ah! liberation made me rebuke my mates at school. They could have been by me now" (37). Having bought into a radicalized version of Western feminism, Nnomo had spurned men to focus on her studies. Now while her female colleagues have men, she describes herself a "stone of the river bed" (38), stuck in one place in her social life and willing to seduce young men like Ngwa and literally throw herself at them. The upright Ngwa, though, refuses to be seduced by a stark naked professor, increasing her infuriation and humiliation.

Though Ndi provides a name for most of his characters, the Narrator remains nameless: The question is why he remains nameless since the author seems to have put some thought and creativity in naming other characters like the protagonist. This lack of a specific name raises interesting issues, for as Frank Nuessel notes, "a name is a *sine qua non* for existence. Without a name, no linguistic means of reference is possible." He further cites another author, Haig Bosmajian, who refers to other forms of identification used for prisoners and slaves, such as numbers, as a "negation of their humanity and their existence" (2-3). To be nameless, then, is to be considered unimportant in the bigger scheme of life, irrelevant to others. This explanation is an apt description of the Narrator's existence as a minority in the imaginary land of Ngoa, a land that resembles the playwright's homeland of Cameroon, where Anglophones have little to no impact on the affairs of state and their existence is not fully acknowledged. In effect, their visibility is reduced to naught.

Remaining nameless can also be a form of resistance to the existing status quo. In looking at namelessness in African American literature, Debra W. King notes, "One way of interpreting namelessness [in Ralph Ellison's *Invisible Man* and James Weldon Johnson's *Autobiography of an Ex-Colored Man*] is a symbolic gesture denoting the nameless characters' inability to assert themselves fully within a world that is hostile or alien to their self-image" (18). Thus to them namelessness becomes a form of resistance to their lack of identity in America. This reading of namelessness definitely helps to explain the Narrator's predicament in *Gods in the Ivory Towers*. He is the eye that observes the political landscape for the people. With the exception of Pa Mbeh and his son Ngwa, he seems to be the lone visionary in the play who cares about the suffering of his people. The Narrator opens the play by identifying himself as the "town crier" who has been crying for his village (4). He is alluding to the tyranny that exists in imaginary Ngoa, modern Cameroon, where Anglophones who have dared to challenge the status quo have faced opposition from the ruling elite. In tracing the life of the author, Emmanuel Doh notes the harsh reality of Ndi's life as a member of the oppressed minority, making him a man on the run (3-4). His characters find themselves in that lonely state. At the end of the play, the Narrator stands alone on the stage, mute, the only one of the rest of his fellow townspeople, very much impacted by the sorrows of his people and the general apathy among them. He is happy that Ngwa's eminence carried him to the top, but at the same time he is sad that his people want the proverbial crumbs from Ngwa's table, but do not want to participate in the process of liberating themselves from the tyranny of their existence.

Finally in resisting naming, the Narrator defies ethnic identification and therefore chooses not to limit himself to anyone.

A name will fix him as belonging to a particular ethnic/linguistic group, something the ruling elite and their representatives like HOD have succeeded in using to divide the country. However, in a land with peoples as varied as their landscape, with multiplicity of tongues and cultures, the playwright deliberately chooses not to participate in that exclusionary practice by refusing his Narrator a name. Naming will also expose him to persecution which is unleashed on those who speak out. Thus being denied a name, the Narrator is not exposed to the persecution that commonly follows those who see and say too much.

In his preface, Ndi attributes any coincidence in naming to an "imaginative nomenclature" (3), and for a one-act play, his imagination was certainly in an elevated mode as he meticulously names his characters. Some names are integral to the plot and its resolution; others reflect the "culture of silence" that has enveloped a group of citizens who feel helpless before their challenges. Other names expose the source of societal problems.

Nomenclatural poetization plays an important role in the works of these two Anglophone Cameroon writers as it provides an important key to unlocking their works and advancing their plots. Were names to be viewed as a simple case of characternyms in the creative act, understanding and elucidating these works will leave much to be desired. A holistic comprehension of these works can only be achieved by a careful reading of the seme incorporated in each name, be it characternyms, toponyms, or names of objects. Both Francis B. Nyamnjoh and Bill F. Ndi will endorse Alastair Fowler's words that names in literature are "often doors to meaning and words giving glimpses of the writer's intention" ("What's in a Literary Name?"). Nyamnjoh and Ndi reveal names could be a means of survival as well as way of resisting the negative forces that seek to keep the oppressed in their place.

Works Cited

Doh, Emmanuel Fru. "Bill F. Ndi's Social Angst and Humanist Vision: Politics, Alienation and the Quest for Freedom in *K'cacy, Trees in the Storm and Other Poems*." In *Fears, Doubts, and Joys of not*

Belonging. Eds. Benjamin Hart Fishkin, Adaku T. Ankumah, and Bill F. Ndi. Mankon, Bamenda: Langaa Research & Publishing CIG, 2014. 3-27. Print.

Fowler, Alastair. *Literary Names: Personal Names in English Literature*. Oxford: Oxford UP, 2012. Print.

———. "What's in a Literary Name?" OUP Blog. 24 Sept. 2012. Web. 16 May 2014.

Hedger, Joseph A. "New York is just New York: An Account of Genuine Proper Names in Fiction." *Review of Contemporary Philosophy* 12 (2013): 43+. *Academic One File*. Web. 30 Apr. 2014.

King, Debra Walker. *Deep Talk: Reading African-American Literary Names*. Charlottesville: UP of Virginia, 1998. Print.

Ndi, Bill F. *Gods in the Ivory Towers*. Bloomington, IN: AuthorHouse, 2008. Print.

Nuessel, Frank. *The Study of Names: A Guide to the Principles and Topics*. Westport, CT: Greenwood, 1992. Print.

Nyamnjoh, Francis B. *The Travail of Dieudonné*. Nairobi: East African Educational, 2008. Print.

Soyinka, Wole. "A Name is More than the Tyranny of Taste." CODESRIA Guild of African Filmmakers FESPACO Workshop: *Pan-Africanism: Adapting African Stories/Histories from Text to Screen*. Ouagadougou, Burkina Faso. 26 Feb. 2013. Address.

"Toubabs in Gambia." Gambia Information Site .n.p. Web. 7 May, 2014.

Vakunta, Peter W. "A Tale of Triple Estrangement."Review of Francis Nyamnjoh's *The Travail of Dieudonné*. *Pambazuka: Pan-African Voices for Freedom and Justice* Issue 423 (Mar. 11, 2009):

Williams, Tennessee. *The Glass Menagerie*. *Backpack Literature: An Introduction to Fiction, Poetry, Drama & Writing*. Ed. X. J. Kennedy and Dana Gioia. 4th ed. New York: Longman, 2012. 969-1022. Print.

Chapter Nine

Names and Nomenclatural Distortions as Dramatic Technique in Anglophone-Cameroon Literature

By
Emmanuel Fru Doh

There is something in a name, even if only at its most superficial, for which reason some time after the supposed end of colonialism, the Gold Coast became Ghana, Congo became Zaire, and Upper Volta, Burkina Faso. In like manner, after the defeat of Germany by the allied forces in WWI, *Kamerun,* which was a German colony at the time, was seized and partitioned into two unequal parts, the bigger given to France and the smaller to Britain, which had so much more already in terms of colonial turf overseas. These parts of *Kamerun* became *Cameroon* under Britain and *Cameroun* under the French. Or, consider again the change of the name of one of Cameroon's cities from Victoria (the name of an English queen) to Limbe, supposedly the local name of a river in this same city. Yes, there is something in names and the distorting of names, and it lies in the way it affects those doing the naming, those named, and those hearing or using the names. Paul L. Leslie and James K. Skipper Jr. are saying the same thing when they declare:

> Names are not just arbitrary symbols; they signify status, achievement, privilege, and meaningful social organization. They may communicate ethnicity, social status, and social prestige all understood as meaningful within social contexts. (273)

In the worldview of virtually every ethnic group located within the geographical space belonging to those Cameroonians whose colonial linguistic affiliation identifies them as Anglophone, names are of great significance as is the case in most of Africa at large. One's name can reveal a lot: one's parentage, one's ethnic group, one's place in society, and even more depending on the ethnic group. This, however, is becoming a little complicated than before with inter-ethnic marriages and the attendant complications as certain names are now going across ethnic lines and in the process shedding some of their cultural values. Even then, names remain a major indicator in these societies and the practice of naming, beyond everyday life, has flavored literature from this part of Cameroon, yet as a literary phenomenon, this has remained unstudied in the main. Abu Shardow Abarry makes the same observation with relation to the African continent as a whole:

Naming has colored the writing and artistic works of Africans, from the earliest generations to contemporary times. What is lacking, though, is a systemic study of the nature and qualities of such nominal colorations as they arise from the various parts of the African world. (157)

My experience of names in literature, then, has left me with the feeling that, along with authorial intentions, names and their distortions seem to exude diverse emotions that possibly characterize and influence the mood, tone, diction, pervading spirit, and so much else of the moment, era even, and the society that conjured them into existence. This is a conviction given birth to by experience, an overwhelming realization that for different reasons—to ridicule, excoriate, or free themselves from potential persecution—authors deal with the exercise of naming their characters seriously. This is the case even if the degree of seriousness varies from author to author, given that in some works the names of characters resonate more serious and equally more important facts or implications than others. My convictions and desire to explore further the role played by names in the works of certain writers were buttressed by Leonard R. N. Ashley's observation with regards to literature and nomenclature:

> You don't have to become a literary critics [sic] but if you are going to be a consumer of poetry, novels, plays, and literature, you will get more out of it if you play the name game with or on the author. You are fully entitled to react, or to research. You can add a lot to your appreciation of or analysis of every book you read, every play you see, every movie or television program you watch if you pay attention to fictional names. You will find there are more 'subtleties of the cultural

matrix' or just that names contribute to plot, tone, and every other literary element. (203)

Roland Barthes is saying the same thing in more general terms when in his study of Proust and the latter's use of names he observes: "*tenir les systèmes des noms, c'était pour Proust, et c'est pour nous, tenir les significations essentielles du livres*" – "Understanding the significance of names was for Proust, and for us, grasping the essential meaning of books" (my translation 132). Accordingly, I have decided to use the works of some Anglophone-Cameroon writers—Victor Epie Ngome, Bill F. Ndi, and Bate Besong—to bolster my point. To understand better the importance and significance of the names used by these chosen playwrights, the plot of their works or their concerns need to be examined.

To begin with, Victor Epie Ngome's *What God Has Put Asunder* (*Asunder*), is double-tiered when it comes to meaning, for there is a surface and an underlying story. At the surface level, *Asunder* is about Weka, a young woman who was raised in an orphanage by Reverend Gordon, the Rector of the orphanage, and his assistant, Sister Sabcth. As Weka matures, two suitors enter her life: Emeka, with whom she has grown up at the orphanage, and a rival and local Member of Parliament (MP), Garba. Weka is virtually forced to choose a husband from this duo as the idea of settling alone out of the orphanage is out of the question. In fact, Reverend Gordon tells her:

> Weka, it was I who administered extreme unction to your mother. And when she handed you over to me, she made me almost swear that as soon as you were of age, I would make sure you were respectably married. So it is completely out of the question for you to talk of being by yourself. (6 – 7)

In the end, in spite of Weka's familiarity towards Emeka, a co-orphan at the orphanage, she is coerced into accepting Garba, the local MP, in marriage. Without the wedding rings, the marriage is tentatively solemnized by Reverend Gordon. The condition is that the couple will live as husband and wife for a decade, after which their union will be revisited by the authorities involved—Reverend

Gordon and Sister Sabeth—to see how the marriage is progressing. If the couple is found to be desirable of each other after ten years of cohabiting, then the marriage would be solemnized.

Alas, even before the decade is up, Weka comes to the conclusion that Garba is a hopeless and unfaithful partner who does not only disrespect her but has wasted her family's wealth which she brought into the union. For these reasons, Weka abandons Garba and takes up residence at her father's now somewhat run-down abode in an effort to rejuvenate the place along with their battered lives—she and her children. Garba's appeal, even his attempt at forcefully regaining Weka back, as his wife, meets with fierce resistance from Weka and her children. As a result of the impasse, the matter is brought to court. The court rules that the couple will remain in separation, while being civil towards each other, even as a final verdict is subsequently arrived at by both parties whose decision would then be ratified by the courts.

At the surface then, Ngome's *Asunder* is the story of an orphan girl fighting her way out of a marital union into which she was pressured by controlling authority figures in her life, granted her status as a child without parents with genuine familial love for her. Beneath this unfortunate plot, however, lies one more horrendous as Weka's marriage, her life as a whole, is a metaphor for the plight of today's Anglophone-Cameroon, Southern Cameroons as it was officially referred to at the onset. Southern Cameroons was in the orphanage when it was a United Nation (UN) Trust territory under British Mandate. However, when her subjects started agitating for independence, like Weka, Southern Cameroons was given the atrocious option to choose between uniting with the Federal Republic of Nigeria or then La République du Cameroun as her only route to independence. She chose La République du Cameroun. The consensus in Anglophone-Cameroon today, in any case, is that the founding fathers of the emerging federal nation were assured that the UN and Britain would revisit the union after ten years to evaluate it. If both parties remained satisfied with the state of the union, then their status as a nation would be confirmed or, on the other hand, dissolved, depending on the findings of the visiting authorities. Even before the ten years, Southern Cameroons had already registered overwhelming dissatisfaction with the union but could only wait for the overseeing authorities' pending fact-finding mission to make known their grievances; the authorities never showed up. Southern Cameroonians were later to find out that the overseeing authorities had hoodwinked them into a position the authorities could care less about. The hope of the authorities was that before the ten years, the minority Southern Cameroon population would have been eliminated, diluted into extinction by the majority French-speaking La République du Cameroun. The appellation and people would then become a mere socio-cultural and historical aberration of years gone by. Things have not worked out that smoothly as the minority Southern Cameroon English-speaking population has turned out to be a most resilient bunch today, struggling like Weka to reinstate the terms of the union which have been violated by La République du Cameroun, or else quit the union.

Informed thus of Ngome's surface and underlying meanings, it becomes at once obvious that Ngome's names in *Asunder* were carefully thought out so as to confirm his underlying story-line; his names are representative of types, in other words. To begin with, Ngome's marriage metaphor appropriately names the socio-political union existing between the former Southern Cameroons and La République du Cameroun. Southern Cameroons' subjection to a UN's trusteeship mandate was analogous to an existence in an orphanage. Ngome's heroine is named Weka, an acronym built by combining the first two letters from West Cameroon, the name by which Southern Cameroons was known when it formed a federation by joining La République du Cameroun. Southern Cameroons was called West Cameroon, and La République du Cameroun, East Cameroon. However, Ngome has used a "K" instead of the "C" in Cameroon as if to recall the days when the nation was a German colony—Kamerun. The "K" became a "C" when this German colony was seized, partitioned, and handed over to France and Britain.

On the other hand, Garba stands for La République du Cameroun and her leader at the time who was from the northern part of Cameroun and a once-upon-a-time member of the French parliament, hence this well-known name from the north of Cameroun and his status as a local MP. Reverend Gordon is given a

Western name, more likely English, as it brings to mind a kind of gin the English supplied in Cameroon in the 60's and 70's, Gordon's Dry Gin. The name suits best the fact that the English were in charge of the UN's Trust territory—Southern Cameroons—just as Reverend Gordon is in charge of the orphanage. French presence in the scene is acknowledged by the existence of a character named Louis, the name of some of France's Kings. Emeka, along with the demotic language attributed to him, is given an Igbo name so as to represent the Nigerian perspective of this saga. Emeka is the alternative suitor to Garba; the suitor with whom Weka grew up in the orphanage just like Nigeria and Southern Cameroons were subject to Britain's administration when the latter was in charge of these UN protectorates. Ngome's names then are effective tools in that they are loaded with meaningful socio-political overtones that best expose and authenticate the allegorical value of his work.

Another playwright whose use of names is richly significant is Bill F. Ndi as is the case in his *Gods in the Ivory Tower*. From Ndi's title, it is obvious that he is looking at intellectuals who have transformed themselves into gods, not of mercy and compassion, but gods who have carved out for themselves a comfort niche from which their pursuits are embarrassing and disgraceful as they have little or nothing to do with intellectual activities. These are pseudo-intellectuals who have transformed themselves into monsters determined to destroy the academic dreams of budding scholars if their whims are not satisfied.

When the play opens, Narrator, in the manner of a Greek Chorus, acquaints the reader with the state of affairs in Ngoa. Through Narrator's comments, the geographical setting is identified and the audience accorded a brief but revealing historical background to the status quo. Our location is the village of Ngoa, with a revealing but obnoxious history:

Everyone passing through here, a boy, a girl, a man or a woman has to make a match with the young or old of his/her direct opposite; a thing cherished by most and abhorred by a handful. This tie is to guarantee one's success through the village college where all these lots meet! (4)

Through Narrator, one hears of Pa Mbeh who is said to be a lunatic, maddened by trends on this hill and village Ngoa. We learn he named his son Ngwa, who, against all odds, has succeeded in climbing to the top of this hill. The value of Ndi's names intensifies as one begins associating them with different settings and geographical locations within Cameroon. One's thoughts, with regards to these names, are endorsed when Ngwa turns out to be a potential graduate about to "enroll for a postgraduate degree course in sociology" (24). Although it is by now obvious that Ndi's protagonist is out to combat existing corruption within a given locale, digging further into the obvious and implied social, cultural, and ideological reverberations surrounding their names will unearth so much that would otherwise go unnoticed if some degree of onomastics was not practiced with regards to the names in this play.

To begin with, Narrator does what is expected of a narrator by telling and running comments about events in the play. From Narrator we get the toponym Ngoa, the name of the village for which he has spent all his life lamenting. To a Cameroonian, especially one who has lived or studied for any length of time within Cameroon's political capital, Yaoundé, this toponym immediately echoes the name of the hill or neighbourhood on which the University of Yaoundé I is lodged. This is the case so much so that Ngoa is now a metonymy for the University of Yaoundé. Ngoa, then, is no ordinary village; it is in reality the University of Yaoundé I that is being referred to thus. Hence, we hear of sociology being studied here, with students looking for professors to direct their research effort?

Still from our first contact with Narrator, one encounters an aptronym—Pa Mbeh. It is not for nothing that his name is preceded by the epithet, "Pa." In most cultures within Cameroon, especially the Bamenda Grassfields, from where Ndi hails, this epithet is indicative of the amount of respect accorded whomever is thus addressed. This is usually respect brought about primarily by the advanced age of the addressee or his mature way of behaving. At once then, it is obvious from his name that Pa Mbeh is an elderly man respected for his age, at the very least.

Beyond the epithet "Pa," this character's name "Mbeh" is also charactonymic in light of certain traits engendered by the resonating sonic effects of the name "Mbeh." To the Bamenda Grassfielders of Cameroon, with an ancient and equally rich royal tradition, the leader of an ethnic group is not spoken to directly by just anyone; it is the same for gaining his attention. Those qualified to communicate directly with such a leader address him "Mbeh."[1] In this light, by giving this insightful character such a name, Ndi is elevating his status in the presence of all those in the village of Ngoa. It must be remembered here that beyond the hill or university campus, Ngoa, the village also represents a nation, in this case Cameroon. Interestingly, Pa Mbeh is considered a lunatic, but this, in my opinion, is because of his passionate love for Ngoa, a setting which the rest are determined to exploit as best as they can regardless of the plight of the exploited lot. He is then the true leader and royal personage, even if unacknowledged, the only one of his generation who sees and identifies with the suffering masses as a true leader should. As if to confirm this man's royalty, the reader or audience only hears of him but never gets to see him or hear from him in person; it is his doctrine that is alive and spreading. His son and potential successor whom he appropriately names Ngwa, after his love for the village, Ngoa, is expected to realize his dreams for his people like Joshua did for Moses: he will lead Ngoa into an ideal future of which the citizens will be proud.

Ngwa, the name of the protagonist, is a pun on the name of the village Ngoa, and it is not for nothing that his father, Pa Mbeh, gave his son such a name. Ngwa was to personify the village of Ngoa to his father who brought him up with the integrity he wanted to see in the village:

> My name! Yes, it was justice! I mean justice done! Done to me and to entire people of Ngoa! Mbeh shall not live to reap the product of his imagination; the iron with which he moulded me, now mustering like troops on hills, shall crack down this small hillock. And that is the justice he did and to me too, justice done! Done to all the people of Ngoa! (sic 7)

It is not surprising then, that Ngwa is determined to deracinate the ills plaguing Ngoa. He is the true scholar and illumined soul who practices the integrity he preaches and expects from others.

Like his father's name "Pa Mbeh," the name Ngwa is from the Bamenda Grassfields. One cannot help but wonder if Ndi is hinting at the reforming role people from this Anglophone part of the country have and continue trying to bring into a corrupt nation here miniaturized in the guise of a sick university campus tormented by tribalism, promiscuity, and the corrupt practices of marketing services for which the government is already paying these employees to render. The reality in Cameroon yields a resounding affirmation.

Enter Mballa, Ngwa's foil. Without doubt, Mballa's name is from the Centre Region of Cameroon, a people today reputed for spearheading the corrupt practices that have transformed Cameroon into a defiled nation under Paul Biya. Mballa, true to his belonging to the empowered and equally corrupt ethnic group, is nonchalant about the damned state of the village, Ngoa. To him, Ngwa's concerns and goals are laughable as all he wants is to benefit from the existing mess of a village. He pokes fun at Ngwa's dreams of purging society of her ills:

> Ngwa: (*Hitting his chest with
> the pointing finger and with pride*) I
> will bring them down one day! And
> the villagers shall move uphill as if
> they were sailing on a smooth river or
> skating on ice. Have you heard?
>
> Mballa: (spontaneously) Ice skating you
> say…! (*Laughs*) That's what you see
> only on TV. (8)

From a defeatist perspective, Mballa goes onto declare:

> (*Nodding in denial*) You see, there is
> one thing everybody thinks and
> knows, but none of them will ever
> admit to. It is the fact that everybody
> as well as everything is nothing but
> toys and puppets in the hands of the

> gods. So you better not think yourself
> better than any of those grasses or
> rocks that constitute Ngoa. You may
> keep dreaming thinking as the village
> myth holds that you are a god or His
> image, but …. (*Pouts*) Myths are myths…! (9)

Like the defeated soul he is, one without any positive vision, Mballa confirms his status in the mire of corruption by berating Ngwa thus:

> (*Serious*) Don't speak like an
> ignorant fellow! Since both you and
> your ambition is to see you rise to the
> top of Ngoa, you must be ready for
> that! Those young boys and girls you
> see up there passed through that
> prison or did imprison some people to
> get there! So, be prepared for the
> worst…. (10)

Mballa is referring to the prison of being wrapped around by female thighs in a system which employs illicit sex as the dominant currency. He had earlier pointed out to Ngwa as he ridiculed Ngwa's dreams: "Maybe you will end / up imprisoned between some laps / someday! One never knows….! (10). What premonition! Nnomo is later to demand payment in this currency for her to supervise Ngwa's sociology research.

"Ojong" is the name of another character that Ngwa meets in his dealings with the village of Ngoa. Ojong confirms the disaster the village is when he observes: "(*Naively*) Since I succeeded in coming here, I have been having a hell of a rough time" (12), before going on to declare categorically:

> Ojong: (*Prostrates and kisses Ngwa's feet*)
> Nature is wonderful! Ngwa, you are
> the one every tongue in the village
> talks of as being the messiah to undo

Ngoa and his numerous ups and
downs! (14)

Ngwa is still unsure of Ojong. He wonders why Ojong thinks he, Ngwa, should be the one to "help him get a solution to [his] problems." (15). Although he promises to help Ojong identify the solution to his problems, the ease with which Ojong is about giving up to the challenges at Ngoa, is disturbing:

> (*Preoccupied with his problems and
> not listening*) The up and down
> movement here is too much, so much
> that I was already thinking of
> making it back downhill before my
> senses directed me to you this lucky
> morning. (*Regrettably*) O, this place I
> dreamt of as the best is just...!
> (*Heaves a big sigh and curses.*) Oh,
> damn it! (15).

There is, indeed, something mysterious about this character as indicated by the meaning of his name, Ojong, within the different Manyu villages of Cameroon, their differences in pronunciation and spelling notwithstanding: "a mystical person" or "one with mystical strength." In spite of this, Ojong's position in the struggle is unclear, hence Ngwa declares:

> If so, you will have to make it your
> duty to pivoting me or collaborating
> with me in this fight! You see me
> carrying this file (*stretching it out to
> him*) not out of my liking and
> volition .... But I understand the
> problem you are facing. You live in
> ignorance, the type our elders here
> want those below to live in so that
> they would view everything bliss! (17)

Ojong's mysteriousness is heightened, albeit negatively, when he gives one to understand, even with all he has been through, that he does not seem to recognize yet the grave and complex nature of their predicament at Ngoa:

> Do you mean to tell me I can't
> peacefully have things that are mine
> by right? (*Ngwa burst out laughing*)
> Is my question that funny? Or, is it so
> silly? (18)

Yet again, he is the one who asks almost immediately in a conflicting manner:

> How can you dream of that here in
> Ngoa's summit? Are you blind to the
> fact that every possible opening here
> is chained tight (19).

He is later to declare in the same disturbing manner, "I came here decades before you, but I am on the floor so to speak and already growing grey!" (20). And then to crown it all, he promises to be involved in this struggle only in spirit, not physically, even though he has indicated he has been a serious victim of the abuses in Ngoa:

> (*Excited*) Bye! Bye–bye! I'm with
> You in spirit in this fight you are
> Going to put up! (22)

Another name we encounter is Nnomo, the cratylic name of the shamelessly lascivious sociology professor Ngwa hopes will supervise his work. Their meeting amounts to the climactic encounter of vice and virtue in Ndi's play. This loose woman of a professor is already sexually involved with the Head of Department (HOD), yet she is unsatisfied and so continues prowling around campus preying on innocent students determined to excel in the academics that brought them there. Interestingly, the name Nnomo sounds almost as if one is saying "no more," yet not only is this woman a sexual predator, she is determined to destroy all those, like Ngwa, who decide to teach her that her sexuality, contrary to what she may assume because of her beauty and youthfulness, is not a universal currency for every manhood. Ngwa's rejection of her brazen and unashamed sexual approach is a loud "No More" to the ongoing ills in Ngoa. Ngwa refuses to be Nnomo's sex toy like the HOD, a meaning that is embedded in the Francophone head of department's name Guignol which in French is a puppet. Indeed Guignol is Nnomo's sex toy or puppet as he plays the fool strung to Nnomo's sexuality by his own lustfulness.

With a writer like Ndi, it is no accident that the name Guignol reminds one of a once upon a time notorious HOD in the Department of African Studies at the University of Yaoundé I with a name that resonates identically with Guignol. In which light, the fact that Ndi considers the HOD a sex puppet is a damning verdict on the powers that be in the nation, village, or university campus called Ngoa. Like Guignol, in Nnomo's hands, these authority figures are just puppets, brainless idiots manipulated by the whims and caprices of worthless men and women in positions of power dangling prurient baits. Beyond all else, these forces of evil and stagnation have turned the quest for knowledge into a trap for sexual preys and victims, hence Nnomo laments the dawn of a new day ushered in by her rejection at Ngwa's hands:

> My female
> colleagues procure their men in this
> way, so do the men their women but I
> am … I am … (*Interrupted by*
> *hiccups.*) Women of lesser beauty
> have been at the origin of the fall of
> even greater men, greater than this
> idiot…. What has he to prove? And
> to which beauty? (*Pouts*) Well he
> must go back to where he came from!
> He does not belong here! This
> standing is too high for that fool. He
> is not even a man! I doubt! Adam,

> hero of all heroes wouldn't have
> resisted such attractiveness from Eve....
> And this idiotic Ngwa wants the
> world to reckon him father of heroes?
> He shall be ejected and I will respire.
> He will learn the hard way! I have
> been here for years! He came and met
> me here so shall he go and leave me
> here. I am the stone of the river bed.
> An idiot from nowhere can't change
> the status quo! Impossible within the
> four walls of Ngoa! I will not give
> him time to be the first out there …! (42-43).

Beyond the names of Ndi's characters, the names he gives to places have underlying meanings. As already indicated, "Ngoa" is part of the name for the neighbourhood accommodating the University of Yaoundé I, the full name being Ngoa Ekele. In this way, Ndi makes obvious the setting of his work. Beyond Ngoa, when Guignol's sexually frustrated bitch, Nnomo, lies about Ngwa to him in his capacity as HOD, he exclaims and questions revealingly:

> (*Scandalized*) What! Did I not ask
> you from the very first day whether
> he was from your neighbourhood,
> Mvog–Akum? Again whether his
> parents were friends of some kind? I
> knew! These English speakers…! Do
> you think it is for nothing that we
> label them in our tongue, I mean
> French as "Les gauchers"? (45)

The word "Mvog" means "neighbourhood" in the local language around Ngoa, and Akum is an Anglophone village in the North West Region of Cameroon. Through this toponym, Ndi is able to present subtly a boiling topic or practice of concern within Cameroon and the University of Yaounde I—the colonial cultural divide which is making it difficult for the university administration or the country's government to function well as Cameroonians are served effectively or otherwise depending on their colonial heritage: Anglophone or Francophone. It is not surprising then that Caroline Sherwood says of names:

> Words and names can tell us much about the origins in consciousness of our world. Our use of words both reflects and *affects* our reality. By tracing derivations of words we find the relationship with the world of the people who first coined them – which puts us in touch with the words' original source and meaning. The same is true of names. A name is a *vibrational symbol*, an embodiment of the person in language. This knowledge … can be used to yield understanding …. (3)

By playing the name game with Ndi and his work, to use Leonard R. N. Ashley's expression, it becomes obvious that this is a practice that can help decode or excavate meaning buried under the weight of a playwright's use of names.

Upon turning to Bate Besong, a playwright who was greatly influenced by the modernists, we encounter the Theatre of the Absurd. The significance of this is that there is no longer an obvious plot and that orderliness in presentation that characterizes traditional plays with a driving conflict, for example, which propels the play causing it to move from the point of attack through the exposition with rising action until it climaxes, followed by falling action and finally the denouement. In Besong's case then, one can only talk of the playwright's concern, and from this one is able to see how name plays go into effect.

In his first play, *The Most Cruel Death of the Talkative Zombie*, Besong's concern is, as is the case with Victor Epie Ngome's *Asunder*, the political journey of Southern Cameroons toward nationhood by reuniting with La République du Cameroun. It is a play with two main characters: Toura and Badjidka. Toura is representative of Cameroon's erstwhile president whose middle name, which was never used in official circles, was Babatoura. Badjidka, on the other hand, is representative of John Ngu Foncha and/or possibly Solomon Tandeng Muna, two Anglophones who were very active during the transactions leading to Southern Cameroon's independence and subsequently became leaders of this part of the union.

Commandante Yaro Amichive, with his merciless techniques as chief of security, is without doubt a reincarnation of Jean Forchive, the security chief under Ahmadou Ahidjo, Besong's Toura, who was notorious for the torture techniques employed by the security police he personally supervised. This far, Besong is only using names to help his readers identify the original characters he is exposing with his fictive versions. He insults this leadership, though, by identifying Toura and Badjidka as lepers on crutches, leprous troglodytes. Through the servile nature of some of Besong's characters, the playwright ushers in name inflations that go to show the foolishness that characterizes the mentality of idiotic dictators like Toura. In fawning acknowledgement of Toura's performance of his duty by presiding over one of many meaningless meetings, Besong floods Toura with ridiculous titles: "Long live His Excellency the Most High Prince of Peace, Dr. El Hadji Toura ibn Adu Al Sallah!...... (19).

Besong's technique is the same in *Beasts of No Nation*: there is a dramatic situation or conflict instead of a plot which is reminiscent of the ongoing stalemate between Anglophone-Cameroonians and the government of La République du Cameroun. In the play, this conflict is between Night-soil-men who are the carriers of fetid waste in Ednuoay City Council area on the one hand, and the Supreme Maximum Mayor of Ednuoay Municipal Council, Comrade Dealsham Aadingingin who is refusing to yield to the Night-soil-men's demands for their rights, here concretized by the identity cards for which they are agitating. Instead, he makes the issue more complicated by asking the Night-soil-men to put in their requests through Chef Gaston Lazare Otshama, himself a former nightsoil carrier lately promoted.

Several of Besong's names in this work show the significance of the art of naming in literary ventures. To call a people Night-soil-men is in itself definitive. These are a people worse off than Frantz Fanon's wretched of the earth. They are night-soil-men with an unmistakable task in society: theirs is to carry fetid waste within Ednuoay City Council. There are none lower in society than these.

Interestingly, this is the status Besong accords Anglophone-Cameroonians in their union with La République du Cameroun; they are the carriers of shit in this union, hence the effectiveness of the label "Night-soil-men".

Then there is the inflated and equally pompous name "Comrade Dealsham Aadingingin." First of all, the term "Comrade," and knowing who is referred to thus in this case, conjures into existence an air of bloated importance reminiscent of several socialist left wing orchestrated revolutions on the world stage and the way those involved in such great ventures referred to themselves. Yet Comrade Dealsham Aadingingin is only a Mayor comparatively speaking. By these names, Besong deflates the value and worth in the title "Comrade" just as in Supreme Maximum Mayor one cannot help thinking of a Mayor functioning as the warden of a maximum prison instead of one overseeing a city even if it is festering in political decay.

In the name "Dealsham," one immediately appropriates Aadingingin's inflated titles which emphasize his leadership at the head of Ednouay Municipal Council to the president of the entire nation of Cameroon. After all, Ednuoay is an anagram of Yaoundé, the capital city of Cameroon. In that case, the Aadingingin of Ednuoay is, or can be equated to the Biya of Cameroon. If this is granted, then one can easily recall that Biya's political doctrine made his followers to claim his tenure and leadership would amount to a "new deal," hence his government was called the "New Deal" government. With the name "Dealsham," it becomes possible that Besong is qualifying and damning the idea of a new "deal" as a "sham," a travesty of a deal because of how woefully it has failed. The absurdity of the man and his country reduced to a mayor and his council is summed up in the foolish and hollow, yet ridiculously high-sounding name Aadingingin. Its outrageousness is multiplied by the outlandish spelling and a worthless onomatopoeic effect that conveys nothing but the stupidity of the name embedded in the jarring but meaningless syllables echoing his woefulness.

Another inflated yet worthless name is "Chef Gaston Lazare Otshama." "Chef" which is from the French "*Chef*" accords this character a certain importance as by being referred to thus, in a way, declares he is in charge, yet he is nothing more than a former

Night-soil-man newly promoted only for him to remain in "Category Nought." He is "Chef" of the nightsoil-soil-men then; still laughable when the irony of his title and position is recognized! The name Gaston, which is from Gascony, a real life place in France, was once a popular name in Cameroon and besides the strength used in pronouncing the name, it is just another common Francophone name. The name Lazare, French for Lazarus, reminds one of Jesus' parable about Lazarus and the rich man. Lazare, therefore, resonates with Chef Gaston's position as a nobody in society, a beggar otherwise, but for his position, which is just above that of a night-soil-man. The name Otshama crowns the joke this character is. This is a name that was popularized in Cameroon by a Cameroonian comedian, Daniel Ndo, also from Paul Biya's region of origin, who called himself Otshama Morbikyè.[2] That Besong accords his character "Otshama" for a surname confirms the fact that he considers him a joke in society. In the play, Otshama brings to mind characters in real life who are exploited by their bosses who make them think they have power when in actual fact they have nothing. They are actually no better than the exploited lot of society who have been fooled into thinking they belong together with the oppressors whereas they are mere pawns in the hands of the rich and powerful. It is in this light that Besong's use of names is reminiscent of M. D. Tschaepe's claims about first names:

> The 'regime' of first naming involves a judgment and type of psycho-sociological bondage, which sustains the personality and idea of an individual as a *specific type of individual* [author's emphasis] within the community in which one is named. (75)

This, to me goes beyond just first names to names as a whole.

In his next play *Requiem for the last Kaiser* (*Requiem*), Besong is worried about the stagnation in Cameroon as a whole, thanks to existing unpatriotic forces of oppression, and then, in particular, efforts at integrating the minority English-speaking population in Cameroon into the majority Francophone population. These are the issues being dealt with in spite of the absence of a standard plot, a characteristic of Theatre of the Absurd as already pointed out.

Armed thus with this issue at stake, the significance of Besong's names can now be explored.

There is nominal inflation at work here again as we encounter a main character, His Royal Highness Baal Njunghu Akhikikrikii of Agidigidi. It is not for nothing that this is "His Royal Highness"; it is a pointer, along with his grotesque name, Akhikikrikii, to the inflated image idiotic dictators have of themselves. Hence out of fear or hypocrisy, his subjects treat him as a deity in a ridiculous nation with an equally absurd toponym, Agidigidi, a name which seems to mean nothing else other than the meaninglessness generated by the echoing of repeated denotatively nonsense syllables—Agidigidi.[3] Again, his royal highness' viciousness as a dictator is brought to light by the name Baal, which, beyond meaning "lord of," is the name of an ancient Semitic god or pagan idol who meant different things to its worshippers. This name, which shows how vain this leader is, is followed by an ordinary name Njunghu, which confirms this character as a Cameroonian, and then the vain yet meaningless name conjured into existence by stringing together meaningless syllables or at best onomatopoeic neologisms—Akhikikrikii. This generates an offending sound reminiscent of the offending chirping of crickets at dusk, hence the nuisance this leader is to his people. "Iduote," the name of the city where Akhikikrikii's Marble Palace is located is equally significant: it is an anagram for Etoudi, the neighbourhood where Cameroon's presidential palace is located. By such backward word play, Besong is able to make obvious his geographical and temporal concerns, along with the personages involved. One can tell with certainty, due to Besong's onomastics, that his concern is about Cameroon, which he calls Agidigidi in this play, and that the time is during Paul Biya's reign, mindful of the sonic similarity in the enunciation of Biya's first name "Paul" and that of Besong's fictive leader "Baal." Again, the location of their palaces has a lot in common. Paul Biya's is at Etoudi and Baal Njunghu Akhikikrikii's is at Iduote, which is Etoudi written backward.

Then there is the character Holy Prophet A. A. Atangana. The playwright hints at the hypocritical nature of this character by calling him "Holy Prophet." A true prophet would be too humble to elevate himself thus. His hypocrisy and vanity come out in the unparalleled "A" rating he has accorded himself which is emphasized by the "a" assonance in his name: A. A. Atangana. The name Atangana tells the local reader the Holy Prophet is from the same ethnic group as Cameroon's current leader, Paul Biya, Baal Akhikikrikii within the play, hence the influence of tribalism in the administration. It is interesting that Atangana the prophet is also referred to as "Monsignor," a Catholic title for a senior prelate. One's mind immediately rushes to a time when there was a powerful Catholic prelate in Yaoundé who was said to have meddled privately in state affairs in a most powerful manner. He later died mysteriously while celebrating Holy Mass. One cannot help wondering if this is the prelate Besong is recreating here and if he was a hypocrite, especially as he is described as a marabout. Was he trying to bring together two irreconcilable practices, which amounts to serving two masters at the same time by being a Holy Prophet and a Monsignor on the one hand while also practicing as a marabout or mingling with them? These are all ideological reverberations brought about by the way Besong plays with names.

In Françoise Hippopo, aka Madame Patriot, one encounters a woman with a Francophone background as revealed by the name "Françoise." She is also extremely obese as given off by her name Hippopo, a shortened form of the word "hippopotamus." Relating these qualities to reality in Cameroon, Besong's fictive Agidigidi, one's mind precipitates to this obese woman whose first name is also Françoise. She belonged to the Wouri Section of the ruling political party of the era, the Cameroon's People Democratic Party (CPDM). It is significant that "Wouri" is also the name of a historically important river in Cameroon, and it is occupied by hippopotamuses, just as Françoise Hippopo is part of the Wouri Section of the CPDM. With this analogy, Besong's insulting of Françoise Hippopo's obesity by comparing her to a hippopotamus is not only complete but becomes glaringly obvious. She was notorious for marching in the frontline during party demonstrations, gasping and perspiring profusely, urging Cameroonians to support a failed political party that had brought untold suffering to the masses. It is very certain this is Besong's target when one recalls that her fictive alter ego is also called Madame Patriot.

In Harl Ngongo, it may seem far-fetched should one suggest Besong might have extracted the name Harl from the female villain in the *Batman* series. Yet as anyone familiar with Besong and his works will agree, nothing is far-fetched when it comes to Besong. These are the practices along with the distant and unfamiliar sources that spiced Besong's opacity as a writer. Ngongo was the palace's "frog-mouthed" laureate, an expression that could mean one of two things: he is French-speaking, since "Frog" is a derogatory term for Francophones in Cameroon,[4] or it could mean a genuinely ugly man with a mouth like a frog's. The former is more likely the case.

Ambassador Cracker Crookster is a crook indeed, one of those foreign diplomats usually present to flatter and manipulate moronic African heads of states so that their countries can get what they need from these victim states. An ambassador with a name like "Cracker Crookster" has to be uncouth and roguish in his ways, given the "crack" and "crook" sounds generated by his name and so is our Ambassador as he lies and flatters Akhikikrikii in a manner that is embarrassing to anyone with a conscience. At one time, and with false humility, according to stage directions, he lies to Akhikikrikii: "It has been a privilege meeting such a distinguished genius of politics" (22), only to insult him when he is not present. He is later to advice Akhikikrikii in a counter-productive manner about a national conference which would have been an opportunity for the citizens of Agidigidi, like Cameroonians, to revisit the nature of their union to straighten things up by claiming that "[a] national conference is an enemy to be killed on sight!" (25).

Etat-Major Andze Abessollo is a name that generates meaning when this character is described as a career toe-breaker and a torturer who is expected to carry out orders no matter what. The French expression "Etat-Major" stands for military headquarters and then the names Andze Abessollo again give away the ethnic origins. One can then understand that Akhikikrikii uses soldiers from his ethnic group to torture those he and his clique consider to be subversive or dissenting. This is very reminiscent of Cameroon under Paul Biya and his cliques from the Centre Region.

The names of other minor characters are simply representative of other parts of the country. "Dr. Akonchong" is from the English speaking part of the country and a progressive. "Mallam Gambari" is from the northern part of the country, as revealed by his epithet "Mallam." "Minority Nnyanyen," Minister of State (oil) is just a figure-head from the minority Anglophone population. The word "minority" is emphasized by the name "Nnyanyen" which in itself is reminiscent of a pidgin or slang word for tiny, "ani-ni," an expression with a sound which is echoed by the repeated syllable "ny-ny" in "Nnyanyen." It is not surprising then that Caroline Sherwood points out: "To name is to acknowledge. It is to identify, single out, distinguish, separate and endow with meaning" (3) A rather challenging task as confirmed by Justin Kaplan and Anne Bernays:

> For the author, finding names like these is a complicated process involving sound, emotion, and associations as well as an awareness of social and political choreography. Sometimes it's accomplished in a flash, sometimes it involves several stages. (182 – 83)

One thing is certain about Besong and his characters' names: Besong takes time to select them, taking into consideration sound effects, music, associative lushness, the things he knows and feels about these characters, his expectations from the audiences in terms of reactions, hence the sometimes grotesque, comic, and the suggestive, often resulting in ridiculous appellations.

Bate Besong's *Banquet* is another play that revisits Cameroon's journey to nationhood, especially from the perspective of Anglophone-Cameroon. In the process he exploits a rich and revealing group of names, acronyms, and toponyms alike. Through these nomenclatural distortions and inflations, Besong adds more meaning and scope to his work. Examples are "Ubae" which is Buea anagrammatically reconstructed as are "Nouayed" for Yaounde, "Adoula" for Douala, "Erooncam" for Anglophone Cameroon and "Erouncam" for Francophone-Cameroun. In a series of other names, Besong uses sound effect to help the reader identify meaning buried deep in them. "Killerand" definitely sounds like Mitterand; "Varis" sounds like Paris; "Vrench," French, "Risky Yzhirag" for Jacques Chirac, "Reginia" for Nigeria, whereas "francefraud" is a newly coined word for France while the "fraud" at the end tells the playwright's opinion of France as a fraudulent nation, especially with regards to her dealings with African nations. Jean-Marie le Pen is "Marie le Guenn," Charles Pasqua is turned into "Caskquoi," and Yvon Omnes, a once upon a time French ambassador to Cameroon, into "Domnes." Besong then was a veritable artisan of names and to good effect.

In practicing onomastics to a certain degree with the works of Victor Epie Ngome, Bill F. Ndi, and Bate Besong, one cannot help agreeing with Ben L. Martin's observation that "…names can be more than tags; they can convey powerful imagery" (83). This is the case because to these playwrights, names, far from being ordinary labels, are employed more like codes with special meanings and implications to which a stranger without their background might not be able to relate completely. Through their works they have shown that names, along with nomenclatural distortions, are the culmination of dense and intricately meshed social interactions, consultations, and concessions that are part of an entire cultural system and beyond even. They have achieved this by their use of names and nomenclatural distortions as ways of uncovering and explicating the workings of a bizarre yet existing realism of an incredulous way of life, an incredulous status quo. Even though Ashley warns that "…terms and names in general must be kept sharp tools of thought" for "inflation cheapens our language as surely as it does our money" (193), these writers effectively create, inflate, and distort names through the use of anagrams, palindromes, backward word play, and more, as dramatic technique to facilitate profound and effective communication with their audiences. In their hands, names and nomenclatural distortions amount to ways of identifying and sustaining personalities and their ways of living. Names to them, then, are psychological and cultural props that hold a character, setting, or location up to scrutiny; to them names are gongs or shackles, as the case may be, that clang out loud the manner of the individual thus nominally identified because of the socio-cultural and psychological values infused in them. To these playwrights, to name then, or distort a name in any way is to acknowledge by singling out and distinguishing by according the bearer a certain status vis-à-vis the name; it is thus a way of empowering or ridiculing a character. Thus names, even when distorted, amount to channels, because of the guiding meanings they generate, leading the reader or audience into different dimensions of a character's essence; hence, the resourcefulness of names and nomenclatural distortions as dramatic technique in Anglophone-Cameroon literature.

Notes

1. To qualify to be able to talk directly to the Fon or traditional leader within this ethnic group calls for the performance of certain traditional rites which are costly in terms of the amount of money one has to pay to the palace.

2. It is worthwhile noticing that the spellings of these names might not be the same since they are not exactly standard in society, yet it is significant that they sound the same. In fact, one can be categorical here that Besong could only have had this name from Daniel Ndo's comedy and nowhere else.

3. The syllables only generate meaning through connotative associations, with the sounds they produce, in this particular society.

4. The word "frog" is a derogatory term used by Anglophone-Cameroonians in reference to francophone-Cameroonians, just as the latter refer to the former as "Anglofous."

Works Cited

Abarry, Abu Shardow. "The Significance of Names in Ghanaian Drama." *Journal of Black Studies* 22.2 (December 1991): 157-67. Print.

Ashley, Leonard R. N. *What's in a Name? ...Everything You Wanted to Know.* Baltimore: Genealogical, 1989. Print.

Barthes, Roland. *Le Degré Zéro De L'Ecriture.* Paris: Coll. Points: Seuil, 1972. Print.

Besong, Bate. *The Banquet.* Makurdi: Edition Ehi, 1994. Print.

_____. *The Most Cruel Death of the Talkative Zombie.* Limbe: Nooremac, 1986. Print.

_____. *Requiem for The Last Kaiser.* Calabar: Centaur, 1991. Print.

Kaplan, Justin, and Anne Bernays. *The Language of Names.* New York: Simon, 1997. Print.

Leslie, Paul L., and James K. Skipper, Jr. "Toward a Theory of Nicknames: A Case for Socio-Onomastics." *Names* 38.4 (December 1990): 273-82. Print.

Martin, Ben L. "From Negro to Black to African American: The Power of Names and Naming." *Political Science Quarterly* 106.1 (1991): 83-107. Print.

Ndi, Bill F. *Gods in the Ivory Tower.* Bloomington: Authorhouse, 2008. Print.

Ngome, Victor Epie. *What God Has Put Asunder.* Yaoundé: Pitcher, 1992. Print.

Sherwood, Caroline. *Naming: Choosing a Meaningful Name.* Gloucestershire: Hawthorn, 1999. Print.

Tschaepe, M. D. "Halo of Identity: The Significance of First Names and Naming." *Janus Head* 6.1 (2003): 67-78. Print.

Chapter Ten

Character Nomenclature, the Bead-string in Thomas Jing's *Tale of an African Woman*

By
Adaku T. Ankumah
Benjamin Hart Fishkin
Bill F. Ndi

The postulation goading this literary analysis is the phenomenological concept positing that the central structure of an experience, a name inclusive, is its intentionality and its being directed toward something, as it is an experience of or about some object. Consequently, the experience is directed toward an object by virtue of its content or meaning (which represents the object) together with appropriate enabling conditions. Thus, character names in this atypical, yet interesting and revealing novel by an Anglophone Cameroonian writer carry with them "worth" that serves both as vehicles for structuring the plot and as carriers of the author's central concerns, the abstraction of which like meaning's brought about by modernity and or foreignness is captured through the treatment of the protagonist. Questioning the *raison d'être* of the names that various characters in Jing's *Tale of an African Woman,* bear and their action both become motifs to investigate the characters' underlying actions and the name as a string holding the beads (i.e. plot structure, theme, characterization, setting, novelistic artistry, etc.) in place. How do names in Jing's novel structure the plot? Are there any chances that the thematic concerns are tied to character names? Is it the name that goads the characters' action? Or, again are the characters' actions inspired by their name?

Craftsmanship in art, be it writing, painting, sculpting or architectural design, has never been surrendered in the hands of hazard, chance or coincidence. Again, neither do the tools for excelling in the craft. For both tools and craftsmanship are major contributors to shaping any art work, i.e. the final product. This concept, once carefully understood and mastered, would originate the finest pieces of art work. It is in this regard that the finest pieces of literature-- poetry, drama, and the novel--are all structured with this in mind. And even though Henry James' reason for the existence of a novel advanced in his *Art of Fiction* is an attempt to compete with life, once well crafted, a novel only mimics life and its representation is fascinating in ways unimaginable. And this surely is what prompted his assertion that "[i]t is a proof of life and curiosity--curiosity on the part of the brotherhood of novelists, as well as on the part of their readers" (Web). Jing's novel, *Tale of an African Woman* is a typical exemplar of such a piece structured with ingenuity and with the perfect tool used to build a narrative that would stand the test of time in its appeal to life and curiosity in the manner of the oldest piece of written literature, the Sumerian text, *The Epic of Gilgamesh*. What is this perfect tool and what is its connection to Gilgamesh?

In the epic, the Sumerian writer makes a name to become the key to existence. Gilgamesh states: "Gilgamesh, my name I am" (Lambert 469). In a like manner, Jing uses names as the cornerstone that holds the structure of his work together. The mention of structure goads one to investigate how amazingly Jing transforms names into a bead-string that holds together his novel from start to finish. It would not be erroneous to posit that without the name and naming in *Tale of an African Woman,* the novel falls short of one to become a loose collection of disjointed and disparate stories. Nonetheless, in a Jamesian twist, Jing uses names to allow his work to live "upon discussion, upon experiment, upon curiosity, upon variety, and attempts to exchange views…" (Web). This, Jing does not only do as Claire Culleton would have it when discussing Joyce, "to preserve the cultural veracity of his fiction…" with selected names that not only enhanced the reading of his plot, but reflected on Irish culture…" (14). He uses names as the foundation of the narrative plot and structure of his novel. How do names account for the conflict(s), climaxes and denouements? In short, how do names structure the plot of Jing's novel?

Jing's novel follows the tradition of great creation narrative. He writes as Henry James would have it from the experience of one on whom nothing is lost and from experience alone (Web.). However, the novelty in Jing is his judicious use of this aspect which seems to be lost to many, viz. names and naming. This novel opens with a hint at Jing's "heteroglossic creative process." (Bakhtin 292) He cages in names many fascinating clues that would raise exciting issues and help his readers reconsider their approach to his novel. Culleton hints at this in her book, *Names and Naming in Joyce*. In this case, the protagonist is first presented to the reader as she reacts to the mention of the name of a newspaper, *The Dubliners*. This reaction not only leaves the narrator confused but the reader as well. It sets the tone and points to the startling route the narrative would follow. Is her hesitation about the way she wants to be addressed going to make or mar the plot? Building on suspense, the novelist is at the same time revealing the reputation the newspaper has certainly acquired as a result of its name as well as the power that a name carries with it. It is none but the power of a name that compels the protagonist to change her attitude towards the Irish journalist who has come to interview her. The name also affects the course and approach to the conversation to be held. As if to confirm that a name is what it does, it is through the subtle use of names that Jing creates an environment whereby the characters can interact with neither intimidation nor fear of each other as a result of rank or position. In this guise, exercising this understanding, the protagonist points out:

> It made me feel bad because I did not want her to be intimidated by my position. I wanted us to build not on sentimental but solid intellectual and rational grounds and this could only happen if our discussions were conducted in a free and fair atmosphere.
> "Shannon," I addressed her by her name and smiled to let know I meant well. (2)

By meaning well, the protagonist acknowledges the essence of Shannon's being and existence. She addresses Shannon by name. She has come to grips with the fact that names have affect and can either create an amicable atmosphere conducive for the interview that is in view or one that would end the interview even before it starts. Conscious of the fact that this interview, which is the basis of their meeting, must be conducted and failure of which will forever leave this great story dormant, Jing has Yaya argue her story. She tries to argue that the story associated with her name is no more than that of multitude of women. She also forgets that the story associated with her name has come to represent more than just another story dealing with feminist oppression. She is reminded by the Irish journalist of this:

> Your story isn't about tears but rather about hope. Hope for millions of women across the world who tremble before their men as we talk, who live constantly in fear and stoically face brutalities of the worse kind; women on the verge of giving up. For those women who have already fallen, your story will strengthen their resolve to stand up, and for those who feel like giving up, your account will provide them with the ammunition to continue to struggle. Hope is a powerful weapon and, if you want to know, it's the main reason for my presence here today, asking you to recount your own story. (4)

Structuring the interview and facilitating its occurrence through the use of names is not the only strong point in Jing's novel. The complexities of the novelistic organization through nomenclature are also reflected in the setting of this novel. Ancestry can only be traced by names. So the Narrator states:

> The village was made up of many large families whose ancestries went far back in history. The most notable of them were the Konchus, the Gings, Bamus, the Forsuhs, the Mbis, the Ndas, the Pefoks, the Abamukongs, the Ayaahs, the Fombuhs, the Wankis, the Atuches, the Abongwas, the Akenjis, the Tamajungs, the Ndifordehs, the Ndumus and many others. (7-8)

The Narrator/protagonist also informs of the hierarchical structure of Bankim. She points out how the elected council of elders came under the authority of a wise man. The title of "Tabih" conferred upon each who ascended this position sets them apart as the wise, and the author notes how impactful the "Tabih" were and would not come as a surprise that shock wave brought to Bankim as a result of Yaa's pregnancy would be from one of these "wise men" who herald the worst form of alienation on its daughters. This narrative device Jing uses in an effort to have his structure depict Bankim life accurately and has the narrator state:

> Under successive Tabihs, Bankim enjoyed some stability and prosperity; but it was when Ngwanueh of the Abongwa family had assumed the much coveted leadership position that the village became the stuff of legends. Its barns could hardly contain the foods which had been hauled in from the fields and so newer and larger ones had to be built. Trade with other groups expanded and almost every family was blessed with many newborns. (8)

In spite of Jing conferring this title to the rulers of Bankim, he does not forfeit structuring and heightening the import and marks of specific Tabihs who distinguished themselves among all others, and this through their names and not just the title of "Tabih." As such Jing has the Narrator mark the height of glory for Bankim. She specifically emphasizes by name "Ngwanueh" and traces his lineage to the Abongwa family. Here the name marks the apogee of the village pride.

The tragedy that befalls the protagonist/narrator's ancestors is all because of a name. The fact that Yaa's father, Tadu, dies before she is born, becomes a cause for concern as the entire village would rather the departed had left or leaves behind a boy who would guarantee the survival of the name. So anything short of a boy from a pregnant woman made widow before she puts to bed spells doom for the departed and both the newborn as well as the widowed mother. Tadu's sudden departure therefore heaps such responsibility, one beyond any human capability, on her shoulder. Even if child up-bringing in a village follows the proverbial collective responsibility in the saying, "it take a village to raise a child," in Yaa's mother's case, the expectation of her having "an extraordinary male child" (9) is one she has absolutely no control over. Here, Jing uses names to structure his narrative and give it the desired effect. Note must be taken of the fact that he introduces Tadu's prospective wife, wife, and widow without any mention of her name(s). The most the narrator tells the reader is "a girl who was the daughter of Tangang, the head of the Mbawa family" (9). This nomenclatural effacement becomes a clear indication of societal views of women and or girls. It is reminiscent of George Eliot's answer to the question: "What does that signify?" in *The Mill on the Floss:* "We don't ask what a woman does; we ask whom she belongs to" (377). Most importantly, in Jing's novel, it is an indictment of the fate to befall her as a result of whom she belongs to.

After her husband's death, the crowd gathered outside, around the delivery home, hypes in anticipation of a male child to be born. Nothing would quieten the screaming crowd, singing and dancing all night. They chant the expected good news: "We want a male child" (10). This seems to be the only thing to appease and calm the crowd. Their expectation would be confirmed or disillusioned come the morning. The birth of the girl is greeted as a slap in the face as indicated by the exclamation heaved by the crowd as well as the narrator's comment on the attitude of both the midwives and expectant crowd:

> "A girl!" they all exclaimed at once as though they had been rehearsing this line when this information was murmured. The singing and dancing immediately stopped and the talking drums went dumb. They too all heaved one big sigh of disappointment and, one after the other, they began to walk away from the hut in the same way they had come. Finally, the poor girl was left alone with her baby to face her very sad fate (10).

However, Jing, as if to acknowledge this ostracized widow as a being, makes the narrator to mention her name for the first time as she is in the process of dying: "Things became so terrible for Biayuh, especially when wild and malicious rumors went around attributing the death of her husband to her" (10). With Biayuh out as soon as she is mentioned by name, her child is left with a fate unbeknownst to any. The narrator draws attention to Jing's nomenclatural structuring poetization and highlights the import of the orphaned child's name. The mother has died without having told the child's name to anyone. So her fate, her nomenclatural identity, calls for recourse to tradition. Thus, "the Tabih was called upon to christen her and he named her Yaa" (11). It is thus the child is given formal existence as claims Milne in "Naming in *Beloved* and *The Poisonwood Bible*" : "a child is not alive… until it is named" (357).

The narrator's comments on the ambivalence of the chosen name as a structuring device make evident the curiosity that a name like that heard or pronounced once in a while in the village would spark. Drawing on the meaning of such a name, the narrator points to the *double entendre* of the name:

> It was one of those curious names which appeared in the village once in a while and which often bore a double meaning, depending on how it was pronounced. In this case, the common meaning of the name was loner but the same word pronounced with a deep inflection had another connotation, the great one. (11)

The mention of the morpheme and sememe of "loner" and "great one" co-existing in "Yaa" redefines and restructures Jing's narrative as the protagonist/narrator ends up as an oddity of a "great one" at the head of a male-dominated society, i.e. the first and only (lone) woman. Yaa as a name thus become a suitable and convenient tool that structures and holds the narrative/storyline together. Jing takes cognizance of the primordial importance of structure in a work of art and frames the architectural conception of his work by letting the reader see through names, the end in the beginning and the origin of the beginning at the end. He "never loses sight of this and in every part is conscious of the rest till the last sentence does but, with undiminished vigour [sic], unfold and justify the first…" (Buckler xviii). Jing's narrator explains:

> Loner or great one, from the very christening of the child, her appointment with destiny seemed to have begun. Condemned by the misfortune of being born a girl as first child into a great family and burdened with the scar or maybe luck of name, she began the dance of life on the wrong foot, so most people believed. (11)

With a name defining Yaa's ostracism, for either way, Yaa's life is that of a loner. She ends up with an ostracized foster mother, Chacha. This leaves one wondering if the prize exacted from her is as a result of this *double-entendre* in her name. Fishkin contends that "[t]he psychological penalty of … imposed exclusion creates incalculable damage. It shapes and molds the recipient who is not genuinely welcomed" (107). Little wonder, Yaa also does things that challenge Bankim male hegemonic society.

In yet another episode, Yaa, the loner, takes to challenging the status quo during a wrestling match marking the rite of passage for young men. The narrator taps from names to point out what a name does. In a previous study on names in the higher education sector, the authors argue that "what became evident for us was that a student's name is an agency of learning. Significant in this agency is the power of name" (*Framing My Name* 3). This illustrates the agential and actualizing potentials of a name as the narrator says:

> Even before the name had been uttered, the crowd started to boo. Never before in Bankim had a person gone on to live the true meaning of his name after birth. Bungah in the local language stood for smoked tilapia. In a pot of soup, this fish had time and again proved to be the most treacherous ingredient, usually concealing or disguising sharp, strong bones which sometimes got stuck in the throats of unwary guests. He was the son of a conman and turned out to be one himself. He often indulged in a series of petty thievery such as fowl snatching and egg poaching and for all these acts he earned the not-too-undeserved nickname of Achagwukwaki, the fox.
>
> In spite of his tender age, he had appeared more than a hundred times before the Council to be tried for one or the other of his endless peccadilloes and seemed to relish in that reputation. Sinister and dangerous, he was the very symbol of untrustworthiness and wherever he went people hid their belongings. Built strong like a buffalo, he would have been one of the best wrestlers in the village if only he could put behind him his devious ways. (31)

It is during this same episode that when it is Yaa's turn to wrestle, she is introduced in a crowing voice as "the one and only Yaa, daughter of Chachaaaa." But as a guise of encouragement, Yaa's foster mother identifies her daughter with deities and royals as she yells out:

> Goddess of the savannah
> Queen of the mountains
> Angel of the woods
> Amina! Nzinga Mbandi! (32)

Such nomenclatural attributes and soubriquets prepare readers through their association with Yaa as the one to emerge victorious over the ordinary folks. More so, she is, like these deities and royals, capable of beating all odds. Jing achieves this by using names and naming as the ultimate means of providing the reader with formal challenges and further making his work anchored in resistance and "the redemption of the oppressed" (Buckler xix) rather than a mere narrative built on ideas and ideas alone.

In the same vein, the author uses names to bring human meanspiritedness to the forefront. The name exerts a force on someone when used without due consideration for its consequences on the bearer. Names as plot structuring devices are used here by Jing to elucidate and let reflect character interaction from start to finish. In the encounter between Nkoh, the town crier, and the old recluse, Bangsiboh, names and naming become the anchor of their discussion. Nkoh thinks that "sometimes it was good to damn the consequences and try things" (53) while Bangsiboh reveals the origin of his name which to him is a way "humanity [has] crafted to remind [him] of [his] troubles" (53).

Yet again, central to Jing's plot are issues of names and naming which the narrator does well more often than not to intimate on the significance and meaning of the names of some major characters. This is brought to bear on the reader following Yaa's pregnancy, the suicide of the Tabih, and the birth of Yabu as well as the child's naming. Naming Yabu, the narrator states, is the first assignment the newly appointed Tabih has. He has to choose a name for the newborn orphaned child. The choice of name, "Yabu" which echoes the Greek mythological long-lived bird that is always reborn from its ashes, refers to the newborn child as the "Ashes" of the "Mad" Yaa, one whose madness has its roots in nothing but her bravura (66-68). This is a telling reference cum allusion to the mythical phoenix. Yabu's name, in this instance, brings to mind what Derrida considers "an adjunct, a subaltern… not simply an additive… but as a substitute whose place is assigned in the structure by mark of an emptiness" (qtd. in *Framing my Name* 36).

The name becomes a technique for this author to anticipate and foreshadow what will happen to the deceased "Yaa" now reborn from her own ashes. She will certainly exact answers from the society or put the same society that has so alienated and pushed her to insanity and consequently madness and death, to shame. The fact that "Yabu" retains a syllable from "Yaa" is indicative that this actualizing agent, Yaa's name, is not dead simply because Yaa had been left to die. Accordingly, "Yaa" will accomplish in Yabu and Yabu in Yaya and Yaya in Yakiri what the society did not give her the opportunity to realize in her lifetime. The mention of Yakiri should be seen as the author's polyphonic play[9] on the name "Yaa" and the French "qui rit" (pronounced: /kiːriː/ and translates into the English language "who laughs"). This is the result of Yaa laughing after all the trials, tribulations and humiliations at the hands of society and for several generations. The setting thus becomes a place where Yaa has not only the last laugh but the best laugh.

In short "Yaa," the name, the morpheme, and sememe in "Yabu" and "Yaya" i.e. the Narrator and in "Yakiri" i.e. the setting of the story, captures the plot as a mover and a pass-on. Curiously the reader finds "Ya" in "Yamade" i.e. the city where Yaya is trained upon the Gnukwabe's advice that she will come back from that city as a big chief, bigger than even the one in Kimbo, a very powerful and rich woman, and will help the village grow. The curiosity provoked by this name *Yaa* and *Made* stems from the clever toponymic coinage by Jing, to inform the reader where Ya is made. She turns out to be made the "great one," for she could not

---

[9] Note must be taken that Jing is a French<->English accredited and practicing Translator. Here, Jing must be tapping into his linguistic expertise in the French language.

have been made such in the village with its stifling and oppressive values and tradition ready to transform her, like it did to her ancestors, into a loner. It remains the author's hope that gender disenfranchisement shall be halted not by a man but by the disenfranchised themselves. It is therefore no surprise that through nomenclatural poetization, Jing's narrator/protagonist whose name contains twice of such actantial and agential properties (i.e. Yaa times two = Yaya) will end up accomplishing the feat of being the first female president just like her ancestor who became the first and only woman recorded in Bankim history to wrestle with men and become part of the Manjung, an all-out male cult.

Jing transforms names into a metaphor that will make no sense to those readers who did not conceive the name in the light of any other thing than a primary identity marker. Names, as a metaphor, are a poetic narrative depicting amongst other things the plight of a woman in Jing's novelistic space. This explains Jing's painstaking narration, woven around names and naming, of the ascendency of this particular character at the helm of the postcolonial state of Mungo. Thus names and naming take form through Jing's attempts at getting to the truth of the intricate, hard-to- identify and unpredictable arbitrariness in the micro Mungo society of Bankim. It is a novel deeply rooted in an anti-intellectual philosophy of life fitting Jing's character nomenclature as well as his theory of names in a cadre that accommodates perfectly well the author's central concerns, thoughts, and feelings to language. So, how do character names string the author's central concerns, thoughts, and feelings?

In the opening chapter of Thomas Jing's *Tale of an African Woman*, the author makes it clear that the novel contributes to the on-going struggle for justice and equality for women in a patriarchal community, Bankim. The female ancestor of the women in the novel, Yaa, is mistreated by the men. Other women who follow her do not fare any better until several generations later when one of her progeny, Yaya, appears on the scene by changing this culture of repression of the female and charting a new course for women to follow. To expound on this theme of repression and its redress, the author has recourse to nomenclatural poetization. Using Yaya as the epitome of a younger generation of women, the author tends to direct a caustic critique at a cast of characters in a society which has become increasingly materialistic and cares less for its own daughters. It is against this backdrop that educating a female in Yakiri is reduced to a cost-benefit arithmetic equation. The obsolescence of argument advanced by the people of Yakiri is that Yaya as a woman shall one day get married, and there is a probability that she might end up marrying out of her clime and taking a foreign name. These conditions make the venture of schooling her to be questionable by the elders who do not, in the least, hide their dubiousness and double-standards when it comes to caring and educating their daughters as opposed to their sons. Oppression of the female in this society is a long standing tradition, and the author gives an historical account and traces the earliest case of such mistreatments.

The first female character to challenge the status quo about female repression is Yaa, a child who begins life with several strikes against her, for her father, an enlightened man and "a man of remarkable humility, integrity and genius" (8) was killed by lightning one month before she was born, and her mother died after she was born, before she could name her daughter. Her father having died before her birth, the villagers had anticipated the birth of a male child to guarantee the survival of the name of the dead man. All, including the midwives, were disappointed when a female baby came out. A name, though, is necessary, even for an undesirable child. As one critic notes about African cultures, naming is viewed as a "sacred act because it brings a person into being or makes real and actual what was considered only figurative or inanimate prior to its naming." The author adds that a baby not named in a naming ritual "remains in the category of 'living object'" (Handley, qtd. in Hayes 675). How does an orphaned girl get a name? This question is the first challenge Yaa faces when she is discovered. The villagers who find this screaming baby had to fall on the tradition of allowing the Tabih, the head of the Council of Elders, to name the baby.

Tabih decides to call the orphaned baby "Yaa," a name that the narrator tells us could mean loner or great one, depending on pronunciation (11). This last observation is common to most African languages which tend to be tonal, with various inflections changing the meaning of words. The issue, though, is why the male head of the village will not give a straightforward name but would use a name that embodies ambiguity, depending on intonation. This name is not an accidental one imposed on the orphaned baby. This is indicative of what Elizabeth Hayes notes: "To name is also to claim dominion; naming children, slaves, domestic animals, or real estate is an announcement of figurative, if not literal, ownership of the named, as well as an indication of the namer's relationship to or sentiments about the named" (669). In this case, it is a patriarchal act, and it underscores women and their ambiguous treatment in society and the determination of a few to overcome their marginalized position in society. Women could be marginalized if they overstep their boundaries and thus become "loners," or they could be great if they defy patriarchal notions of greatness, which involves subordination to their traditions, the acceptable codes of behavior. Yaa chooses the former when she challenges accepted roles of females and moves from the margins of patriarchal society to compete with the best the gender has to offer. She aims for the moon, and even when she misses, she lands among the stars as she distinguishes herself among the women of Bankim by coming second in a wrestling match with males her age. Eventually, she becomes a loner, having met opposition from males and some females and driven to insanity after her adopted mother Chacha has died.

Prior to colonization, surnames were not common in Africa; thus these characters do not possess them. Yaa uses just her first name; however, as Richard Alford observes, first names, not surnames, are markers of personal identity since last names are shared with others: To him, first names declare, "I am an individual" (141-2). Personal names, according to Alford, serve two functions: they send a message to the rest of the society about an individual and secondly, "they provide messages to the named individual about who he or she is or expected to be" (51). He notes that those two are achieved in a number of ways, one being the components of the name providing messages about identity (52). In the case of Jing's female characters, the components are found in the prefix the women share: "Ya." Thus personal names do not simply distinguish one individual from another but as Alford suggests, they "reflect ethnopsychological conceptions of the self" and family continuity (54). These women have their identities tied to that of their first foremother, Yaa, and it will take the last one Yaya, to complete the identity battle began by their foremother. These names, as one critic notes, may provide "appropriate qualities or models"for these named and so help achieve the "desired reality" (Alford 63).

Tradition, the author informs us, is the reason women are "loners," marginalized in a society that benefits from women and their labor. Men have been in charge at the decision-making level, and they are not ready to admit women into their ranks. Yaa's adoptive mother who challenges men's domination is labeled a rebel and isolated by all, including women. A tall, tough and beautiful woman with a free spirit, Chacha challenges the notion of the woman as helpless and in need of males to stand on her feet. Her name, which sounds foreign, underscores her isolationist state. It could also refer to an "energetic modern dance" (Cambridge Dictionaries Online) from South America. And Chacha seems to dance to a feverish rhythm not understood by any in Bankim. This proto-feminist refuses to be bullied or subdued by men and their traditions. Her husband divorced her after many years of marriage using the excuse that she is a "barren woman." This view is generally taken by African men that women are to blame in childless marriages. Yet, scientific research reveals that men are equally at fault in some cases of infertility. Chacha does not accept responsibility for their lack of children; on the contrary, she blames the husband. The narrator notes that she is not afraid of the Council when she appears before them and appeals to reason and logic to show them that she is not the party to blame for childlessness. She diagnoses her husband's problem as having plenty of liquid but without seeds. She consequently challenges the inherent sexism of the group: "The moment a person doesn't have two nuts swinging underneath, the person instantly becomes a fool in the eyes of this Council" (13). Even the men are amazed at the strength of her logic! As one writer notes, "The single woman who manages her affairs successfully without a man is an affront to patriarchy and a direct challenge to the so-called masculinity of men who want to 'possess' her" (Oduyoye 5). Indeed, Chacha has made it as a loner, "as if the community did not exist" (14) and even her detractors admit that the orphaned child will fare better in the care of such a hardworking and strong woman.

Her daughter Yaa, a precocious child with masculine inclinations, becomes a "loner" too when she insists on joining the all-male group of goatherds. She abandons "female" chores like fetching water to carrying bow and arrow and hunting for rats and squirrels. She faces opposition not because she is incompetent or weak, for she beats other young men to come in second place in the group's annual wrestling match; the men deny her entry initially because she is a woman. When she proves herself again on a hunting expedition by saving a man who complained about women, her act goes unmentioned. Yaa's isolationist existence in society, especially after the death of her mother Chacha from a snake bite, pushes her to a mental breakdown; she walks around unkempt, half-naked. At her lowest point, she is raped by no other than the Tabih and she becomes pregnant. This final act of degradation on a woman on the fringe of society decries the inhumanity of one group towards another, especially a disturbed member of society. Thus, Yaa's name capitalizes on the dualities of female existence in society. She chooses to live out the part of greatness, but in so doing, she finds herself on the margins of society, a loner.

The Tabih's act, though, belies his name and function, for the Tabih is the head of the ruling council of elders, "the father of the people," "the wise" who is supposed to protect them, not harm them. Yaa's pregnancy is considered "an abomination, a severe breach of tradition which was punishable by death in the old days" (45-6). The Tabih, a very outgoing man, remains in cowardly silence during the deliberations to find the man who raped Yaa, knowing very well that he is the culprit. In the end, this father of the people, who ends up committing suicide, brings untold hardships to them because he rapes a mad woman. Bangsiboh, the gnukwabe who is consulted by the acting Tabih, will tell him: "See the act of an individual as an extreme expression of what prevails in the community" (56). The dead Tabih may have committed the act, but the people are not innocent either when it comes to trampling on female rights.

Women are treated as "loners" not only by men but also by women who uphold patriarchal structures in society. When Yaa opts to join the goatherds, the women were vocal in their criticism of her move, as exemplified in one woman's comments: "Who does she think she is!" (22). In the course of the Grand Migration of the village to their new settlement, Yakiri, the daughter of Yaa, Yabu, talks with her village people, upbraiding them about their "appalling treatment" of her mother in Bankim: She reminds them that "no human community could survive in the midst of prolonged injustice, especially one which tended to exclude others, not because they were bad but because they were of the 'wrong' sex and too good" (81).

Thomas Jing does not ignore Yaa and her horrific past at the hands of her fellow citizens; instead he forges a connection between the past, the present and the future by maintaining a morpheme "Ya" from Yaa's name to add to the names of subsequent female descendants. Thus her daughter is named Yabu—the ashes of Yaa. The author makes it clear that the villagers have not heard the last word about the Yaa whom they mistreated, the woman who challenged the status quo to live up to the greatness of her name but whose upward climb was curtailed by patriarchal forces. It is the author's way of acknowledging Yaa's unfinished agenda which must be completed by Yaa's female descendants. No wonder one critic notes that in some texts, naming becomes a "socially and politically charged act" (Hayes 676). Yabu, like the mythical bird phoenix, rises from the ashes of her mother to become a symbol of hope for the many women who have lost hope. Yabu continues where her mother Yaa left off, vocalizing her objections to her mother's treatment at the hands of the villagers of Bankim since Yaa was unable to articulate her oppression at the hands of males. Yabu challenges her mother's contemporaries whose silence about her mother's treatment was tantamount to acquiescence with her treatment. Even female voices were in conspiracy with the patriarchal ones. Yabu thus becomes the voice of her late mother, a voice from the dead to castigate the villagers for their inhumanity towards her mother.

Yaya, the name of the last descendant, is further anchored in history as it means "little Yaa," proverbially "the chip of the old block." She is not named after her mother Mayemfon, a tall and pretty seventeen year old woman who is "sold" into an arranged marriage to a man of questionable character and mores. The same happens in Henry James's *The American*. She perceives marriage as the source of her ruined career. Like Biayuh, Yaa's mother and Yaa, Mayemfon dies after childbirth. These women go through pregnancy and give birth, but they do not live after the birth of their daughters. Instead, they live vicariously through them. In fact, the gnukwabe had prophesied that the marriage between Mayemfon and Goran would be a disaster but the baby girl that would come out of this union would "take on the character of the renowned forebear by defying many odds to become very great" (211). Yaya, doubling the "Ya" morpheme, becomes the embodiment of all her female ancestors as she achieves what they could not due to societal repression of females.

Just as Yaa challenges masculine exclusivity in raising goats, her progeny Yaya will challenge masculine domination in academics. She does not subscribe to the notion that education is the province and prerogative of males and that females are to stay at home and oversee domestic chores. Her mother Mayenfom had subjected herself to her parents' whims, marrying against her wishes and dying at a young age. Little Yaa competes with Forche in elementary school, ending up tying with him for first place. She refuses to be described as Forche's "wife" since she does not want to sacrifice her career dreams for domesticity. In high school, Yaya finds herself at the top at the end of the year, and she receives many prizes as her grandparents and Father Sean are there to celebrate her achievements. The teacher who hands her the math prize jokes with the boys who are unhappy to have been beaten by a female. She has become the embodiment of Yaa, the great one as she excels to go to college, against the wishes of her grandfather and even her strong grandmother who is still not convinced about the pragmatic use of education for females. Yaya will eventually end up in the highest position in the country, president, fulfilling the dreams of all her foremothers who wanted to move out of female repression to self-fulfilling positions in society.

Of all her female predecessors, Yaya is the only one with a Christian name, Monica. This is no accident in the thematic concerns highlighted in Jing's novel. Yaya looks up to the church, especially to Father Sean to help her deal with her oppression. At her confirmation she has to choose a European first name. Father suggests "Monica," and when her grandfather asks, "Who's Monica?" he explains, "She's a saint and also the mother of St. Augustine. [...]. St. Augustine is one of Africa's greatest saints" (214). The name is thought to be derived from a Latin word which means *counselor* or *advisor* or from a Greek word which means *single* or *only*. Father Sean, though, links this name with that of the mother of St. Augustine, a woman noted for her perseverance and faith in the face of challenges to her faith. A Christian woman, Monica found herself married to a hot-tempered non-believer who did not want his children baptized and who was a womanizer. She persevered in prayer and saw the conversion of her mother-in-law, husband and son Augustus, who would become an important pillar of the church. Just as Monica overcame her trials to be honored as a saint, her Yakiri namesake will have to maintain her focus and purpose in the face of oppression and opposition to succeed as the first female president of her country.

Jing contends that female emancipation will come when both males and females cooperate to remove obstacles by way of traditions in the path of women. As such, he introduces some men of goodwill who are eager to overturn decades of female repression. Men like Asanbe and Ngufor are men of "integrity and intelligence," men who have the "reputation for fairness and perspicacity," men who have been around females long enough to know that if given the chance, women would excel at everything men did (20). Ngufor warns his male colleagues about tradition and its role:

We mustn't come across as a sentimental bunch only eager to uphold tradition, even when it doesn't serve our aims anymore. We mustn't forget that men put the tradition in place. So why should women even play by the rules they didn't contribute to formulate? (20)

The problem is not women's lack of ability; the problem stems from traditions put in place by men to prevent them from progressing. As Yaya admits, this "collection of habits" called tradition has become the major means of excluding women from advancement in society.

Another such male who challenges the acceptance of male dominance and female subservience is the Irish missionary Father Sean, who arrived in Yakiri as a young twenty-year old. His name Sean, a variant of "John" or the French "Jean" means God is gracious. Of all the male sympathizers, he is the most outspoken about equality and the promotion of females. Indeed, a positive addition to the community, a gift to the community, Father Sean warms up immediately to the community and the work he has set out to accomplish. Unfortunately, his name presents a challenge to the Africans, some of whom call him "Farar" (Father) or Son, "Sun, Sign, Sin" (147) for Sean. Their difficulty in pronouncing his name is not a sign of rejection; they are enthusiastic about this man who beats their best in dancing and who (to them) may have missed his calling in becoming a priest (167). The various pronunciations reflect his position among them. Like the sun that is at the center of the solar system and the source of light and warmth, Father Sean becomes the source of inspiration, change, and progress for the village of Yakiri. He has to be taught many things by the villagers, and so he is a son, but he is also Father to them, guiding them to reach their full potential. He becomes a sign to them, someone whose presence indicates that something positive will happen.

His coming to Yakiri was not accidental; Kwakala, the gnukwabe, had prophesied long before of the arrival of "a very strange man" from a strange land "so cold that human urine sometimes becomes as a hard rock" to assist the community (92). Father Sean is described as man of "great compassion, courage and learning" (97). He lives up to his name of God being gracious to the people of Yakiri, especially the women as he notices that the status of women lags behind that of men.

Some readers may be concerned about the fact that a white man, not an African, champions the course of women and societal reform in Yakiri, suggesting that Africans need help from the West to progress. Father is not the only male in Yakiri who supports

Yaya's endeavors in education. Takwabe, the gnukwabe who functions like a religious guide for the community, when consulted by Tafon, Yaya's grandfather, endorses Father's decision for Yaya to go to college: "Father is right. Send her to Yamade, for she'll come back a big chief, bigger than even the one in Kimbo, a very powerful and rich woman, and will help our village grow" (314). He is unequivocal in his wholehearted support of Yaya, and Yaya attributes her transition to the university to both Father and Takwabe (315).

Again, Father Sean is unlike the typical colonizer and does not come from one of the colonizing countries. He is from Ireland, and as the narrator tells us, "Good news in Ireland has often meant good news for humanity" (97). While on the boat to Africa for the first time, he reflects on his mission and discards the colonizers' top-bottom approach for an all-inclusive, collective approach involving the people (107). He is aware of customs and traditions that act as stumbling blocks to progress in society and for women in particular; thus he chooses the school and church as foundational to his goals. However, he does not reject the history of the people. When he decides to challenge the Amidou Ngong dance troupe in baya dancing, barely six months in Yakiri, he composes music for his troupe, which includes the names of two women, based on the Wotikars' "greatest ancestor Yaa" (166). Mercy Oduye concludes that religious leaders need to be involved in the eradication of female oppression: "Doing right by women, of course, places responsibilities on all religions to be a voice that calls for promoting more humane social structures and for safeguarding or reviving life-affirming traditional structures" (15). Father may have been a catalyst for other males to support females; however, he is not alone since men of goodwill in the community also recognize that they are hindering progress with structures that limit women's advancement.

In Jing's novel, names ultimately hold the key to unlocking meanings, especially the theme of female repression which he delves into so well. To effect this thematic feat, Jing's nomenclature does not only unveil the negative, but it also becomes the means of infusing hope as the last woman, Yaya, leaves the margins to inscribe herself into the center, thus fulfilling the aspirations of several generations of women who longed for the promised land of justice, fairness and equity, but could only see it from afar. Jing uses names to deliver a powerful message for breaking down barriers and obstacles in the way of female empowerment and against repression of the female. This use of names by Jing explored so far draws attention to be tilted to the import of how Jing's nomenclature relates to characters, their deeds, actions, psychological portraits as well as all that which is beheld of them. Is it the name he gives his characters that goads the characters' action? Or, again, are the characters' actions inspired by their name?

In the nineteenth century, when authors such as George Eliot, Charles Dickens, and Oscar Wilde were producing works that defined the epoch that they were immersed in, there were limits for women who sought freedom, authority and independence. There was precedence for the woman who had no advantage, no wealth, and all sorts of restrictions that placed weights upon her feet. At least, one might say, she had her family. At least she knew where she stood in a world where traditions, however harmful, were unambiguous. Gwendolyn Harleth knew the circumstances of her family's financial reversal, Nancy knew the consequences of being a prostitute and Lady Windermere knew the consequences of infidelity because her mama had done so and paid the price. If independence is compromised in the Victorian era, there was solace in the fact that every other female was equally hindered. In short, women knew what not to expect.

All of this changes when we meet Yaa who, a century later, has even less to aspire to than the meekest, poorest Victorian girl. From the moment that an Irish missionary appears in Yakiri, a small hamlet in the fictional country of Mungo, it is clear that even the impoverished streets of James Joyce's Dublin have something more than their tradition can completely fathom. Whereas the transatlantic novel went from innocence to experience (often from America to Europe) here the roles are transposed. Europe comes to Africa, not necessarily with malice but surely without an engraved invitation. The firm belief is that the female, *the African female*, cannot possibly be in a position to know best. Someone else, like a financial portfolio manager, is in a better position to control other peoples' lives and spend their emotional capital.

Early on in Thomas Jing's *Tale of an African Woman* our narrator states precisely how she is thrice afflicted; once in terms of race, twice in terms of gender, and thrice in terms of nationality.

For centuries, the story of my life has already been told in different ways by different women in different parts of the world. In other words, I don't think that the challenges I've faced are peculiar to me and so need to be recounted…the cries of women echo throughout the generations and seem all through to have always fallen only on deaf ears. (Jing 4).

This is a sad inadequacy, what literary thinker Patricia Beer calls a "dutiful, unenthusiastic acceptance…" (177). In other words, the personality of the female is depleted. Even before she begins to spell, her character is shaped and her expectations curtailed. Self-despair is universal, pervasive and relentless.

In something akin to a gendered call to arms Shannon, like the city near Limerick, travels to Africa as a journalist hoping, without any evidence, that things have gotten better. Her interview subject, a simple woman whose unique character exists to revive and give hope to others without expectations, describes herself as "…an orphan at birth, lost in distant and unknown Africa, with a voice which counted for little" (Jing 5). Thomas Jing begins with the oral tradition and plays the storyteller, asking the patently absurd question: "should an intelligent girl be educated?" Does a girl, on any continent, have intrinsic values? The inner workings of the names, the culture and the economy of the village respond with a deafening silence.

The collective and communal disappointment at the gender of Tadu and Biayuh's only child is similar to the birth of Queen Elizabeth in 1533. Both occurrences were initially thought to be disastrous. No one wants a female baby. The family name is lost unless there is a male sibling. Property is lost. In the latter case, the only hope for Princess Elizabeth was to marry quickly and count on her husband for support and stability. Instead of a legitimate male heir England and Bankim have disappointment. Shannon's journey of thousands of miles is to refute, in print, such meaningless and insincere talk. Just as William Shakespeare's *As You Like It* refutes the principal of primogeniture and seniority in order to develop and display a girl's resourcefulness, *Tale of an African Woman* is, in its own way, a pastoral involving exiles who are cut out of the officially sanctioned life of the hamlet. Rosalind and Yaa must adapt and take on the characteristics of the anti-hero. They must survive on the margins and have their identities tested, reforged and reformed. "I may not be a lion, but I am a lion's cub and I have a lion's heart" (Queen Elizabeth I). The baby Yaa, like "The Virgin Queen" who was motherless at age three, must also take what is erroneously perceived to be a poor hand and play it into strength. In both cases news of a girl was not welcome. This is how the names of women in Jing's novel shape their characters and those of other characters. "The singing and dancing immediately stopped and the talking drums went dumb" (Jing 12). The baby's sad fate was no different from that of the Brooke sisters in Eliot's *Middlemarch*, Cecily in Wilde's *The Importance of Being Earnest* and Sissy Jupe in Dickens' *Hard Times*. All were orphans with uncertain futures who were associated, solely by their gender, with unmet needs and unfulfilled expectations.

No one in the village, when the novel commences, even knows what to call the baby. That is a symbol of her absence of value. She began "…the dance of life on the wrong foot" (Jing 14). What we are left with are a series of criticisms leveled at the novel's female characters over circumstances not of their own making (Jing 14). A woman, at birth, is poorly assessed, placed at a disadvantage, considered foolish, and financially troublesome. This is the traditional premise that *Tale of an African Woman* is there to attack, dilute, and refute. This is a new way of looking at interpersonal relationships. And it happens we have an exceptional baby. The girl is brazen, precocious, and what I would call "overreaching" in the eyes of the people in Dawa. Yaa's "…vigor and energy were too much for a female …" many would say and, like an anonymous Greek chorus, the people in town made clear their disapproval and hasten tragedy. A girl is not *supposed* to be so good at so many different things. It is not natural, although all of the village's ideas about medicine seem to be based more on emotion than hard medical fact.

In a modern-day version of the famous work by the Danish poet Hans Christian Anderson the child who is subject to abuse surprisingly turns (or metamorphoses) into a figure that is lovely, with all of the problems inherent with such a classification. The attractive female, going back to Helen of Troy, has a series of tragedies laid at her doorstep. "La donna e mobile" says Verdi in the third act of the opera *Rigoletto*. That means she is not constant and not to be trusted. What's more, and perhaps more threatening, she is confident, upbeat, enjoying herself—rightly demanding a place at the table and a voice in the debate with males her own age. This will not come to fruition without a fight. The privileged do not often make concessions unless it is compulsory. Just as Ella Fitzgerald, the jazz and blues singer, once sang, "Every woman has misery/ Every woman is crying," Yaa, and girls like her, are set up to suffer. This is intentional. The deck is stacked. The contract is cooked. The penalty is meted out in a form of lack of involvement. Is this not a continuation of her new adopted mother's open show of defiance "with her hands on her hips and the upper part of her body thrust forward" (Jing 30)? This is the same female, antecedently potent connection that exists between Alice Walker and Zora Neale Hurston. The same "patrimony" is shared by Virginia Woolf and Aphra Behn. When it comes to displaying female power, even Rudyard Kipling, the greatest author and champion of the concept of Empire, presents a "Mother Wolf" taking down a masculine tiger in protection of an adopted child. The female is a force to be reckoned with. Men fear her. "And it is I, Raksha [The Demon], shall live to run with the Pack and to hunt with the Pack; and in the end, look you, hunter of little naked cubs– frog-eater– fish-killer–he shall hunt thee!" (9).

The Manjung ceremony is something of a commencement exercise. An elaborate rite of passage and at seventeen, it is among the first of Yaa's tests; her goatherd skills are impeccable. Some of the men on the Council, to their credit, show what Jing calls "perspicacity" (24). They see her argument. This psychological fissure says something about the male thought process, firstly (thank God) that there is one and secondly that its reasoning can be deductive, meticulous and measured. The name "Yaa" means great one and no one doubts her talent. That is why she is so threatening, thus explaining why society wishes to ostracize her, making her a loner. Even with Yaa's exceptional qualities, she has supporters on the Council, Asanbe and Nguforh, who have their work cut out for them against a defense that does not have even "…one good reason why females should not become members" (Jing 20). This is the passive or what we term "resting" argument of habit and tradition. The Council, as a collective, wants to maintain balance. The tired old, untested men are more concerned about keeping up appearances in the village than dispensing justice to womankind.

Thomas Jing's look at the Grassfields that surround Yakiri reveal a dying tradition. Not only does it not want to change, but it has forgotten the very directives crucial to its formation. A capable woman, one who is too hard to handle, threatens to upend the fragile equilibrium within the community. What is one to do with such a bold upstart? Prior to German, British, and French administrations, the status quo within the small village of Bankim is valued above all else. Yaa's very name is an indication that she will not be able to be compartmentalized or pigeonholed. Her name propels and goads her to act. Her moniker means and it informs. Education, from this vantage point, is a negative. It is the enemy of a docile character. It is a way of acting, thinking and processing information that is better shunned. In an argument forwarded by personalities such as George Sand, who similarly to Yaa, became mistress of her grandmother's estate when she died, and Mary Wollstonecraft, who made a career out of writing about confined women, the very qualities of strength, brutishness, forcefulness, and persistence that are extolled in men are terrifying in women. Strength of character in a woman is something to fear. It is something that can emasculate. This is what causes people to sweat and shift uncomfortably in their seats.

The baby Yaa's precociousness is a problem discussed in whispers and veiled actions. The subtext of the novel is that the name "Yaa" makes the characters in the village so very uncomfortable. Her skills as a wrestler and the watcher of her mother's goats are unsettling. She is holding Mungo's structural inconsistencies and double-standards up to the light. No one in Africa wants to look at this image. No one wants gender bias to be illuminated, let alone examined. Thomas Jing's Tale of an African Woman is a feminist tract in a portion of the globe which has never had one before the thirties and forties when the book commences .

No African author, male or female, has ever challenged, in print, the mischief that men have been causing from time immemorial.

Yaa's name and the interplay of words such as great, lone, and grandmother so dominates this gendered argument and ties the novel to the thematic concerns discussed above. While names are pointers to ancestry, females' ancestry can only be traced to abuse. Yaa's daughter, who is her ashes, will equally suffer and be discarded like her mother before her. She will tremble in direct proportion to the opposition she vocalizes. The notion of the female (how she will fare, how she will survive, and if she will have justice) is at the heart of how characters act in Tale of an African Woman. Her very existence becomes a mechanism of commerce, bringing in the language of "...bright prospects...", "...big price...", and "...excellence and independence..." in relation to crops, harvests, and fertility (Jing 41). Will future generations of girls rise out of the smoldering kindling like the phoenix bird? Yaa's maturity means that not only must she hold her own as a farmer, hunter, and wrestler, but that these roles and her choices have generational economic consequences. Whether she marries, whom she marries, and whether she has children of her own are crucial to keeping her adopted mother and her biological mother's legacies alive. This is Jing's representation of the matriarchy. Without Yaa's obedience, both her parents' names (her dad's too), and the village's investment in her, will disappear. Jing's point is that not only must Yaa confront pressure, but that her burdens are motivated by names and gender. This is an enormous and cursed combination. She is female, she is an orphan, she is poor, and she is alone. Is it any wonder that without any support once Chacha dies, she buckles under this unrelenting and unasked for exertion of force? A modern feminist critic, Julia Kristeva, argues that to combat these overwhelming problems women need to reconceive identity. The identity is built on the solid, or not so solid, rock of the birth name. They must reinvent their own characters in order to be well. The modern world of the nineteen forties in which the novel is set does "... not have the civilized splendor of the Greek city state. The modern political domain is massively, in totalitarian fashion, social, leveling, exhausting. Hence madness is a space of antisocial, apolitical, and paradoxically free individuation" (Kristeva 235).

Charles Dickens would say in Oliver Twist that, as a crying newborn, if Yaa could have known the fate that awaited her "left to the tender mercies of church-wardens and overseers, perhaps [she] would have cried the louder" (6).

Yabu, Yaa's daughter, is also given very little chance to thrive in her African community. Things have not changed much (Jing 81). Like Oliver in Oliver Twist, both have mamas who die after giving birth. The famous orphan of nineteenth century Britain may be masculine in biology, but he is feminine in character and is excluded for it. These are figures who, as Jing puts it, "...lived on its [society's] margin and was [were] treated very unfairly" (Jing 80). Both the village and the ultimate colonizer of the village treat their own badly. Tellingly, the missionary, who intervenes in Yakiri, is from neither.

From the moment Father Sean appears in Chapter Seventeen of Tale of an African Woman, it is clear that he is to stop the madness. His name is a character structuring device. The name Sean, in a case that is not onomatopoeia, loses its source and its resemblance. "Sean" in the African village is mistaken for "sun." He is a source of "light" and understanding. The verbal gymnastics continue when one realizes that the word "sun" and "son" are pronounced the same way. How can a celibate priest, who has no son, be called Father? The priest travels from Bristol to Dakar to Monrovia to Freetown to Victoria to disavow "...ignorance and some customs... [that] ...always proved to be stumbling blocks" (Jing 107–108). He is there, in the gentlest possible way, to push and to modernize. The fact that he is from Ireland, the only European nation not to colonize Africa nor be present at the Berlin conference of 1884, is a hint that he is there to meddle, but that his meddlesomeness is well-intentioned. His arrival in Victoria, a hustling and bustling commercial center of the Cameroons, before heading inward, smacks of something akin to most English language stories about Africa. The visitor arrives and journeys into the forest to change things by the way he carries himself and by the content of his character. The danger in those very British stories is that those very things he hopes to change will change him instead.

In a land clearly characterized by male chauvinism, it is ironic that Father Sean has a particular fondness for pigs. "I love pigs," he states and with that remark he is given five piglets on his first day in Abakwa (Jing 126). The pigs are placed in baskets that are tied onto horses for the purposes of travel. The horses, like their rider, are decidedly out of place. This use of livestock is a subtle form of confrontation. Like two clouds ("black clouds") that collide in the sky, a storm is coming with lots of neighing and squeals to usher in a season of discontent (Jing 128).

Once in his new home the meteorological references continue. Father Sean and Kikakilaki, on their way to consult a gnukwabe, literally "kick[ed] up a storm" as they travel by foot upon a dusty and unwanted road (Jing 139). Kikakilaki, or Kiki, is one of the men in Yakiri who assists the priest and helps him by "…opening boxes and unpacking things" (Jing 136). Note this unsettling and disturbing, yet necessary step, identical to giving one's butt a kick. Kiki is an interpreter and a conveyor of conundrums and difficult choices, and this explains the cacophonic nature of his name. In order to liberate Mungo, the old customs must be untied. In "untying" (or forgetting), the nation becomes vulnerable and susceptible to new ideas from the West. You can't win. This is a spiritual skirmish and a cultural war. Tale of an African Woman is a novel about disintegration, penetration and encroachment. Yaa's name, meaning "great one" or "loner," fits into this paradigm. She exists to overstep the boundaries that are circumscribed. She is there to create collisions. She is there to cause mischief.

With the principal characters meticulously positioned on stage, the conflict that has been simmering can truly be brought to a boil. Will people embrace the new ways of modernity and Christianity or will they resist Father Sean's teachings and cling to the past and ancestral worship? Furthermore, will women "…continue to be left behind" (Jing 159)? This is a contest that reaches back generations to Chacha's challenge to the Council. It is still uncertain as to whether or not this fictional version of the Cameroons is ready for logic and European logic at that.

Through Jing's novelistic craft and adherence to nomenclatural traditions of the Grassfields of the Cameroons, character names do not only betray their agential capabilities but also reveal the author's central concerns as a lover of a dying tradition attempting to resist change brought about by extraneous forces in an effort to redeem it. These forces seem to abridge or cut things short and the author seizes the opportunity to birth through his nomenclatural craft, such characters as Yaa, an abridged version of Yaya, i.e. little "Yaa" or Greek for grandmother. This is not withstanding the fact that Yaa is the foremother of Yaya. Yaa is, therefore, only a fraction of what a grandmother stands for. And indeed, throughout the novel, Yaa and her female descendants in the views of the elders as well as according to ancestral tradition are nothing short of "half-baked" humans in the society of Bankim. Bankim cannot contend with women of their caliber. Yaa, like her offspring, is difficult to be caged. Their names ring an ominous bell that no one in Bankim wants to hear. Thus, as the foregone analysis illustrates, Jing's poetization of names structures the plot, themes and character in the context in which Yaa, Yabu, Chacha, Yaya, etc. find themselves relegated as women to the role of housewives and child-bearing agents.

Works Cited

Alford, Richard D. *Naming and Identity: A Cross-Cultural Study of Personal Naming Practices*. New Haven: HRAF, 1988. Print

Bakhtin, *The Dialogic Imagination*, (Ed.) Holquist M. Austin, U. of Texas P., 2004. print

Beer, Patricia. *Reader, I Married Him*. New York: Barnes & Noble Books, 1974. Print.

Buckler, William E. *The Prose of the Victorian Period,* Boston, Houghton-Mifflin, 1958. Print.

Culleton, Claire *Names and Naming in Joyce*. Madison: U of Wisconsin P, 1994. Print.

Dickens, Charles. *Oliver Twist*. London: Penguin Classics, 2009. Print.

Eliot, George. *The Mill on the Floss,* New York: Harper. 1860. Print.

Fishkin, Ankumah and Ndi, (Eds.) *Fears, Doubts, and Joys of not Belonging*. Mankon-Bamenda: Langaa-RCIPG, 2013. Print.

Fitzgerald, Ella "Happy Blues" in *Ella in London* Germany, Pablo Records, 1974. Vinyl.

Hayes, Elizabeth T. "The Named and the Nameless: Morrison's 124 And Naylor's 'The Other Place' as Semiotic 'Chorae.'" *African American*

Review 38.4 (2004): 669-681. *Academic Search Premier*. Web. 22 May 2014

Hurston, Zora Neale *Mules and Men*. New York: Harper Perrenial, 1990. Print.

James, Henry. "The Art of Fiction." *Longman's Magazine* 4 (September 1884). Print. Rpt. in *Partial Portraits*. London: Macmillan, 1888. Web. 18 May, 2014.

Jing, Thomas. *Tale of an African Woman*. Mankon-Bamenda: Langaa-RCIPG, 2008. Print.

Joyce, James. *The Dubliners*. Boston: Longman, 2011. Print.

Kristeva, Julia. *Black Sun: Depression and Melancholia*. New York: Columbia UP, 1989. Print.

Kumar, Margaret, Supriya Pattanayak, and Richard Johnson. *Framing my Name: Extending Educational Boundaries*, Altona, Victoria, Australia: Common Ground, 2010. Print

Lambert, W.G. *Babylonian Creation Myths*. Winona Lake: Eisenbrauns, 2013. Print.

Milne, Leah. "The Importance of Naming in *Beloved* and *The Poisonwood Bible*." *CLA Journal* 55..4 (June 2012): 352-369. Print

Oduyoye, Mercy Amba. *Daughters of Anowa: African Women & Patriarchy*. Maryknoll, NY: Orbis Books, 1995. Print.

Shakespeare, William. *As You Like It*: Mineola, NY: Dover Thrift Editions, 1998. Print

Verdi, Giuseppi. *Rigoletto*. Richmond, England: Overture, 2011. Print.

Walker, Alice. *The Color Purple*. New York: Pocket Books, 1985. Print.

Wilde, Oscar. *Lady Windermere's Fan:* Mineola, NY: Dover Thrift Editions, 1998. Print.

Wollstonecraft, Mary. *A Vindication of the Rights of Woman and A Vindication of the Rights of Men*. Ed. Janet Todd. Oxford: OUP, 1993. Print.

INDEX

Abeng. 35, 37, 38, 39, 46, 47, 49, 54, 55
Abu Shardow Abarry 170
Achebe, Chinua........... 37, 94
Achilles 14, 16
Adams 74, 76, 81
Adichie 83, 84, 85, 87, 91, 93, 94, 96, 97
Afikpo 109
Africa... 3, 23, 37, 39, 43, 47, 58, 62, 64, 67, 71, 72, 73, 76, 78, 81, 88, 89, 91, 96, 102, 103, 106, 107, 108, 109, 111, 112, 113, 115, 116, 117, 118, 119, 120, 145, 158, 169, 207, 212, 214, 215, 216, 219, 221
Africanness 43
Ahidjo, Ahmadou 184
AIDS 158
Alfred Saker 73
Alice Walker 218
Amadiume, Ifi 101, 118
Amir Baraka 91
Ana Njinga 107
Anglophone-Cameroon . 172, 190
Ankumah . 34, 145, 168, 195, 223
Anne Frank 52
Aphra Behn 218
Appiah, Bernard........... 2, 18
aristeia 15
Aristotle 14, 33
Asaluhi 8
Audra 128, 139
Babylonian .. 6, 8, 17, 19, 224
Bakhtin . 1, 3, 4, 18, 197, 223

Bakhtinean 1, 4, 5, 7
Bangolan 123, 124, 125, 126, 127, 128, 129, 139, 140
Barry, Peter 35
Barthes, Roland 171, 193
Bate Besong ... 171, 183, 190, 191
Belgian Congo 78
Ben L. Martin 191
Bernhardt, Sharon 23
Beverly Hills 76, 148, 149, 159
Beyala, Calyxthe ... 83, 84, 88, 90, 91, 92, 93, 94, 96, 97
Beynon 114
Bismarck, Otto von 74
Blake, William 70, 81
Bob Marley 65
Bolton, Carol 27
Booth 24, 33
Bosmajian, Haig 165
Bosnia 100
Bourdieu 124, 130, 139
Britain 169, 172, 173, 174, 221
Bronze Age 6, 10
Brown, James 66
Bubenechik, Milena 50, 55
Buckler 201, 203, 223
Burkina Faso 168, 169
Burnard 99, 115, 118
Burning Spear 65, 66
Cameroon 18, 60, 65, 73, 78, 106, 131, 134, 137, 147, 149, 150, 166, 167, 169, 170, 171, 172, 173, 174, 175, 176, 177, 179, 182,

183, 185, 186, 187, 188, 189, 190, 192
Cameroun .. 89, 169, 172, 173, 183, 184, 185, 190
Catholicism 76, 89
Charles Grant 107
Charles Pasqua 191
Chaucer, Geoffrey............ 72
Chicago Mercantile Exchange 75
Chimamanda Adichie .. 83, 97
Cliff, Michelle 35, 37, 53
Cohen 108, 111, 118
Coleman 109, 118
Coleridge, Samuel Taylor .. 26
Colonialism.... 37, 41, 54, 55, 106
Congo................. 169
Conrad, Joseph 78, 79, 81
Corinth 17
cosmogonic........................ 7
Culleton, Claire A. 63, 64, 69, 81, 196, 197, 223
Currie, Gregory................ 35
Cyclops . 7, 11, 12, 13, 14, 15
D'Alisera......................... 103
Dahomey 51
Daniel Ndo 186, 192
Davis, Clive...................... 73
Dennisss, Richard 73
Derrida 33, 125, 136, 139, 204
dialogized........................... 4
Dickens, Charles 57, 61, 215, 217, 221, 223
Dijksterhuis............. 99, 119
Diomedes 15, 16
diplomacy 2, 3
Doh 2, 18, 21, 25, 26, 27, 28, 29, 30, 31, 32, 33, 34,

123, 130, 139, 164, 166, 167, 169
Droz, Yvan 102, 103, 119
Duckworth....................... 36
Dunkerley 114
Dylan, Bob....................... 73
Ebeogu 93, 97
Ebeogu, Afam.................. 83
Emerson, Ralph Waldo 59, 81
England ... 41, 47, 49, 51, 77, 82, 94, 216, 224
Enuma Elish 6, 7, 9
Ervin...................... 113, 114
Europe..... 52, 100, 117, 120, 136, 153, 215
Evans 1, 3
Expinoza................. 116, 119
Falola, Toyin 37
Fanon, Frantz........ 40, 55, 184
Fearon..................... 105, 119
Fishkin 34, 57, 168, 195, 202, 223
Flaubert, Gustave.............. 70
Foster....................... 7, 8, 18
Fourie 102, 119
Fowler.... 68, 69, 72, 81, 154, 158, 167, 168
Framing My Name.... 1, 2, 3, 6, 14, 17, 18, 19, 70, 131, 140, 202
France.... 169, 173, 174, 186, 191
Frazer, Sir James 69, 70
Freeman, Kitty 39
Freud, Sigmund..... 71, 72, 82
Gachuhi 104, 119
Galtung, Johan 48
Garvey, Marcus 66
Genesis 6, 9, 80
George Eliot 200, 215

George Sand 219
Germany 169, 223
Ghana 104, 140, 169
Giddens 112
Gilgamesh 17, 196
Glaukos 15, 16
Glissant, Édouard 85, 97
globalization ... 2, 63, 64, 103, 112, 113, 114, 117, 118, 123, 125, 129
Gold Coast 39, 169
Gottlob Frege 21
Graham Greene 76
Greek 6, 11, 15, 17, 140, 174, 204, 212, 217, 220, 223
Greenfield. 91, 92, 94, 95, 97
Gutman, Herbert 23
Hahn 102, 119
Handley 206
Hans Christian Anderson 217
Hanumaan 9
Harding 107, 119
Hartman 26, 33, 41
Harvey 116, 119
Hawthorne's 17
Hayes ... 10, 11, 18, 206, 207, 210, 223
Heart of Darkness 78, 81
Hebrew 6, 9
Heidegger, Martin 26, 34
Henry James 57, 196, 211
hermeneutical 4
heteroglossia 1, 3, 6
Hill 116, 119
Hinduism 76
Hitchcott 89, 94, 97
HIV/AIDS 58, 72
Holocaust 41
Homer 11, 15, 16, 18
Homeric 11, 15

Hopkins, Gerard Manley ... 76
Huntington, Samuel . 99, 119, 121
Igbo 83, 93, 96, 97, 174
Iliad 14, 15, 16, 18
Imbusch, Peter 46, 48, 55
intercultural communication 2, 3, 4
inter-ethnic 4, 170
Jamaica ... 40, 41, 47, 99, 115, 118
James K. Skipper Jr. 169
James Weldon Johnson ... 166
Jean Forchive 184
Jean-Marie le Pen 191
Jeismann 105, 120
Jespersen 105, 120
Jesse Jackson 100, 151
Jing 195, 196, 198, 199, 200, 201, 203, 204, 205, 207, 210, 212, 214, 216, 217, 218, 219, 220, 221, 222, 224
Johannes Krapf 106
Johnson, Richard 1, 18, 19, 106, 120, 126, 134, 137, 139, 224
journalism 2
Joyce, James 77, 81, 196, 197, 215, 223, 224
Judaism 76
Judeo-Christian 6
Julia Kristeva 220
Kalu 106, 120
Kamerun 169, 173
Kasser, Tim 74, 82
Kelsey Wood 49
Kennedy, John F. 155, 168
Kiely 114, 121

King... 17, 25, 34, 44, 55, 75, 145, 151, 152, 163, 166, 168
king Ur-Nammu 10
King, Debra Walker ... 23, 43, 145
Klose, Fabian 37, 40
Kolle 99
Kono 109
Kripke, Saul 21
Kumar, Margaret.... 1, 18, 19, 126, 134, 136, 137, 139, 224
Kyallo Wadi Wamitila 38
Laitlin 105
Laius 17
Lattimore 12, 18
law 2, 51, 111, 212
Lechner.................. 113, 120
Lederer 49, 55
Leonard R. N. Ashley..... 170, 183
Livingston, David 106
Lo Bianco 131, 133, 134
Lugaldimmerankia................ 8
Macbeth 59
Mann, Michael 37
Manneh, Hawah.............. 101
Marduk 7, 8, 9
Martin 18, 34, 100, 103, 120, 193
Marukka......................... 8
Marutukku 8
Mary Wollstonecraft 219
Mauron, Charles.......... 25, 34
Mayes.................... 74, 76, 81
Mayfield, Curtis................. 66
Mbiti, John..... 101, 104, 108, 120
Mbundu 107

McAllister, Vance.............. 77
memorialization 11
Menelaus 11
Mercy Oduye 214
Mershakusu........................ 8
Mesopotamian 10
Mimboland..... 59, 60, 64, 66, 70, 71, 72, 73, 74, 75, 77, 78, 80, 81, 147, 148, 151, 155, 156
Mortesen, C. David 48, 49, 56
Murdoch, Rupert............... 71
Ndi. 2, 6, 14, 17, 18, 34, 123, 124, 129, 130, 134, 135, 137, 139, 145, 146, 149, 150, 163, 164, 165, 166, 167, 168, 171, 174, 175, 176, 177, 180, 181, 182, 183, 191, 193, 195, 223
Ndongo........................... 107
Ndũngi wa Mũngai... 70, 127, 130, 133, 135, 140
Near East 10
Near Eastern 6, 11
Newell............... 106, 120
Newman, John Henry 76
Ngoa Ekele 182
Ngugi wa Thiong'o............ 25
Nicolaisen, W.F.H....... 44, 56
Nigeria ... 33, 37, 55, 94, 106, 118, 172, 174, 190
Nnam.................... 108, 120
Nuessel, Frank 151, 152, 165, 168
Nyamnjoh, Francis B.. 57, 58, 59, 60, 61, 62, 63, 64, 65, 66, 67, 68, 69, 70, 71, 72, 73, 74, 75, 76, 77, 78, 79, 80, 82, 145, 146, 151, 154, 156, 167, 168

Nyanzi, Stella 101, 120
Oduyoye 208, 224
Odysseus..... 7, 11, 13, 14, 16
Odyssey. 11, 13, 14, 15, 16, 18
Oedipus 17
Ogaga Ifowodo 50
Ogwude 87, 97
Okpewho, Isidore 30
Oliviu, Felecan 44
Onyeoziri 83, 87, 97
Orwell, George 74
Ottenberg 109, 120
outsidedness 4, 5
Patricia Beer.................... 216
Pattanayak 1, 3, 9, 10, 18, 19, 126, 128, 130, 134, 136, 137, 139, 224
Paul Biya 177, 186, 187, 188, 189
Paul L. Leslie 169
Phillipson.......................... 76
Pinchoff.... 91, 92, 94, 95, 97
poetization 123, 132, 137, 167, 200, 205, 223
polyglossia 6, 18
polyglossic 18
Polyphemus 7, 11, 13, 14
Poseidon 14, 15
Proust, Marcel................. 171
pseudonym 7
Quakerism 76
Queen Elizabeth 216
Ralph Ellison 166
Reece 11, 12
Renan 105, 120
Rhetoric 14
Richard Rorty.................... 22
Robert Phillipson 74, 76
Rudyard Kipling.............. 218
Rwanda 100, 106

Saint Augustine 76
Saussure, Ferdinand de...... 21
Savage, Clare .. 37, 38, 39, 41, 43, 44, 49, 50, 54
Schwarz............................. 38
Searle, John 21, 22, 34
Second World War.... 52, 100
Shakespeare, William .. 59, 61, 82, 152, 216, 224
Sheats, Paul 27, 34
Sherwood, Caroline 183, 190, 193
Shuey 114, 121
Sisyphos 16
Smith 110, 113, 114, 121
Soames................... 22, 34
Socrates............................. 21
Somalia 106
Sophocles.................... 17, 19
Southern Cameroons...... 172, 173, 174, 183
Soyinka 32, 123, 125, 126, 130, 132, 133, 137, 145, 154, 168
Switzerland...................... 105
Telemachus 11
tetragrammaton....................... 6
The Dubliners 197, 224
theogonies 7
Tirop Simatei 37
Tschaepe 186, 193
United States.... 77, 100, 105, 115
Upper Volta 169
Vakunta....... 2, 18, 23, 24, 34, 123, 124, 127, 128, 129, 135, 139, 140, 144, 153, 154, 155, 168
van Knippenberg 99, 119
Vedder 102, 119

Verdery 112, 121
Virginia Woolf 218
Walraven, Gijs 101
Wamitila....................... 38, 43
Washington DC 103, 116
Wells 114, 121
West, Cornel 8, 23, 40, 51, 64, 73, 76, 82, 102, 119, 120, 127, 128, 132, 153, 155, 173, 182, 213, 222
Wilde, Oscar 68, 82, 215, 217, 224
Williams .. 128, 139, 150, 168

Wilson, E. O. 79, 82
Wojcicki 104, 121
Wordsworth, William . 26, 27, 28, 29, 33, 34, 130, 145
xenia 11
Yaoundé. 147, 148, 164, 175, 181, 182, 185, 188, 193
Yugoslavia 106, 117
Yvon Omnes................... 191
Zaire 169
Zeus 12, 15
Zora Neale Hurston 218

www.ingramcontent.com/pod-product-compliance
Lightning Source LLC
Chambersburg PA
CBHW051609230426
43668CB00013B/2042